emissions trading & competitiveness

ALLOCATIONS, INCENTIVES AND INDUSTRIAL COMPETITIVENESS UNDER THE EU EMISSIONS TRADING SCHEME

EDITORS:
Michael Grubb and
Karsten Neuhoff

Published by Earthscan in 2006

First issued in paperback 2014

Earthscan is an imprint of the Taylor & Francis Group, an informa business

Copyright © Earthscan, 2006

ISSN: 1469-3062
ISBN: 9781844075942 (hbk)
ISBN: 9781138002074 (pbk)

Typeset by Domex
Cover design by Paul Cooper Design

Responsibility for statements made in the articles printed herein rests solely with the contributors. The views expressed by the individual authors are not necessarily those of the Editors or the Publishers.

For a full list of Earthscan publications please contact:
Earthscan
2 Park Square, Milton Park, Abingdon, Oxfordshire OX14 4RN
711 Third Avenue, New York, NY10017

Climate Policy is the leading international peer-reviewed journal on responses to climate change. For further information see www.climatepolicy.com.

Contents

Contents

Preface

Tom Delay[*]

The Carbon Trust, 8th Floor, 3 Clement's Inn, London WC2A 2AZ, UK

The European emissions trading scheme (EU ETS) is a driving force for business interest in reducing CO_2 emissions. In capping emissions from power generation and much of heavy industry in Europe, it gives value to their efforts to reduce emissions and has created a market with an asset value worth tens of billions of euros annually. Putting a price on carbon has been an achievement of global significance, as a focal point also for those seeking to invest through Kyoto's international project mechanisms of CDM and JI.

Like any market, price is central and the key to prices is scarcity. The most fundamental difference between emissions trading and any normal market is that the amount available depends directly on government decisions about allocations. Recent events have underlined the need for robust allocation as the system moves into the Kyoto phase, and investors are already starting to look beyond that to the post-2012 period. Yet governments also have a duty not to undermine the competitiveness of their industries, and there are fears that the two aims could conflict.

Recognizing the central importance of competitiveness concerns, in 2004 the Carbon Trust conducted a pioneering study on the competitiveness impacts of the EU ETS.[1] Building upon this work, in 2005 the Carbon Trust sponsored an international collaborative study with the European research network Climate Strategies, led by our Chief Economist, Michael Grubb. The work aimed both to build upon our earlier study, and add to this much deeper analysis of the issues surrounding allowance allocation, costs and incentives. The full results are presented in this special issue of *Climate Policy*.

As a lead investor in this research, the Carbon Trust has taken a strong interest in the work, but does not itself hold any responsibility for the views expressed in the individual articles. We do firmly believe that UK and European policy can only be improved by such detailed and relevant analyses by independent researchers, published for open debate, as represented by the articles here. The Carbon Trust has taken this work as the evidence base for its own position on the EU ETS, published as a separate report in late June 2006.

We are pleased to have helped support this work through to completion, and are also grateful to the co-funders in UK and European industry and governments for matching the Carbon Trust contribution, and for their substantive input along the way. On behalf of all the sponsors we also thank all the researchers involved for their intensive efforts, Climate Strategies for managing the

---

[*] Corresponding author. Tel.: +20-7170-7000; fax: +20-7170-7020
E-mail address: tom.delay@carbontrust.co.uk

project and the review process, and Earthscan for producing this special issue in such a timely and professional manner.

Tom Delay
Chief Executive
The Carbon Trust

Note

1   Published as The European Emissions Trading System: Implications for Industrial Competitiveness, 2004 [available from http://www.carbontrust.co.uk/Publications].

www.climatepolicy.com

Allocation and competitiveness in the EU emissions trading scheme: policy overview

Michael Grubb*, Karsten Neuhoff

Faculty of Economics, Cambridge University, Sidgwick Avenue, Cambridge CB3 9DE, UK

Abstract

The European emissions trading scheme (EU ETS) has an efficient and effective market design that risks being undermined by three interrelated problems: the approach to allocation; the absence of a credible commitment to post-2012 continuation; and concerns about its impact on the international competitiveness of key sectors. This special issue of *Climate Policy* explores these three factors in depth. This policy overview summarizes key insights from the individual studies in this issue, and draws overall policy conclusions about the next round of allocations and the design of the system for the longer term.

- **Allocations for 2008–2012.** Allocations defined relative to projected 'business-as-usual' emissions should involve cutbacks for all sectors, in part to hedge against an unavoidable element of projection inflation. Additional cutbacks for the power sector could help to address distributional and legal (State aid) concerns. Benchmarking allocations, e.g. on best practice technologies, could offer important advantages: experience in different sectors and countries is needed, given their existing diversity. However, a common standard for new entrant reserves should be agreed across the EU, based on capacity or output, not on technology or fuel. Maximum use of allowed auctioning (10%) would improve efficiency, provide reassurance, and potentially help to stabilize the system through minimum-price auctions. These measures will not preclude most participating sectors from profiting from the EU ETS during phase II. Companies can choose to scale back these potential profits to protect market share against imports and/or use the revenues to support longer term decarbonization investments, whilst auction revenues can be used creatively to support broader investments towards a low-carbon industrial sector in Europe.
- **Post-2012 design.** Effective operation during phase II requires a concrete commitment to continue the EU ETS beyond 2012 with future design addressing concerns about distribution, potential perverse incentives, and industrial competitiveness. Declining free allocation combined with greater auctioning offers the simplest solution to distributional and incentive problems. For its unilateral implementation to be sustainable under higher carbon prices over longer periods, EU ETS post-2012 design must accommodate one of three main approaches for the most energy-intensive internationally traded sectors: international (sectoral) agreements, border-tax adjustments, or output-based (intensity) allocation. If significant free allocations continue, governments may also need to follow the example of monetary policy in establishing independent allocation authorities with some degree of EU coordination.

* Corresponding author. Tel.: +44-1223-335288; fax: +44-1223-335299
E-mail address: Michael.grubb@econ.cam.ac.uk

Such reform for the post-2012 period would require the Directive to be fundamentally renegotiated in relation to allocation procedures. Such renegotiation is neither feasible nor necessary for phase II operation. Rather, phase II should be a period in which diverse national approaches build experience, whilst the profits potentially accruing to participating sectors can be used to protect market share and jump-start their investments for a globally carbon-constrained future.

Introduction

The EU emissions trading scheme was launched in 2005 to cap CO_2 emissions from heavy industry. Covering almost half of all EU CO_2 emissions, it forms the centrepiece of European policy on climate change. Trade in these emission allowances gives value to reducing CO_2 emissions and has formed a market with an asset value worth tens of billions of euros annually. Putting a price on carbon has been an achievement of global significance, through the linkages to emission credits generated under the Kyoto mechanisms: indeed, in response to the unexpectedly high prices of 2005, a flood of such projects started coming forward.

Although unprecedented in its scale and scope, the main pillars of the EU ETS were built on many years of economic research into theories of emissions trading, combined with practical experience of emission trading schemes principally in the USA. Yet the analogies are far from exact, and the emerging experience with the EU ETS is beginning to highlight the profound nature of the differences – many of which have thus far been under-appreciated in economic and policy analysis.

Like any market, the key to prices is scarcity, and the price depends on both the absolute quantity of allowances available and expectations about the future. The most fundamental difference of emissions trading from any normal market is that the amount available depends directly on government decisions about allocations; and expectations about the future are largely expectations about future emission targets. The large reduction of EU ETS prices in Spring 2006 is the first tangible sign of the scale of the problems around allocation in the EU ETS. Equally, some of the initial responses give a foretaste of numerous other possible problems:

- Suggestions to 'bank' surplus allowances forward into phase II (the Kyoto first period), without understanding and correcting the cause of the initial problem, may simply exacerbate similar problems in the next, crucial, Kyoto phase;
- Plans to withdraw allowances from the market risk being seen as penalizing abatement. Indeed such *ex-post* adjustment runs the risk of undermining the basis of a stable market upon which industry feels confident to invest;
- Proposals to use 2005 as the base year for phase II allocation risk a perverse 'updating' incentive; a belief that higher emissions today will be rewarded with bigger allocations in future periods.

Due in part to the sheer scale of the EU ETS, governments are subject to intense lobbying relating to the distributional impact of the scheme, and are constrained by this and by concerns about the impact of the system on industrial competitiveness. Few academics understand the real difficulties that policy-makers face when confronted with economically important industries claiming that government policy risks putting them at a disadvantage relative to competitors. Yet attempts to manage the consequences – by giving allocations based on projected needs, by *ex-post* adjustments after the real situation becomes clearer, or by updating allocations based on most recent data – are loaded with the potential to weaken the system with perverse incentives that undermine the original objective. The same is true of many other 'fixes' to meet the pressures of lobbying and competitiveness concerns. Allocation is at the heart of the EU ETS; it is also potentially its Achilles heel.

This special issue brings together the most complete analyses of these core issues yet conducted:

- Three articles apply economic modelling to focus directly upon how the EU ETS and allocation decisions may affect sector profits, pricing, market share and incentives: an overview study of five key sectors, complemented by finer-grained modelling of the electricity and cement sectors, to study the incentive aspects of different allocation approaches.
- Three articles look at issues arising from these economic conseuences of the EU ETS. One study presents initial empirical evidence about the system's impact on electricity prices and profits. A legal study highlights how the scale of profits generated under the ETS may itself bring contrary pressures to bear on the allocation process through State-aid considerations. Both of these then inform an analysis of the issues surrounding auctioning of emission allowances, including the extent to which auctioning might help to address some of the difficulties identified in other articles.

This overview also draws on several other studies, including a related analysis of how the modelling studies of aggregate sectors 'in equilibrium' relate to the diverse nature of key sectors across Europe, and the likely dynamics of economic impacts and mitigation potentials over time (Grubb et al., 2006).

This policy overview is in two parts. Part A draws directly on these component studies to clarify and emphasize five ways in which the EU ETS differs from previous emissions trading systems:

1. The economic scale of the scheme, which drives heavy lobbying around allocation and competitiveness concerns, yet which paradoxically is the source of profit-making incentives unprecedented in the history of environmental policy;
2. The consequently small nature of cutbacks relative to 'business-as-usual' and the resulting instabilities in the system;
3. The corresponding large proportion of free allocation, which underlies legal stresses and the scope for distortions;
4. The multi-period nature of allocations, which drives dependence both upon post-2012 decisions and the risk of perverse incentives;
5. The devolution of allocation responsibilities to Member States and the way this affects the development of viable solutions.

Part B then examines the 'bigger picture' policy implications that flow from this: the implications for allocation during phase II; the options for longer-term continuation; and the implications in terms of the existing Directive and related institutional considerations.

Part A: Why the EU ETS is different – and what that implies

A1. Scale, costs and competitiveness

In terms of economic scale, the European emission trading scheme is the biggest such scheme in the world by an order of magnitude. At allowances prices in the range €10–30/tCO$_2$, the value of allowances issued every year is €22–66 billion, compared with the USA's East Coast NO_x trading programmes (€1.1 billion) or SO_2 trading schemes (€2.8–8.7 billion).[1] The sheer scale of the EU ETS means that it could affect the costs of key industrial sectors more than any previous environmental policy – perhaps more than all the others put together. Yet part of the problem in the debate over the EU ETS is the tendency to make sweeping generalizations, not least about costs and competitiveness impacts.

Two aspects drive competitiveness issues. First, the level of international competition for a specific product and, second, the direct and indirect CO_2 emissions associated with the production. Figure 1 provides a sense of scale for both dimensions.

As an indicator for the cost exposure, the vertical axis of Figure 1 depicts the potential *value at stake* for major industrial sectors. It is defined as the potential impact of the EU ETS on input costs relative to sector value-added, before any mitigation or pass-through of costs onto product prices. The horizontal axis shows the current trade exposure of these sectors. The data are for the UK, which in many respects is one of the most exposed countries in Europe to external trade effects, and in which most sectors (with the exception of pulp and paper) are plausibly representative of the situation facing many European producers.

The **lower end** of the vertical bars shows the *net value at stake* (NVAS) if the sector participates in the EU ETS and receives free allocations equal to its 'business-as-usual' emissions, takes no abatement

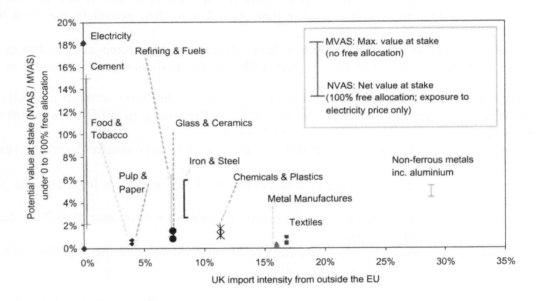

Figure 1. Value at stake over range 0–100% free allocation. The chart shows value at stake (see text) relative to total value-added by sector, plotted against UK trade intensity. The bars span the range from (NVAS) 100% free allocation, to (MVAS) the theoretical impact of zero free allocation or equivalent carbon tax. Results are for a carbon price of 15€/tCO_2 and an electricity cost pass-through that increases power prices by €10/MWh, consistent with a coal-dominated power system (CCGTs could roughly halve this rate of electricity price impact for the same carbon price). Scaling the electricity price moves the lower point of the bars in proportion; scaling the carbon price scales the length in proportion.

action, and does not change product prices: the NVAS then represents the sector's exposure to indirect costs through electricity price impacts only, since all direct emission costs are covered by free allocations. The most striking feature of the graph is that only three sectors have NVAS exceeding 1.5% of sector value-added. If exposed to the full impact of electricity price rises, NVAS is estimated at 2.1% for Cement, 2.7% for Iron and Steel, and finally 4.4% for Non-ferrous Metals (principally aluminium).

The high value attributed to non-ferrous metals reflects dependence on electrical input for processes, particularly for aluminium, which sometimes result in it being termed 'solid electricity'.[2] For cement, iron and steel, the figure is around 2%; refining, which uses hardly any electricity from the grid and has NVAS with 100% free allocation, is 1.3% of its total value-added. The pulp and paper sector does not have significant cost exposure in the UK, although other EU producers may have. The impacts could be non-trivial for a few other individual subsectors – notably in glass and ceramics, and in chemicals, both of which have average sector NVAS exposure (at 100% free-allocation), close to 1% of value-added. In all cases, the actual net impact depends on the extent that industries can undertake cost-effective emissions abatement measures or pass on CO_2-related costs to product prices.

Box 1: Five principles underlying the economic impacts of emissions trading

The aim of emissions cap-and-trade is to secure emission reductions at the lowest possible overall cost: the trading allows companies to seek emission reductions to meet the aggregate cap wherever and however it is cheapest to do so. Five principles underlie the practical economic impact of an emissions trading system applied to CO_2:

1. In general, CO_2 constraints generate economic rents, and free allocation of allowances to industry gives the *potential* to capture this value and profit, subject to:
    (a) degree of alignment of allowances with costs (e.g. not sectors outside EU ETS or affected primarily by electricity pass-through costs);
    (b) constraints on cost pass-through due to imports and other factors.
2. Profit and market share are not synonymous, and *for internationally traded goods they are frequently in opposition*: the more that companies profit by raising prices to reflect the opportunity costs of carbon, the greater the possible erosion of their market share over time.
3. The details of allocation methods matter: new entrant, closure, and incumbent allocation rules all affect the incentives, pricing and efficiency of the scheme.
4. The power sector can and does pass through the bulk of marginal/opportunity CO_2-related costs to the wholesale power markets, as expected in a competitive system, resulting in substantial profits and downstream costs where retail markets are competitive.
5. Other participating sectors also have the potential to profit in similar ways, but the net impact is complicated by details of electricity retail market regulation, by international trade, and by downstream company, regional and product differentiation.

The **upper end** of the bars shows the theoretical impact on sectors in the EU ETS if there were no free allocations – equivalent to 100% purchase (on markets or through auctioning at the market price). This forms a potential *maximum value at stake* (MVAS) that would arise from such allocation, or an equivalent carbon tax, if product prices were held constant and no abatement undertaken.

The significance of the upper level (no free allocation) is that *it also gives an indication of the impact on marginal/opportunity cost for producing an additional unit of output*.[3] As long as increasing or decreasing production does not change the amount of free allowance allocation, the incremental decision to produce more (or less) faces the full cost of extra allowances (or the opportunity cost of not selling allowances). Thus the upper end of the bars gives a rough indication of the potential relative impact on output prices, if firms pass through these opportunity costs. As discussed below, such pricing can lead to large profit gains from the EU ETS.

However, passing through the opportunity cost impacts of the EU ETS would increase prices relative to imports from regions outside the EU ETS.[4] This forms the main constraint on the ability to pass CO_2-related costs on to customers. The chart also shows (horizontal axis) the existing degree of imports from outside the EU. The quite exceptional position of aluminium, as noted in Smale et al. (this issue), is readily apparent – not only is its NVAS potentially twice that of any other sector, but the same is true of its import intensity.

In contrast, hardly any cement is currently imported from outside the EU. This does not imply that changes in production costs cannot create opportunities for international trade. Its *maximum value at stake* (MVAS) – and the relative significance associated with marginal/opportunity cost pricing – is comparable with electricity itself, at more than twice that of any other sector. This explains the high leakage rate associated with profit-maximization mentioned in Demailly and Quirion (this issue): if the sector passes through most of its marginal/ opportunity costs, the price differential simply becomes so large as to overcome the barriers that have traditionally kept foreign imports out.

The equivalent MVAS impact on refining and fuels, and iron and steel, is about 6% each and both have existing trade intensity around 7–8%. For the UK, no other sector in aggregate has marginal value-at-stake impacts above 2%, even for zero free allocation.

Several points flow from this. Allocation and competitiveness in the EU ETS is a tale about a few key sectors. At the prices and allocations plausible in phase II (considered briefly below) the *net* cost impacts are not large relative to sector value-added. If impacts on marginal costs were passed through to prices, while the sectors still receive mostly free allocations, as detailed below the sectors will profit substantially but with an erosion of international competitiveness over time. Moreover, differences in allocations between Member States would affect the cash flows of their companies (the length of the vertical bars gives an indication of sensitivity to this), and many have far greater trade within Europe than outside it (discussed further in Grubb et al., 2006, which presents equivalent data for trade within the EU). In reality these *internal* dimensions do far more to drive lobbying and allocation decisions than the external competitiveness considerations, and we now turn to consider some consequences.

A2. Small cutbacks and price instabilities

The scale of the EU ETS, combined with the relative difficulty of reducing CO_2 emissions compared to many other pollutants, has two immediate consequences: cutbacks imposed in phase I – and under discussion for phase II – have been small; and prices have been volatile. Cutbacks in phase I of EU ETS amounted to about 1% of projected needs, contrasting, for example, with the US SO_2 programme, which involved cutbacks over 50% of historical emissions, and additional reductions later.

The evolution of prices is illustrated in Figure 2. In the few months after its launch, prices, initially around €10/tCO_2, rose to unexpectedly high levels. This was due to two main factors: European Commission resistance to larger allocations in some outstanding disputes with Member States; and soaring gas prices that drove electricity production back to coal and raised the CO_2 price that would be required to reverse this. After tracking the coal–gas price differential up to close to €30/tCO_2, prices decoupled from gas prices and varied in the range €20–30/tCO_2, as emitters focused on other opportunities, before crashing in Spring 2006.

The price crash occurred as data on actual 2005 verified emissions were released, and this displays the extreme sensitivity arising from the small cutbacks of EU ETS allocations. Figure 3 shows the actual emissions,[5] compared to the corresponding initial allocations, and a few different estimates made by market analysts. Even as late as Spring 2006, there were retrospective estimates from a leading provider of market intelligence that turned out to be completely wrong. The uncertainty in projections upon which NAPs had originally been based was, of course, far wider.

Some excess of allocations over verified emissions, which led to the large price reductions, was predictable.[6] Moreover, as indicated, the higher gas prices shifted some power generation back from gas to coal-based operation, *increasing* emissions compared to initial power sector projections. Thus the error, and the excess of allocations, could easily have been bigger, and this was the case in most other sectors. Both evidence and theory suggest that projection-based targets and allocations tend to be biased upwards.[7]

The key difference between the EU ETS and other trading programmes is that the *cutbacks negotiated have been well within the range of projection uncertainty*. This inevitably creates price volatility if, as has been the case before, emissions turn out to be lower than the projected basis upon which allocations are made.

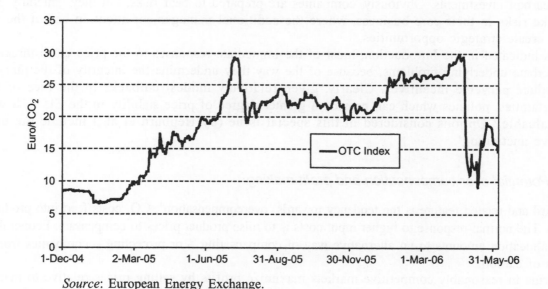

Source: European Energy Exchange.

Figure 2. EU ETS trading prices from Dec 2004 to May 2006.

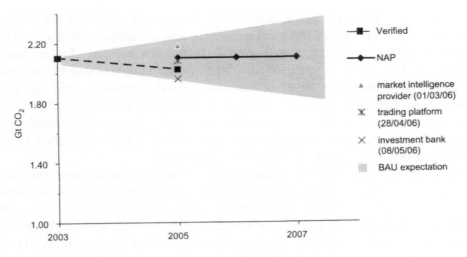

Figure 3. Uncertainty of emission projections from installations covered by the
EU ETS. The chart shows best estimates of total CO_2 emissions from EU ETS
sectors in 2003 and 2005 (connected by dotted line), compared to allocations
(flat line 2005–2007), and two estimates of 2005 emissions provided by market
analysts in the months leading up to the release of the verified emission data.
The shaded area indicates a plausible range of uncertainty in emission
projections for the phase I period at the time of initial allocation decisions.

Price volatility carries a cost. Difficulties in predicting future allowance prices are delaying
investment decisions. By waiting, a company can gain more knowledge about future CO_2 prices,
and thereby make better decisions. Furthermore, in the presence of price uncertainty, risk aversion
is also likely to reduce investment.[8] The risk of low CO_2 prices represents a significant hurdle for
low-carbon investments. Obviously, companies are prepared to bear risks, but they generally prefer
to take risks in their core business, where the additional management attention can at the same
time create strategic opportunities.

As indicated in the Introduction, most of the immediate responses to the price crash threaten to
exacerbate underlying problems, because of the way they undermine the integrity of the market or
introduce perverse incentives. Clearly, given relatively modest cutbacks in the face of large
uncertainties, policies which can provide a greater degree of price stability in the EU ETS would
be valuable.[9] Options considered in this special issue (by Hepburn et al.,) include the use of
'active auctioning'.

A3. Potential over-compensation and profit-making

A third and related feature is the tendency towards 'overcompensation'. CO_2 costs feed into production
costs. The normal response to higher input costs is to raise product prices to compensate. Economically,
free allocation amounts to an alternative way of compensating – or protecting – companies from the
costs of carbon.

Firms in reasonably competitive markets maximize profits by setting prices relative to marginal
cost of production. These marginal costs now include opportunity costs of CO_2 allowances, even
if allowances are received for free – in which case there is potential 'double compensation'. This

creates the potential to make substantial profits, as found in the modelling studies in this issue by Smale et al., and analysed more fully for electricity by Sijm et al. and for cement by Demailly and Quirion.

The empirical situation is mixed (Sijm et al., this issue). In countries with liberalized power markets, generators have passed through most of the opportunity costs, as expected, with aggregate profits totalling billions of euros. There are notable exceptions, including France and Spain, where the retail price levels are set by government contracts or regulation.[10] However, whilst consumers may welcome such protection from the real costs of CO_2, all these approaches create distortions that can prevent entry from third parties and undermine the intended incentives for companies to reduce CO_2 emissions and for consumers to reduce electricity consumption.

In other sectors, pricing responses may be influenced by competition from outside Europe. This is not an 'all or nothing' constraint: if firms maximize profits, they will still generally pass through much of the opportunity cost, making profits at the risk of some loss of market share (Smale et al., this issue). Granting free allocations is thus highly imperfect as a protection against foreign competition: companies still face the full costs in their marginal production decisions. In most products, the price rise required to recoup the net exposure (NVAS) alone is trivial (Carbon Trust, 2004; Grubb et al., 2006); the marginal cost incentive is to go beyond this, and firms will end up both making profits from the system and losing some market share.

The more robust justification for free allocation is that it compensates existing assets for the impact of environmental regulation that was not foreseen at the time of construction. This interpretation would create clear criteria for the amount and basis for allocation, and indicate that free allocation is part of a transitional process towards a strategic objective of fully internalizing CO_2 costs.

Free allocation of allowances probably qualifies as State aid under the State Aids Directive (Johnston, this issue). Countries may thus have to make State aid declarations (otherwise, allocations could be challenged in national courts). State aid could be justified as a compensation for forgone profits due to the environmental regulation, but in this situation the proportionality principle applies – the amount of State aid should be proportional to the forgone profit. To the extent that profits may be deemed to amount to excessive compensation, this may create considerable legal pressures to reduce the scale of free allocations.

Free allocation can distort incentives. If installations cease to receive free allowances when they close, the withdrawal of over-compensation creates a perverse incentive to keep inefficient facilities operational.

If the objective of free allocation is to compensate existing assets for the impact of new regulation, it should not be required for new entrants. In practice, most governments set aside free 'new entrant reserves', which economically amount to an investment subsidy. If the volume were unlimited, such subsidies might reduce the product price – which may be part of the aim, but is not actually achieved.[11] Governments use NERs to help support new construction, but giving free allowances in proportion to the carbon intensity of new plants, can bias the incentive towards more carbon-intensive investments (Neuhoff et al., this issue). When projected forwards, such distortions are amplified by the multi-period nature of the EU ETS, to which we now turn.

A4. The multi-period nature of the EU ETS

The repeated negotiations of allocations for subsequent periods create additional challenges for the European emission trading scheme. CO_2 budgets and allowance allocations are only determined for a limited time period, initially 3 and 5 years. Even beyond 2012, the need for flexibility to adapt to learning in both climate change science and mitigation may make it difficult to commit credibly to much longer allocation periods. The complications of international negotiations put further constraints on such commitments.

As indicated above (and see note 9), uncertainty about the future carries a cost, and early clarity about post-2012 continuation would be valuable. The rules surrounding future allocations, however, need to address a number of issues arising from the potential incentives surrounding multi-period allocations.

In negotiating allocation plans for future periods, governments will inevitably find it hard to ignore the latest information on emissions. For example, upon releasing the verified emissions data for 2005, the European Commission suggested that these should be considered in allocation plans for the period 2008–2012. Yet, such 'updating' creates a potential problem, sometimes known as the 'early action problem': if free allocations continue and industries expect future allocations to reflect recent emissions, this undermines the incentive to reduce emissions now.

This is the strongest case of the 'updating' problem. In fact, there are a range of periodic allocation options which introduce different degrees of perverse incentives, as illustrated in a 'pyramid of potential distortions' (Table 1, also see Neuhoff et al., this issue). This illustrates how the distortions

Table 1. Effect of allocation methods to power sector incumbents

	Impacts	More expenditure on extending plant life relative to new build		Increase plant operation		Less energy efficiency investments
Allowance allocation method	**Distortions**	Discourage plant closure	Distortion biased towards higher emitting plant	Shields output (and consumpt-ion) from average carbon cost	Distortion biased towards higher emitting plant	Reduce incentives for energy efficiency investments
Auction						
Benchmarking	capacity only	X				
	capacity by fuel/plant type*	X	X			
Updating from previous periods'	output only	Y		X		
	output by fuel/plant type*	X	X	X	X	
	emissions	X	X	X	X	X

Note: X indicates a direct distortion arising from the allocation rule. Y indicates indirect distortions if allocation is not purely proportional to output/emissions.
* Differentiating by plant type adds additional distortions compared to purely fuel-based distinctions.

increase when moving from auctions (top) to allowance allocation based on historic emissions (bottom). With equal allowances allocated per unit of installed capacity (uniform benchmark, capacity-based), only the closure of inefficient plants is discouraged.[12] The distortion can be stronger if the allocation differs according to fuel type or production process, so that higher-emitting plant types (per unit output) get more allowances. These incentives refer to incumbents, but if the previous period's new entrants expect to receive the same free allocations as incumbents in subsequent periods, these distortions may transfer to the actual investment decision, with the potential for particularly perverse consequences.[13] Allocating allowances in relation to historic production (e.g. of electricity) creates different distortions, this time in relation to plant operation and pricing, but may reduce some of those associated with closure and new entrant rules.[14]

Phase I allocations were, and phase II are expected to be, mainly related to historic CO_2 emissions. If companies expect a continuation of this approach, then in addition to the above distortions, the incentive for companies to improve the energy efficiency of existing or new plants is reduced.

All these effects are created by the expectations about allocation for the period post-2012. Committing to less distortionary methods would reduce adverse impacts, and starting to use such approaches during phase II would make this more credible. All distortions can be reduced if governments credibly commit to reducing the free allowance allocation related to historic data or existence of installation.

Note that these incentives apply to methodologies at *facility level*. Where countries separate aggregate emission allocations from the way they are distributed between facilities, the incentive effects need to be distinguished. For example, taking account of recent emissions in setting aggregate national or sector caps may introduce no operational distortions if the allocations to individual facilities are done on an entirely different basis – but the disjuncture may exacerbate distributional tensions.

Finally, some of the potential difficulties in allocation are exacerbated by the lack of harmonization, if a sector in one country can plausibly argue that the methodology adopted in another is more favourable. We now consider this final characteristic of the EU ETS.

A5. Devolution of allocation responsibilities

The final way in which the EU ETS differs from many other trading systems is in the devolution of allocation responsibilities, in this case to its 25 Member States. This was an essential part of the deal that enabled the adoption of the Directive: Member States would never have ceded to the European Commission the power to distribute valuable assets to their industries. Nor is the EU ETS unique in devolving powers of allocation: it is typical in a number of US systems. Moreover, there are different degrees of harmonization, applicable to different aspects of the EU ETS, and the Commission can and does seek to increase the degree of harmonization through guidance notes (del Rio Gonzales, 2006).

Nevertheless, the devolution of allocation responsibilities does cause significant problems. The most notable area is with respect to new-entrant rules, where free allocation forms a subsidy to new investments. This raises the prospect of a 'race to the bottom' as Member States compete to attract investment – though such subsidies are usually at a macroeconomic cost, in this case exacerbated by the need to then cut back emissions more elsewhere in the economy (or to buy international credits) to comply with Kyoto targets.

In practice, competition on broader aspects of the allocation method to incumbents is also problematic. Politics is largely comparative, and claims by one company or sector that it is being treated more severely than its neighbour can create powerful pressures to weaken allocations. If companies can use recent operational data or projected activities to buttress their case for more generous allocations relative to neighbours, this starts to introduce perverse incentives based around efforts to prove why one's own industry is bound to emit more than neighbouring ones. Significant differences between Member States in allocation and expectations can amplify some of the incentive problems indicated above. The European Commission does not have the legal authority to scrutinize allocation at this level beyond the remit of explicit State-aid considerations.

A sense of proportion is vital in this context. The height of the bars in Figure 1 gives a sense of the real sensitivities to allocation differentials. At a carbon price of €15/tCO$_2$, a 5% differential allocation in the iron and steel, or refining and fuels, sectors would represent just 0.25% change in the sector 'value-added'. Only in cement and electricity could the value of a 5% allocation differential potentially approach 1% of value-added; in both cases, this is also small compared with existing price differentials between different parts of Europe, because of transport costs, and tie-line constraints and losses, respectively. Comparative lobbying, and the case for harmonization, needs to be kept in this context.

Part B: The policy implications

During 2006, the EU emissions trading scheme faces practical decisions in two key areas. The first is the allocation plans for the first Kyoto period of 2008–2012. The second is the conduct of a major review, to lay out options for continuing the system post-2012, and to signal how the Directive may evolve in that context. This part of the article addresses these two dimensions.

Considering post-2012 design may appear to be premature, but is likely to be just as important as getting phase II right. Investment decisions now hinge on projected revenue streams out to well beyond 2012; therefore, the decision, nature, and indeed location, of investment in the case of highly tradable goods, may be as much influenced by post-2012 expectations as by phase II allocations. Operational decisions may be distorted to the extent that operators believe that current emissions may influence future allocations. The price of allowances during phase II will be influenced by expectations about the future, both indirectly and directly, because allowances can be banked into the post-2012 period.

Thus the two dimensions are linked. We start by looking at phase II allocations, then address post-2012 options, and conclude by considering linkages and cross-cutting institutional issues. We do not discuss various dimensions already extensively covered in other studies or ongoing processes, such as:[15]

- technical aspects of implementation, accounting rules, financial reporting standards;
- extension of ETS to cover other sectors, both within industry and others such as transport[16];
- the small installation limit, notably the debate about whether the present 20 MW threshold should be raised in order to reduce transaction costs.[17]

These are important issues, but our focus is upon allocation and competitiveness, and associated issues around price.

B1. Allocation for phase II

The context for phase II allocations: the international dimension

With the Directive as it stands, the allocation *method* is entirely in the hands of Member States, subject to the constraint that governments must give at least 90% of allowances out for free and respect the relevant criteria under the EU ETS Directive. Unlike phase I, they will, however, be making decisions in the context of Kyoto commitments, and using experience from phase I. This involves the knowledge that in countries with competitive markets, the power and potentially other sectors have been profiting from their free allowance allocation. Forecasts for most sectors, particularly outside electricity, have been revealed to have an upward bias, consistent with previous experience of allocation-related negotiations. The sensitivity of power sector emissions to gas prices increased the volatility of CO_2 prices, and this linkage is unlikely to vanish in the coming years.

This suggests that the expected balance of supply and demand, and associated uncertainties, should be an important consideration for phase II NAPs. This must include the potential for credits generated internationally through the Kyoto Protocol mechanisms. The high ETS prices in 2005 led to a surge of investment in projects intended to generate emission reduction credits, particularly through emission-reducing investments in developing countries under the Clean Development Mechanism (CDM). As of March 2006, the projects officially registered or submitted for verification or registration would generate some 825 Mt CO_2-equivalent up to 2012. Box 2 sets out international projections, which indicate a scale of external supply of Kyoto units that would be looking for buyers. This on its own makes sustained high prices during the phase II of the EU ETS period implausible.

Against this background, our analysis leads to conclusions about phase II allocation in three main areas.

Scale of allocation/cutbacks

It is fundamental to understanding the EU ETS that the 'caps' combine with 'trading'. Fears that reducing the free allowance allocation would restrain the ability of companies to produce are misplaced: allowances are freely traded, and companies can acquire additional allowances in the market from three different sources. First, some companies may be able to reduce emissions below their allocation and thus sell surplus allowances. Second, the European Commission currently envisages that up to 8% of allowances can be imported into the European emissions trading scheme from JI and CDM projects. Third, in phase II, governments can auction up to 10% of all allowances. Cutting back on free allowance allocation does not therefore translate directly into a cutback of feasible emissions or output; it simply helps to establish the price and incentives that companies face to undertake cost-effective emissions abatement. In principle, free allocation is a temporary derogation from bearing the full costs of CO_2 emissions.

Recognizing this and the wider context set out above, we reach the following conclusions about phase II allocation.

(i) All sectors should receive less free allowances than projected 'business-as-usual' needs

The evidence that basing allocations on projected 'business-as-usual (BaU) emissions' leads to an inflation of emission projections is consistent, overwhelming, and readily explicable (see above). The recent market collapse is proof either that projections were inflated, or that companies found it far easier than expected to reduce emissions – probably a combination of both.

Box 2. International supply and demand of emission credits and allowances

International project credits. CDM projects already submitted by March 2006 project emission saving credits of 825 $MtCO_2$eq up to 2012; some may not proceed but most are already significantly developed, and of course many more could yet be submitted. Climate Strategies estimates of likely credits available from the CDM span 680–1200 $MtCO_2$ for the Kyoto first period. The contribution of Joint Implementation projects in eastern Europe is more uncertain because the institutions were only set up in December 2005; Climate Strategies estimates span 120–980 $MtCO_2$. The combined projections are a little lower than those of one of the major market analysts, PointCarbon (1000–3000 $MtCO_2$eq); see the table below.

Surplus Kyoto allowances. The potential supply of surplus Kyoto allowances available from eastern Europe (including the new EU states, Russia, and Ukraine), without the need for specific projects, is much bigger (3000–8000 $MtCO_2$eq). The amount made available on terms attractive to potential buyers is subject to political uncertainty.

Supply-demand balance. Japan is likely to need 250–1000 $MtCO_2$ imports to comply with its Kyoto obligations, some of which would be drawn from allowance trading; Canada could also compete but with less certainty. Thus the Kyoto system has a supply of project-based credits already in the pipeline (officially or unofficially) that is likely to substantially exceed non-EU demand, plus a large 'buffer' of surplus Kyoto allowances potentially available. For more detailed discussion and data see workshop report. This will inevitably tend to limit EU ETS prices during the Kyoto period.

	LOW	HIGH
SUPPLY		
CC-Perspectives/Climate Strategies estimates (a)		
Clean Development Mechanism (CERS)	680	1200
Joint Implementation (ERUs)	120	980
Total emission credits	**800**	**2200**
PointCarbon estimates (b)	**1000**	**3000**
Potential supply of AAUs	<1000–3000(a)	8000(b)
NON-EU SOURCES OF DEMAND		
Japan	250	1000
(Canada*)	(700)*	(1300)*

(a) CDM estimates by CC-Perspectives based upon registered projects; CDM and JI estimates debated and adjusted for likely attrition through registration process at Climate Strategies workshop on Kyoto implementation, *http://www.ukerc.ac.uk/content/view/231/115*.

(b) Estimates by PointCarbon presented by Kristian Tangen at PointCarbon conference, Copenhagen, March 2006, *www.pointcarbon.com*.

*Note: Canada could have demand comparable to Japan, but the new government has raised serious questions about its willingness to trade internationally, although it does not have a parliamentary majority anywhere near sufficient to withdraw from the Kyoto Protocol. All figures are cumulative, thus a range of 1000–2000 $MtCO_2$ in project credits corresponds to 200–400 $MtCO_2$/yr over the Kyoto first period.

The psychology of negotiations that give any sector everything that it projects that it would emit, without any CO_2 constraint, places an unhealthy emphasis on lobbying around emission forecasts, which are inherently uncertain, and is a fundamentally unsustainable way of approaching allocations in future periods (see below). Moreover, it risks fostering a focus on compliance without optimization, and creates incentives to highlight the difficulties of mitigation rather than to assess objectively the full range of options (Hepburn et al., this issue). A credible case can be made that giving any sector all that it projects would be emitted under BaU (if defined as if there were no CO_2 problem or policy) fundamentally undermines the motivation to cut emissions and could also be challenged under the EC State-aid rules (Johnston, this issue).

Modest cutbacks carry no significant implications for competitiveness. The 'value at stake' involved in a 10% cutback is about 1% of present sector value-added for cement and electricity, and around 0.2–0.4% for steel and refining (Figure 1: see notes on underlying price assumptions). If the companies maximize profits, competitiveness is about their pricing strategy as influenced by the cost of carbon, not by their allocation, and most of these sectors could be expected to continue to profit even under considerably stronger cutbacks (as explained and demonstrated for the core ETS sectors for cutbacks up to 30% by Smale et al., this issue). In most cases, modest cutbacks would reduce the scale of the profits they can expect to derive as a result of the EU ETS, with no other significant implications for pricing or competitiveness.[18]

(ii) Free allocations to the electricity sector should be cut back by more than other sectors
In the light of the scale of profits made by the electricity-generating sector in countries with competitive markets (empirical evidence set out in Sijm et al., this issue), this proposition is now more widely accepted. The electricity sector is barely exposed to foreign competition and, unlike other sectors, it does not face electricity price increases in inputs. In countries with competitive markets, greater cutbacks for the power sector have no direct implications for other sectors, since the price is predominantly set by the opportunity cost of carbon, not by the profit/loss balance of power generators.

Of the total 2.2 Gt CO_2/year emissions covered by the EU ETS overall, the power sector currently accounts for around 60%. To illustrate the potential magnitudes involved, *after* allowing for forecasting errors:[19]

- a 20% cutback in free allocations to the power sector would generate a 'potential' demand (i.e. relative to 'no control' emissions with no emissions abatement) of about 260 Mt CO_2/year;
- a 5% cutback to other sectors on the same basis, about another 45 Mt CO_2/year.

A maximum 10% of auctioning would make around 210 Mt CO_2/year available through auctions, out of a total allocated of 2100 Mt CO_2. The overall shortfall – to be met through emissions abatement (e.g. fuel switching end-use efficiency in the power sector) and international purchase – would then still be only around 100 Mt CO_2/year, close to the revealed surplus in 2005 and much smaller than the lowest estimates of the total supply of Kyoto project credits.

Method of allocation and new entrant rules
Allocating allowances for the period 2008–2012 to existing facilities based on historic emissions does not in itself create any adverse incentives. However, if companies expect that the allocation for the period post-2012 will be based on their emissions in the coming years, then this distorts their operational and investment decisions – for example, deterring early action. If free allowance

allocation is phased out rapidly post-2012, then this is less of an issue. Otherwise benchmarks based on installed capacity or historic output also reduce distortions. Greater use of benchmarking in individual sectors or countries in phase II could both inform future allowance allocation and signal commitment to these policies.

Giving free allowances to new entrants is being widely considered to help boost new investment, for example to support the security of supply objectives or reduce impacts of CO_2 allowance prices on the electricity price. New entrant reserves should be based on output or capacity, and avoid differentiating according to the CO_2-intensity of the new investment. In particular, giving more to coal than gas plants rewards investment in new coal facilities, which would conflict with objectives to tackle climate change, increase the cost of future emission reductions, and in the long run could lead to higher electricity prices. The damaging effects would be amplified if carbon-intensive new entrants not only receive free allowances for the period 2008–2012 but also receive promises for subsequent periods. This could also undermine various options that governments have to implement European and international solutions to address longer-term competitiveness issues and emission spillovers, as discussed below.

This suggests a sharp contrast between the methods appropriate for incumbents, and those for new entrants. Differentiating allocations to incumbents based on their carbon intensity avoids a large redistribution of rents associated with existing assets; politically, it is unavoidable and does not in itself distort the efficiency of the system, provided the practice is phased out over successive periods. Differentiating allocations to new entrants based on their carbon intensity has no such defence, runs counter to the objectives of the system, and builds up trouble for the future by failing to encourage low-carbon investments.

Price stability and auctioning
As noted above, there are inherent reasons why the phase II market may be volatile, and price instability carries a cost. Greater stability in price expectations would reduce risks and increase investment in low-carbon technologies and energy efficiency improvements.

The Directive enables allowances to be banked from phase II into future periods. Economic analysis tends to assume that this will improve price stability, by reducing exposure to short-period variations. However, this conclusion depends upon the stability of expectations for future periods. In practice, the early years of phase II may be a period of intense struggle over the shape and degree of future commitments, with considerable impacts on expectations about future emission reductions and allowance prices. The net effect of banking on price stability is therefore hard to predict, and it is certainly not a panacea. Suggestions that allow 'borrowing' of allowances from future periods would amplify risks and volatility, and introduce additional problems.[20] Strong intertemporal linkages could also make negotiations about future periods even more political and more complicated, as their impact would be felt directly in the current market.

Linkages between periods have some desirable features in principle by allowing for longer-term smoothing of demand and supply shocks, but the solutions to price instability lie elsewhere.

Our analysis suggests, rather, that auctions could be employed to improve stability and investor confidence surrounding CO_2 prices (Hepburn et al., this issue). The key mechanism would be for governments to release some of their allowances through a joint minimum-price auction. The minimum bid level would then act as a price floor (to the extent that the market needed access to the auction). To avoid competition between Member States, they would have to agree the minimum price and basic auction rules, which could be most simply operated by the European Commission, although Member States would retain the revenues. This process would not conflict with the existing terms of the Directive, and there are several familiar, readily available approaches to conducting such auctions (Hepburn et al., this issue).

If the overall allocation is set such that the market requires at least some of these allowances, then this ensures the price will not drop below the agreed minimum bid price. Excessive allocation, or large inflow of cheap allowances from CDM and JI projects, could of course ultimately overwhelm a price floor set in this way, though the 'supplementarity' criteria does also allow member states to limit the inflow into the system (Article 11a of EU Directive on emission trading, amended 27.10.2004).[21]

Some other analysts express the opposite concern, that prices might rise to levels deemed to pose an unacceptable risk to European industry, and that to prevent this risk the system should contain a price cap or 'safety valve' (e.g. Bouttes et al., 2006). Our assessment of phase II, in terms of both supply–demand balance and the economics of competitiveness over the 5-year period, leads us to be sceptical that this is a realistic concern. It is, however, true that a planned response to any such eventuality would be better than a panic-based reaction such as occurred in the California NO_x trading system. Should prices rise to levels that were judged to pose a credible threat to competitiveness of a particular sector, and State-aid rules prevented auction revenues being used to assist it (or the country concerned had not conducted any auctions), the most obvious first step would be to relax supplementarity constraints, and possibly expand the scope of emission credits that could qualify for compliance purposes. We do not consider issues of price ceilings or safety valves beyond this.

B2. Allocation, competitiveness and design post-2012

As indicated above, early clarity about the existence and nature of the system post-2012 would be extremely valuable to the functioning of the EU ETS. Reduced uncertainty post-2012 would enable more efficient investment and thus reduce ongoing CO_2 emissions and prices. This will not be easy to achieve – but it could still be possible and useful to make certain commitments, and to clarify key elements of design, much sooner.

Negotiations on post-2012 quantified commitments in the framework of the Kyoto Protocol were launched by the Montreal Meeting of Parties in December 2005. Rapid progress is not expected, however, not least because of continued non-participation by the USA. The EU ETS Directive is explicitly designed to continue in sequential periods, and the process of examining this in earnest begins with the Review in 2006.

Given the complexity of the issues, combined with the international political situation, a global agreement on post-2012 quantified reduction targets is unlikely before 2009 at the earliest. This is too late to be of much use in assisting efficient investment under the EU ETS: a credible EU commitment and structure to support EU low-carbon investment needs to be established well before then.

Credibility on post-2012 targets therefore requires clarity and commitment to a design that is:

- *effective* in reducing CO_2 emissions to justify continued policy support;
- *efficient*, for example the structure must achieve acceptably low levels of perverse incentives;
- *economically sustainable*, by avoiding adverse competitiveness impacts and emissions leakage;
- *politically sustainable*, by creating a shared perspective in the public sphere and among key industry sectors that the above objectives are achieved.

The European Emission trading scheme has secured political support for a successful start and the creation of an effective and potentially efficient instrument. After five decades of struggle over European energy and environmental affairs, establishing a free trading market across the EU is no small achievement. It has also secured an environment in which there is now unprecedented management attention devoted to CO_2 emissions. However, beyond phase II the EU ETS needs to evolve. Future design needs to avoid the perverse economic incentives that can result from repeated free allowance allocations, and concerns around competitiveness and leakage must be addressed to allow the EU ETS to maintain higher prices over longer periods.

Allocation will in any case have to move away from projection-based approaches for purely pragmatic reasons. Already in phase II negotiations the attempt to estimate 'what emissions would be during 2008–2012 if there were no CO_2 policy or problem' requires complex speculation to unravel what may have already been influenced by climate concerns, a year of high carbon prices, the impact of CO_2 on gas prices and expectations about the future. After five years of operation and investment based on the EU ETS, constructing a 'no carbon policy' projection as a baseline for the post-2012 period would be an exercise in fantastic speculation about precisely which investments might have been 'attributable' to climate policy, and trying to unravel them and guess what might have happened instead, and then project the implications forward. It is a wholly impractical basis for the long term – consistent with the view that phase II is essentially a transitional period towards a better-grounded and more durable approach.

In principle, the two simplest approaches to maximizing the internal effectiveness and efficiency of the scheme are rapidly to phase out free allocations, or to move to relatively uniform output-based benchmarking of allocations, probably based around the performance of best available technology for the sector.

In either case, the implicit cutbacks probably imply greater use of auctioning. As argued above, this has distributional and State-aid benefits, and could be used in ways that help to stabilize prices, and potentially to support longer term price signalling. This in turn can underpin low-carbon investments directly through greater price security, and also potentially by using auction revenues to support longer term investment instruments (Hepburn et al., this issue).

However, rapidly reducing free allocations may be politically very difficult, and benchmarking is generally far more complex than it appears because of the variety of installation types, processes and products; and neither *in itself* offers ready protection against competitiveness and leakage concerns. If the EU ETS is to be sustained over long periods, and potentially at high carbon prices, we see three main avenues that have the potential to meet all the criteria:

• *International agreement(s)*, covering all major competitors, to implement policies that reflect CO_2 costs in product prices of energy-intensive, internationally mobile goods. Note that fully global participation may not be required, either in terms of countries or sectors: protecting EU industry under the EU ETS may only require agreement involving the principal competing nations covering the core sectors of aluminium, cement, iron and steel, refineries, and perhaps some chemical products.[22] Agreement to reflect CO_2 costs in electricity generation would also be desirable because of its downstream impacts. In theory, agreements with sector organizations themselves could be considered, but the absence of any precedents or institutional authorities for such an agreement would make it highly problematic (Kulovesi and Keinänen, 2006). The more serious proposals for sectoral agreements have focused upon governmental commitments, albeit in consultation with their industries (Schmidt and Helme, 2006).

- *Use of border-tax adjustments* to compensate industry producing in regions with high CO_2 costs for these costs when exporting, with a symmetric tariff being applied to imports. Thus the combination of a stringent emissions policy with border-tax adjustment need not discriminate against industry in either region. The flexibility of WTO rules could be explored to ensure that industry in regions controlling CO_2 are not disadvantaged, though this would probably require the use of auctioning rather than free allocation to allow compensation for average costs incurred (Hepburn et al., this issue). Again, this need not be a universal approach, but rather one addressed to the specific sectors where there may be valid concerns.

- If these two approaches cannot be implemented, the EU ETS could still be continued by enabling *output-indexed allocation*. Sectors exposed to international competition could receive CO_2 allowances in proportion to output (output- or intensity-based allocation). Demailly and Quirion (this issue) illustrate how this would avoid both leakage and profiting from the EU ETS by the EU cement industry. This would require either 'ex-post', or at least 'within-period', adjustments. The current Directive precludes such allocation for good reasons. Fully output-indexed allocation would require retrospective adjustments to allocations, and would shield product prices from the real costs of CO_2. Along with removing the scope for sectors to profit from the EU ETS price impacts, by removing the costs of CO_2 from product prices this would remove incentives for product substitution as means for CO_2 abatement. Within-period adjustments, that update allocations based on recent output, would have similar but less extreme effects. In macroeconomic terms these approaches would thus be less efficient, but would maintain the incentive for individual sectors to reduce the carbon intensity of their operations, and thus protect the value of low-carbon investments within the EU ETS sectors whilst avoiding competitiveness problems. The detailed provisions required for any such allocation are tailored for existing products and processes and thus create barriers for the use of innovative solutions for energy efficiency and low carbon technologies.

In practice, the EU may not face a straight choice between these three options. Where effective sectoral agreements can be secured, these are probably the best first choice; but they are unlikely to be easy or quick to negotiate, and may come down to focusing on particular products or subsector markets. Border tax adjustments, similarly, are unlikely to be 'all or nothing'. They would instead be considered in the context of particular industries and products, where a valid case for competitiveness concern was raised, and for which other solutions appeared inappropriate. Output-indexed allocations, similarly, could be considered in some cases, but the more widespread their adoption, the more deleterious would be the impact on the macroeconomic efficiency of CO_2 controls.

However, any or all of these options would both avoid competitiveness concerns and protect the security of low-carbon investments in the EU ETS sectors. Thus it is neither possible, nor necessary, for the EU to choose between them now. Rather, our conclusion is that solutions are available, and that the EU can unambiguously commit to continuing the EU ETS, recognizing that three avenues are available to support this decision in the event of failure to secure a truly global agreement. The next few years can then be used to engage industry and other stakeholders in dialogue about which would be the most appropriate avenue to follow, perhaps on a case-by-case basis, given the limited number of sectors at stake.

B3. Implications of post-2012 options for phase II and the Directive

We conclude our analysis by considering briefly the implications of this analysis in relation to phase II, the EU ETS Directive, and related institutional considerations.

All three of the options above for long-term design would probably require amendments to the EU ETS Directive, or other complex bodies of EU legislation:

- in the case of international sectoral agreements, to accommodate the specifics of such agreements;
- in the case of border-tax adjustments, to implement the necessary tariff legislation;
- in the case of output-indexed allocation, to enable *ex-post* adjustment or within-period updating based upon industry output.

These observations raise the question of whether such measures, and associated amendment, should be considered for phase II. We unambiguously conclude not, for two strong reasons.

First, the economic analysis in our studies underlines that competitiveness is primarily a *strategic* issue, not an *immediate* one. Most participating sectors can expect to profit from the EU ETS in phase II: but those for which this involves significant price rises on internationally traded products may start to see erosion of exports, and/or import penetration into domestic markets, if product price impacts are high enough and sustained (Demailly and Quirion, this issue; Smale et al., this issue). Similarly, decisions on the location of major investment by multinational companies will not be made primarily on the basis of carbon costs to 2012: they will be based on strategic evaluation of the costs and benefits of locating in different regions over periods of decades (Grubb et al., 2006). Indeed, phase II could be considered as a transitional period in which the profits accruing to several sectors as a result of free allocations could be used to build up investment in low-carbon technologies and associated expertise, enhancing their position for a carbon-constrained world.

Second, the changes that may be required for post-2012 continuation are all complex. Sectoral agreements would require extensive international negotiation; so, in practice, would any sensible approach to border tax adjustments. Even output-indexed allocation would require extensive redesign of trading markets and evaluation of the appropriate basis to be used. Moreover, the sectors are not homogeneous and the EU does not have homogeneous industries; on the contrary, diversity of products, processes, and national circumstances is the norm when these sectors are examined more closely (Grubb et al., 2006). Any attempt to reopen the Directive to make such adjustments quickly for phase II would rapidly risk unravelling. The only possible exception might be for adjustments driven by, and confined to, the explicit legal basis of State-aid considerations – which itself allows for the continuation of existing arrangements while alternatives are developed (Johnston, this issue).

Indeed, the relative simplicity of the system as it stands, and the flexibility it gives to Member States, should to some degree be considered as an opportunity for experimentation. For example, benchmarked allocations in a range of sectors *may* be an attractive approach for the longer term; but this is far from certain, given the complexities. If phase I was mainly about establishing the market, phase II offers the chance for national experimentation with some of these allocation possibilities.

There is one significant caveat to this. Allocations during phase II should not create promises about allocations post-2012 that foster inefficiency, or undermine the options post-2012. The risk of perverse incentives arising from expectations about continued free allocation has already been illustrated (and detailed in Neuhoff et al., this issue). Moreover, WTO law (and arguably EC State-aid law) may allow border-tax adjustments that compensate for actual costs incurred, but not for opportunity costs; consequently they may be most effective in combination with very limited or no free allowance allocation. Output-indexed allocation might offer free allowances, but not against a historic baseline or an *ex-ante* commitment. For phase II this is relevant if countries make promises about future allocations, for example in the context of new entrants. This not only risks the distortions already indicated; it could also undermine Europe's scope to evolve the EU ETS to a system that uses sound economic principles to secure efficient emission reductions whilst avoiding competitiveness distortions.

Finally, managing the future allocation of allowances, which will be increasingly valuable at higher carbon prices over time, will require stronger institutional foundations. Allocations designed to compensate sectors for average costs incurred would require far more sophisticated approaches than are currently being considered, which might have to be differentiated much more according to specific sectoral characteristics. Long-term credibility is crucial; yet greater sectoral differentiation of approaches could make it even harder to resist pressures to tweak allocations for short-term political convenience. There may also be more need to harmonize allocation methods across Europe. Faced with these conflicting pressures, governments may need to learn from monetary policy, in which the need for credibility of commitments to tackle inflation led to the establishment of independent central banks with clear mandates, and ultimately the creation of the European Central Bank (see Helm et al., 2003). Establishing a long-term, clear and credible foundation for allocating allowances under the EU ETS, and managing its diverse international linkages, could require thinking of a similar order.

The EU ETS is a remarkable achievement. Current debates, in the light of the first verification results, the allocations for phase II, and the launch of the Review for phase III, offer important windows of opportunity to improve the scheme for both phase II and beyond. Member States need to look beyond the immediate short-term pressures of allocation negotiations, and seize the opportunities on offer.

Acknowledgements

Climate Strategies would like to express its sincere gratitude to the following organisations for sponsoring and supporting this study: The Carbon Trust; Department of Trade and Industry, UK; Department for Environment, Food and Rural Affairs, UK; Ministry of Economy, Netherlands; BP; and Ministry of Sustainable Development, Sweden. Financial support from the UK research council under grant TSEC is also gratefully acknowledged.

For more information about Climate Strategies, the EU Emissions Trading Scheme study and work on national implementation, contact: Beverley Darkin, Convenor, Climate Strategies & Senior Research Fellow, Chatham House, *bdarkin@chathamhouse.org.uk*, tel: + 44 (0)20 7957 5741.

Notes

1   CO_2 – 2.2 billion tonnes of annual CO_2 emissions in phase I (EC, 2005), at prices between €10 to €30/tCO_2. SO_2 10 million t at \$270–850/short ton, NO_x East Coast, 640,000 t at \$2000/short ton.

2   Note that this is a complementary treatment to that presented in the Carbon Trust analysis (Carbon Trust, 2004) which focused on the variation in value at stake for a range of electricity price pass-through and a modest range of allocation cutbacks (0–10%). The intent in Figure 1 is also to give an insight into the marginal cost impacts that can drive imports under profit-maximizing behaviour. In addition, the chart in Carbon Trust (2004) was indexed on total sector turnover, rather than value-added.

3   If the marginal carbon intensity equals the average carbon intensity, the MVAS as indicated here is equal to the marginal cost divided by the sector value-added per unit output. In most sectors, in most countries, there is not much divergence between the marginal and average carbon intensity.

4   Sectors outside of the EU ETS would face the cost impact at the bottom of each bar (electricity price exposure) and an equivalent incentive to change the price of their products; there would be no divergence between average and marginal/ opportunity costs, and no resulting scope for profiting from such divergence.

5   Based on preliminary data from the EC for verified emissions for 21 of the 25 countries covered by the EU ETS, released on 15 May 2006. It is assumed that Poland, the main unknown, has an 18% excess allocation, similar to Hungary and the Czech Republic. The data suggest that market was 86 $MtCO_2$ (long) in 2005. See the article on auctioning (Hepburn et al., this issue).

6.   And indeed had been predicted on the basis of simple aggregate trend statistics and the experience with previous target-based systems such as the UK ETS and Climate Change Agreements (Grubb et al., 2005).

7.   This is for three reasons. First, business, like the rest of humanity, tends towards optimism. No business sets out its store based upon pessimism, contraction, or projected failure. Second, linking allocations to projected needs creates a huge incentive for businesses to inflate forecasts. Third, assumptions that cutting emissions would take time and capital underestimate the scope for some basic housekeeping measures: companies 'don't know what they don't know' about mitigation possibilities until they find out.

8   These are classic results of real option theory. See Baldursson and von der Fehr (2004) for a more sophisticated discussion of this issue.

9   Obviously industry is exposed to volatile prices for many other input factors, but if all producers use similar technologies, then they can pass on changes in input prices to product prices. In contrast, if two competing technologies, e.g. with different levels of energy efficiency, can be used to manufacture the same product, then cost differences that only affect one technology are more difficult to pass to the product price. Risk-averse investors then prefer the solution with lower capital costs – which is usually not the energy-efficient approach. Reducing uncertainty about post-2012 can thus accelerate investment in low-carbon technologies, reducing emissions and CO_2 allowance prices.

10   In these countries, domestic bills are not affected despite an increase in wholesale price levels, and the vertically integrated companies cross-subsidize their retail costs with the profits from the free allocation. In other countries, dominant power generators might anticipate government intervention and thus refrain from passing on CO_2 opportunity costs to wholesale price levels.

11   The amounts available in most allocation plans are limited, and the response of new construction too slow; and once operational, carbon-intensive new entrants face the same incentive as incumbents to factor-in opportunity costs of production.

12   Of course, discouraging closure might be considered as an aim of policy, particularly in the power sector, where many European countries are worried about adequacy of generating capacity. But it is using the ETS for purposes – to implicitly support extending plant lifetimes – contrary to that for which it was designed, and such extension could be at the expense of new investment in lower emitting plant.

13   The modelling studies of Neuhoff et al. (this issue) include an example where technology-specific new entrant reserves, extended into technology-specific incumbent free allocations in future periods, result in coal plants being constructed that would not have been economic in the absence of the EU ETS.

14   An allocation that is not differentiated between different fuel types (uniform benchmark, output-based) reduces opportunity costs of emitting CO_2 and thus reduces the impact on the product price. This reduces incentives to substitute less CO_2-intensive products, e.g. from cement to wood as a building material, or from electricity consumption to investment in energy efficiency; but there is not an incentive to keep plants operating above some minimum threshold purely to get allowances. If such 'output-based updating' allowance allocation is differentiated between production processes and fuel types, then additional distortions create an incentive to increase operation of more CO_2-intensive fuels and production processes.

15   See also the forthcoming ECP Report No. 2: The EU ETS: Taking Stock and Looking Ahead [available at http://www.ceps .org/].

16   This issue was a major focus of the LETS study, 'LIFE Emissions Trading Scheme' (AEA Technology Environment, Ecofys UK et al., 2006). This concluded that the EU ETS coverage could readily be expanded to include CO_2 from some chemical sectors (production of ammonia, fertilizers and petrochemicals); methane from coal mines; and CO_2 and PFCs from aluminium production. These would increase emissions coverage of the EU ETS by about 9%, resulting in it covering almost exactly half of EU total CO_2 emissions. Overall, however, 'there is limited scope for modifying the current Directive to include additional sectors and gases in the scheme for practical reasons. Many sectors either consist of a large number of small emitters or their emissions are too uncertain. Other measures may be more appropriate for tackling emissions from these sectors.'

17 Whilst the wider political debate is calling for more sources (such as aviation) to be included, the debate within the EU ETS is about precisely the opposite: whether the 20 MW threshold for small facilities has been set too low, causing high administrative costs across thousands of installations that contribute only a small fraction of the total emissions covered (e.g. Schleich and Betz, 2004).

18 The only exception would be where energy-intensive operations engage in 'limit pricing' designed explicitly to exclude foreign competition in the most exposed markets, rather than seeking to maximize overall profits, i.e. where companies already cross-subsidize operations to exclude cheaper imports. Even cement, with by far the highest relative 'value at stake', the magnitudes are not large compared with the present costs and with integrated cement companies, the profits accruing to the more shielded inland cement operations would more than fund continuation of such cross-subsidy if the companies choose to adopt that strategy over the phase II period (see Demailly and Quirion, this issue).

19 If the upward bias of aggregate forecasts over the period were estimated to be 5%, for example, the corresponding cutbacks relative to these forecasts would be about 25% and 10%, respectively.

20 In addition to uncertainty about future prices, this would inject into the phase II market uncertainties about the terms of borrowing from future periods that do not yet exist, against allocations that are not yet defined, with no legal clarity around penalties for non-compliance in future periods, and with much scope for lobbying future allocations based upon the size of the 'debt' accumulated.

21 For example, the German draft NAP2 allocation plan indicates a limit on imports of 12% of allocation (Draft NAP, and statement by Jurgen Landgrebe indicating he expected this limit to remain, cited in Point Carbon 02 June 06.

22 Nor, in fact, is the converse true: a global agreement on national CO_2 targets would not necessarily protect industrial competitiveness, if other countries sought to meet their targets through action on domestic or transport sectors whilst still protecting their internationally mobile industries from CO_2 costs. This further strengthens the case for designing the ETS to be viable for the long term in ways that do not hinge upon an all-encompassing global agreement.

References in Climate Policy Special Issue, Volume 6(1) Allocation and Competitiveness in the EU ETS

Demailly, D., Quirion, P., 2006. CO_2 abatement, competitiveness and leakage in the European cement industry under the EU ETS: grandfathering versus output-based allocation. Climate Policy 6(1), 93–113.

Hepburn, C., Grubb, M., Neuhoff, K., Matthes, F., Tse, M., 2006. Auctioning of EU ETS phase II allowances: how and why? Climate Policy 6(1), 137–160.

Johnston, A., 2006. Free allocation of allowances under the EU emissions trading scheme: legal issues. Climate Policy 6(1), 115–136.

Neuhoff, K., Keats Martinez, K., Sato, M., 2006. Allocation, incentives and distortions: the impact of EU ETS emissions allowance allocations to the electricity sector. Climate Policy 6(1), 73–91.

Sijm, J.P.M., Neuhoff, K., Chen, Y., 2006. CO_2 cost pass-through and windfall profits in the power sector. Climate Policy 6(1), 49–72.

Smale, R., Hartley, M., Hepburn, C., Ward, J., Grubb, M., 2006. The impact of CO_2 emissions trading on firm profits and market prices. Climate Policy 6(1), 31–48.

Other references

AEA Technology Environment, Ecofys UK, et al., 2006. A report produced for the LETS Update Partners [retrieved 26 May 2006, from http://www.environment-agency.gov.uk/business/444217/590750/590838/1294204/1295326/1291719/1291949/?version=1&lang=_e].

Baldursson, F.M., von der Fehr, N.-H.M., 2004. Price volatility and risk exposure: on market-based environmental policy instruments. Journal of Environmental Economics and Management 48(1), 682–704.

Bouttes, J.-P., Leban, R., Trochet, J.-M., 2006. A Low Carbon Electricity Scenario: A Contribution to the Energy Policy and Climate Change Debate. DDX-06-10.

Carbon Trust, 2004. The European Emissions Trading System: Implications for Industrial Competitiveness, Carbon Trust, London [available at http://www.carbontrust.co.uk/default.ct].

del Rio Gonzalez, P., 2006. Harmonization versus decentralization in the EU ETS: an economic analysis. Climate Policy 6, forthcoming.

EC, 2005. Further guidance on allocation plans for the 2008 to 2012 trading period of the EU Emission Trading Scheme. European Commission, Brussels.

Grubb, M., Azar, C., Persson, U.M., 2005. Allowance allocation in the European emissions trading system: a commentary. Climate Policy 5(1), 127–136.

Grubb, M., Sato, M., Cust, J., Chan, K.L., Korppoo, A., Ceppi, P., 2006. Differentiation and dynamics of competitiveness impacts from the EU ETS. Climate Policy 6, forthcoming.

Helm, D., Hepburn, C. and Mash, R., 2003. Credible Climate Policy. Oxford Review of Economic Policy 19(3), 438–450.

Kulovesi, K., Keinänen, K., 2006. Long-Term Climate Policy: International Legal Aspects of a Sector-based Approach. Finnish Environment Ministry [available at http://www.ymparisto.fi/download.asp?contentid=29397&lan=fi].

Schleich, J., Betz, R., 2004. EU Emissions trading and transaction costs for small and medium sized companies. Intereconomics/ Review of European Economic Policy 39(3), 121–123.

Schmidt, J., Helme, N., 2006. Sector-based approach to the post-2012 climate change policy architecture. Climate Policy 6, forthcoming.

The impact of CO$_2$ emissions trading on firm profits and market prices

Robin Smale[1]*, Murray Hartley[2], Cameron Hepburn[3], John Ward[2], Michael Grubb[4]

[1] Vivid Economics, The Old Dairy, 13B Hewer Street, London W10 6DU, UK
[2] Oxera Consulting Ltd, 40/41 Park End Street, Oxford OX1 1JD, UK
[3] St Hugh's College, Oxford University, St Margaret's Road, Oxford OX2 6LE, UK
[4] Faculty of Economics, Cambridge University, Sidgwick Avenue, Cambridge CB3 9DD, UK

Abstract

The introduction of mandatory controls and a trading scheme covering approximately half of all carbon dioxide emissions across Europe has triggered a debate about the impact of emissions trading on the competitiveness of European industry. Economic theory suggests that, in many sectors, businesses will pass on costs to customers and make net profits due to the impact on product prices combined with the extensive free allocations of allowances. This study applies the Cournot representation of an oligopoly market to five energy-intensive sectors: cement, newsprint, steel, aluminium and petroleum. By populating the model with empirical data, the results are shown for three future emissions price scenarios. The results encompass the extent of cost pass-through to customers, changes in output, changes in UK market share, and changes in firm profits. The results suggest that most participating sectors would be expected to profit in general, although with a modest loss of market share in the case of steel and cement, and closure in the case of aluminium.

Keywords: Emissions trading; Firm behaviour; Market structure; Competitiveness; Grandfathering; Cournot

1. Introduction

The EU Emission Trading Scheme (EU ETS) has been hotly debated since the publication of the European Commission's Green Paper in 2000 (Commission of the European Communities, 2000). At the forefront of the debate are concerns that:

- by acting unilaterally, the EU's economy might be damaged and its firms might lose out to non-EU firms;
- by allowing Member States to determine allocations of allowances for their industrial sectors, with only broad guidance on harmonizing approaches across the EU, some Member States

* Corresponding author. Tel.: +44-7753-984051
E-mail address: robin_smale@yahoo.co.uk

might use the allocation as a means of state aid, providing their firms with a reserve of cash with which to compete against firms in other EU Member States;
- emission reductions may be limited;
- prices, particularly those paid by household consumers of electricity, will rise.

A public debate has engaged both government and business. UK government ministers have said that the UK's draft National Allocation Plan 'recognises the need to preserve the competitive position of UK industry' (Defra, 2004a), while some industrialists were voicing concern about a threat to UK jobs. Strong differences in views were held at the time, in the first quarter of 2004. More than two years have passed since those early stages of debate, but the question of the impact of emissions trading on the competitiveness of UK firms has not diminished in importance.

In the academic literature, commentators have observed that there are likely to be increased profits from the introduction of emissions trading schemes. This conclusion, which may at first appear counterintuitive, is nevertheless founded upon conventional economic assumptions of profit maximization and the Cournot competition model, discussed below. The underlying reason is that although emission cap-and-trade schemes increase marginal costs, these costs are largely passed on to the consumer, and at the same time the free allocation of emissions allowances represents a large economic rent to firms. Based upon this logic, Vollebergh et al. (1997) recommended partial grandfathering of allowances (or taxes with partial credits) for carbon policy in the European Union. Bovenberg and Goulder (2000) came to similar conclusions in research on the coal, oil and gas industries in the USA. They proposed that no more than 15% of allowances needed to be grandfathered to preserve profits and equity values. Quirion (2003) similarly found that only 10–15% of allowances need to be grandfathered to achieve profit neutrality.

This article examines the impact of the EU ETS on UK competitiveness and addresses the potential changes in the prices, volume of sales and profits of UK firms and those of their rivals, as a result of the trading scheme. It encompasses research carried out by Oxera under contract to the Carbon Trust over the period 2004–2006, and a report published by Oxera (2004) containing an initial set of results. Later results are presented here.

2. Background

It is estimated that the industrial activities within the EU ETS were responsible for releasing 46% of all CO_2 emissions from the UK in 2002 (Defra, 2004b). However, the number of sectors involved, as classified by the Department of the Environment, Food and Rural Affairs (Defra), is small. In the UK, 12 sectors together represent 98.8% of all the emissions covered by the trading regime, but only approximately 11.1% of UK value-added in 2001 (National Statistics, 2002). Furthermore, these sectors tend to have several characteristics in common. They are all energy- and capital-intensive relative to the UK average. Energy is an important input into production, and the production plants tend to be large because of the associated economies of scale. Moreover, these firms are often vertically integrated into companies that produce the raw materials for their production process, or consume or retail their product. In combination, these factors result in sectors comprising relatively few firms, and entry by new firms into the sector is relatively uncommon.

This research was designed to show the consequences of the EU ETS on business. The sectors were selected expressly to make apparent the variation between:

- those in which exposure to international competition is a particular concern and those that are more insulated from overseas rivals;
- those for which energy expenditure constitutes a high proportion of their production costs and those for which it constitutes a relatively low proportion of production costs.

2.1. Defining the market

The economic model used to explore these questions delineates the behaviour of individual firms competing against each other in a market. Hence, it is necessary to define the relevant markets represented by the model.

Economists have devoted considerable attention to defining the relevant market, particularly in competition law investigations. Essentially, a market can be defined along two dimensions: the product market and the geographical market. For both dimensions, the issue concerns whether other products/regions provide an effective competitive constraint on the production of the particular product or on the region of production under examination. In short, a market may be defined as something worth monopolizing.

A number of tools have been developed to test the scope of the relevant market. However, it has not been necessary to use these tools in undertaking this study since, in all cases, an appropriate market had already been defined in competition law investigations at both the UK and the EU level. The products chosen within these sectors, and associated geographical markets as established in competition cases, are set out in Table 1. Since all these decisions were arrived at recently, there is little reason to believe that the nature of the markets will have changed substantially since then.

2.2. Choice of model

As mentioned earlier, many of the sectors in the EU ETS contain a relatively small number of large firms.[1] This suggests that it is appropriate to consider the markets as oligopolistic rather than perfectly competitive. There are important differences between oligopolistic and perfectly competitive markets in the way prices are determined. In a perfectly competitive market, prices are set by the marginal cost of production (the cost of producing an extra unit of output), and firms make profits equal to their cost of capital. In an oligopolistic market, the process is more complicated. Marginal cost still plays an important role, but the presence of fixed costs often means that prices are above marginal costs, allowing for the recovery of these costs and, potentially, if there are barriers to entry, significant economic profits to be made.

A number of theoretical models seek to explain the behaviour of firms in oligopolistic markets, including the classic Stackelberg, Bertrand and Cournot models.

In a Stackelberg equilibrium, the firms in the industry compete on quantity in a sequential fashion. One firm moves first, and then each moves in turn until the last. Working by backwards induction, the last firm seeks to maximize its profits, given the output decisions of all the other firms. The Stackelberg model was rejected because it is more complicated to implement and in most, if not all, of the markets being represented, there were no firms with a leading market share.

The Bertrand model of competition assumes simultaneous price setting between firms. This results in a zero economic profit equilibrium, where price equals marginal cost. The pure Bertrand competition model obviously cannot apply to an industry with fixed costs, as a price equals marginal cost rule would, in the long run, lead to closure of the entire industry. The pure Bertrand model would appear to be inapplicable to all the industries under examination here, as they all have significant fixed costs. A modified price-setting model, such as under monopolistic competition, however, could be employed.

The Cournot model is a standard oligopoly model, and it is often used in competition policy as a first approximation of how competition works (Martin, 1993). For our modelling purposes, the Cournot oligopoly model offered the best combination – faithful representation of market cost structure and behaviour, and flexibility to incorporate a mixture of profit-maximizing and sales-maximizing objectives – as well as tractable conversion into a spreadsheet modelling application.

The key assumptions of the Cournot model, as it is applied here, are as follows:

- firms are profit-maximizing
- firms compete on quantity rather than price
- the output that firms produce is homogeneous
- the cost structure consists of a fixed cost and a constant marginal cost, although the levels of these costs within this structure may, and in this model do, differ across companies
- the relationship between consumer demand and price is constant for all price/quantity combinations (i.e. there is a linear demand curve).

Using these assumptions, a model was constructed to predict market price, total sales, individual firm output, and individual firm profits. At first glance, the assumption over which there may be greatest concern is that firms compete on quantity. Experience suggests that, in many markets, firms compete on price. However, the economic literature has shown that the outcome predicted by the Cournot model may also be realized when firms first choose their capacity levels and then only later compete on price (Kreps and Sheinkman, 1983).

However, one important feature has been introduced in order to reflect a greater degree of compromise between profit maximization and long-term market share, specifically to ensure that price increases do not stimulate the entry of new firms to a degree that would reduce the incumbents' profits (see Ventosa et al., 2005).

This feature took the form of a parameter representing the degree of revenue-maximizing behaviour. The value of this parameter (between 0 and 1 within the mathematical framework of the model) was set so that, where there was a possibility of companies increasing their profits as a result of the policy levers, this would never be implemented in a manner such that it would attract new entry and therefore be self-defeating, i.e. that the firms exhibit limit pricing (see later discussion on profit maximization). As a result, new entry was only assumed to take place when companies did not have the opportunity of increasing their profits as a result of the policy levers introduced.

Having solved the Cournot equilibrium for a set of incumbent firms, any company that is no longer profitable is assumed to exit, and the Cournot equilibrium is re-calculated. Also, data from abatement curves is used to assess whether companies would profitably undertake any abatement, given the prevailing market conditions.

3. Operation of the model

Initially, the model assumes that the market is populated by a number of identical, 'typical' firms. All of the firms choose the same volume of output to maximize their individual profits. If, at this optimal level of output, the firms cannot pay their fixed and variable operating costs, including providing a 'reasonable' return to providers of finance, at least one firm would close. As a consequence of the closure (exit) of a firm, the individual outputs of the remaining firms would increase and their profitability would improve. The model automatically reduces the number of firms in the industry until the remaining firms cover their costs and achieve a reasonable profit.

The EU ETS affects costs (both fixed and variable), prices, and quantities in the market. It is helpful to divide these impacts into marginal and fixed effects: marginal effects determine the impact on the price or quantity sold; fixed effects do not alter these 'allocative' decisions, but have a direct impact on the profit made and hence on the number of surviving firms.

Under the EU ETS, CO_2 emissions become a factor of production that has to be paid for, in the same way as labour or raw materials. It is assumed in the modelling that marginal costs are constant across the range of output considered, i.e. that each additional unit of output has the same marginal impact on costs. The introduction of the EU ETS leads to two potential changes in the marginal cost of production:

- the direct CO_2 cost – the amount of CO_2 emissions from producing an additional unit of output multiplied by the market price of allowances. This affects EU ETS participants only;
- an increase in the price of electricity – the amount of electricity consumed in producing an additional unit of output multiplied by the change in wholesale market price of electricity caused by the EU ETS. This will affect all companies within the EU.

An increase in marginal cost has an impact on a firm's profits in three ways:

- the level of production is reduced – as the costs of production increase, quantity supplied is reduced, regardless of whether prices are changed;
- some costs are absorbed by the firm – this does not lead to an increase in price, but the margin achieved on each unit is eroded;
- some costs are passed on to customers – this does not erode margins, but the increase in price leads to a decrease in volumes and hence revenues.

The first of these impacts, which always takes place, reflects the fact that, as each unit of production is now more costly, the level of output at which marginal cost equals marginal revenue will also necessarily be lower. The extent to which this factor results in lower output depends critically on the number of other firms in the market that also face the marginal cost increase.

The second and third impacts depend on the extent to which the marginal cost increase is passed on to customers, and occur in inverse proportions. In the Cournot model, the extent of this pass-through is determined by each firm pursuing a profit-maximizing strategy (Varian, 1992, p. 290). Under certain assumptions, including the assumptions that demand is linearly related to price (each quantum of price rise reduces demand by a fixed amount), the extent to which a change in cost leads to an increase in price is given by the formula $X/(N + 1)$, where X is the number of companies affected by the cost change, and N is the total number of companies operating in the market.[2]

For example, for the extreme case of a monopolist, $N = 1$, and therefore X also $= 1$. As such, a monopolist facing linear demand passes through half of any increase in costs. However, as the sector becomes more competitive, and the number of firms increases, the amount of cost pass-through to customers rises until it is close to 100%. In other words, the more competitive the industry, the greater the cost pass-through. This is explained by the fact that, as an industry becomes more competitive, prices become more aligned with costs. This rule also shows that the smaller the proportion of firms in the market that are affected by the marginal cost increase, the lower the level of cost pass-through. Thus, a lower proportion of costs will be passed through if a larger proportion of demand is satisfied by small or overseas firms not affected by the EU ETS.

The same basic idea can be applied if demand is assumed to be isoelastic, i.e. demand is related to price with constant elasticity (ε) in which case the cost pass-through rule is:

$$dp/dc = N\varepsilon/(N\varepsilon + 1)$$

where N is the number of firms (Varian, 1992, p. 290).

For a monopolist ($N = 1$) facing a constant elasticity demand curve, the cost pass-through rule is thus $\varepsilon / (\varepsilon + 1)$, which corresponds to that found by Bulow and Pfleiderer (1983). Note that because $\varepsilon < -1$ for a monopolist, isoelastic demand therefore implies cost pass-through of more than 100% of any price change, and the pass-through would decline towards 100% for more competitive markets.

For the purposes of the analysis in this article, we assume a linear demand, partly because the higher rates of pass-through under isoelastic demand are inconsistent with the claims and concerns of many industries regarding the difficulty of passing through cost changes.[3] As shown below, even assuming linear demand, it can be shown that significant pass-through occurs along with resulting profit-making from the EU ETS; adopting the isoelastic assumption would simply tend to make these effects even greater.

Once the proportion of cost increase that is passed on to customers is known, the impact on profits from a decrease in margins can be established relatively easily. The magnitude of this effect is given by the sensitivity of demand to price, the 'own-price elasticity of demand'. Estimates of this elasticity are available in the economic literature.

The final impact is on the fixed costs of firms. A firm's fixed costs may rise as a result of abatement investment undertaken to reduce exposure to the marginal cost impact of the EU ETS. Knowing the cost of CO_2 emissions, a company can decide whether to invest in abatement technology to reduce emissions. Using published abatement cost curves, the model estimates the level of abatement investment for both CO_2 emissions and electricity consumption. For simplicity's sake, it is assumed that the cost associated with the introduction of new technology is entirely a capital cost, and that the new technology does not change the fixed or variable operating costs of production, except to the extent that marginal costs are reduced due to the lower intensity of electricity or CO_2 consumption.

More important than abatement investment (in financial terms) is the free allocation of allowances to firms. This is equivalent to a fixed, lump-sum revenue transfer to the firm, because the revenue that the company could generate from selling these allowances is independent of its own production volumes.

While, in the short run, the number of companies in the sector is fixed, in the long run firms can enter or exit. The model shows the financial impact of the EU ETS as though it were distributed equally across all the firms in the market. If the reduction (increase) in profitability is sufficiently great, it is expected to cause firms to exit (enter) the market. This alters the degree of cost pass-through (through the $x/(n+1)$ rule), and requires further iterations of the model, giving a new financial impact estimate. The iterations continue until a long-run equilibrium number of firms in the industry is established. The treatment of firm entry and exit is discussed further below.

4. The assumption that firms pursue profit-maximization

The assertion that firms maximize profits is so common in economic analysis that it might seem surprising to question it. Yet it is widely discussed, and its importance in the context of modelling the EU ETS is that it determines the fundamental trade-off that firms face between maximizing profits in the short term, and maximizing market share (and hence gross revenues) and thus potentially maximizing profits in the longer term. Raising product prices increases profits but leads over time to loss of market share.

Generally, shareholders have a shorter time horizon than the investment cycle of firms, and thus the assertion that firms maximize profits (in a given period of analysis, such as 5 or 10 years) is based upon the implicit set of assumptions that (1) shareholders seek profit maximization; (2) management aims to best achieve shareholder objectives; and (3) management is able to achieve its aims. All three assumptions have been questioned, as discussed below.

4.1. Do shareholders desire profits?

It can hardly be denied that shareholders seek profits. It is an open question as to whether they have motivations other than profits. In recent times, there has been an emergence of an ethical investment sector, where managed funds pursue profits in conjunction with additional ethical objectives, such as environmental protection. These additional objectives are often satisfied simply by placing constraints on the types of firms these funds will invest in. On other occasions, the fund is a more active participant in guiding firm policies. Even so, however, the question of most interest in the popular press is whether the ethical sector is more or less profitable than other sectors. In short, the focus is still squarely on profits, and it is safe to proceed on the assumption that shareholders seek profit maximization (see Baumol, 1958; Jensen and Murphy, 1988; Murphy, 1985).

4.2. Do managers seek to achieve shareholder objectives?

The crux of the debate concerns the divergence between the incentives of shareholders and managers. This debate is not new. Over 40 years ago, Koplin (1963) stated that the 'profit maximization assumption has long been under attack, chiefly on the grounds that it lacks realism'. The attack was largely begun by Baumol (1958, 1959), who conjectured that managers' salaries appeared to be more closely correlated with total sales revenue rather than bottom-line profits. As such, he asserted that managers induce over-expansion of firms, not for reasons of profitability, but because managers see expansion as a means to obtaining higher salaries.

All firms consist of several distinct groups of stakeholders (employees, managers, shareholders and customers) and each group has different objectives. The dominant groups are generally the owners and the managers. As Stiglitz (1991) encapsulates it: the fundamental problem of owners of firms is how to motivate their managers to act in the interest of the owners. This, of course, is just an example of the classic principal–agent problem.

Baker et al. (1988) noted the relatively stable empirical finding that managers' salaries increase by 3% for every 10% increase in sales and, perhaps more importantly, Murphy (1985) showed that this relationship is causal, and not merely a matching of more productive workers to larger firms, implying that pay can increase with firm size even if this reduces firm value. Stiglitz (1991) agrees that managers often behave to the detriment of shareholders, pointing out that managers sometimes prevent takeovers that would be in the best interests of their shareholders by taking 'poisoned pills' (entering the firm into contracts costs that would impose costs on the new owners) and 'golden parachutes' (entering the firm into commitments to pay high levels of financial compensation to managers who are ousted during a takeover). Given that managers have an incentive to increase sales as well as (or even instead of) profits, sales maximization appears to be empirically plausible.

The implications from this are that firms should be expected to maximize the dual objectives of profits and sales if (1) managers are powerful relative to shareholders, or (2) the market structure is oligopolistic and quantity leadership provides a profit advantage. It follows that managers might find it optimal to use the lump sum represented by their grandfathered allowances as a 'war chest' with which to reduce prices and increase sales in the output market, in an attempt to take Stackelberg leadership, as outlined earlier.

4.3. Can management achieve its aims?

The final argument used to question models based on profit maximization centres on the claim that managers are incapable of determining the profit-maximizing strategy. Instead, managers operate by rules of thumb. The intellectual background for this view is to be found in the concepts of satisficing and bounded rationality, and this is increasingly being expounded in the economic literature concerned with behaviour. Several rules of thumb are now considered.

Average-cost pricing, also known as markup pricing or cost-plus pricing, is where a markup is added to the average unit cost of production. This appears to be particularly common in the retail sector, where the proliferation of products implies that a careful study of demand for each product is uneconomic.

Survey evidence suggests that this practice is particularly widespread. Govindarajan and Anthony (1983) concluded that most firms in the Fortune 500 price their products based on average cost, and Shim and Sudit (1995) found that 69.5% of the 600 US manufacturing companies surveyed claimed to base their pricing decisions on full costs, with only 12.1% using a variable cost method. Lucas (2003) presents a useful survey of the various econometric and case study evidence for and against average cost pricing, and suggests that both average cost and marginal cost pricing are plausible, and that further empirical research is required before any conclusions can be drawn.

Limit pricing consists of pricing to ensure that no additional firms will find it profitable to enter the industry. It is a long-run profit maximization strategy for monopolistic or oligopolistic firms. In a survey of 54 industries in the USA, Koutsoyiannis (1984) found evidence against short-run profit maximization (and sales maximization) and evidence for limit pricing. He substantiated this view by citing 37 industries where the evidence is consistent with limit pricing, while in the remaining 17 industries the evidence is inconsistent. The model parameters were set to achieve limit pricing in those circumstances where limit pricing was a profitable strategy.

Profit maximization and other assumptions: lessons for modelling

As discussed in the text, although it is clear that shareholders desire profits, it is unclear whether managers seek to maximize profits. In particular, there is good evidence to show that they seek to maximize sales instead, although sales maximization is actually a profit-maximizing strategy in some oligopolistic industries. Sales maximization results in the conclusion that managers would not keep all the rents from grandfathered allowances, and would instead use them to reduce prices and increase output.

This has implications for model design. A model in which firms maximize a weighted average of profits and sales may provide a more realistic representation of markets than one which purely maximizes profits. The weights on sales and profits would determine how much of the economic surplus is spent on increasing revenues, and how much is retained as profit.

There is a final popular argument which should also be taken into account. Irrespective of whether the three assumptions are fulfilled, Friedman (1953) has argued that in a competitive environment, firms must maximize profits or they will eventually be driven out of the market. Thus, he states that 'under a wide range of circumstances individual firms behave *as* if they were seeking rationally to maximize their expected returns'.

However, Dutta and Radner (1999) have rigorously examined a model similar to that which Friedman puts forward and have arrived at the opposite conclusion. They say that if innovating firms in a stochastic environment are subject to competitive pressure, the result will be that the profit-maximizing firms will eventually go bankrupt and, after a period of time, practically all the surviving firms will not be maximizing profits. The Dutta and Radner (1999) setting does not apply here, but it does question the legitimacy of the 'as-if profit-maximization' of Friedman (1953), which is commonly encountered in the literature.

Furthermore, Nabil et al. (2004) consider an oligopolistic market with product differentiation where firms adopt real-world accounting practices, including practices where fixed (and sunk) costs are bundled in together with variable costs. With the assumption that firms follow adaptive learning in adjusting prices, they find that pricing above marginal cost predominates, and all firms end up showing a sunk cost bias. This provides further evidence against the Friedman (1953) hypothesis.

5. Initial market conditions

With the number of companies in the market established, the actual profits made by each company can be calculated. A check is performed to ensure that all companies that enter remain profitable. Therefore, a company that enters the market 'first' and makes high profits could end up making losses due to the subsequent entry of other companies. Thus, the model finds an equilibrium where all the companies in the market are profitable and any company that is not in the market would not make profits by entering. Note that the geographical scope of the market is either the UK, Europe or global, as set out in Table 1. Since the EU ETS changes the production costs of EU firms relative to global firms, where it has an effect on the market share of UK or EU firms the effect is that market share is gained by non-EU firms.

Table 1. Sectors, products and geographical markets

Sector	Product market	Relevant market	Selection of European Commission Cases
Cement	Grey cement	UK	Lafarge/Blue Circle (Comp/M.1874, 07.04.2000)
Newsprint	Newsprint	Europe	
Petroleum	Refined products	Europe	
Steel	Cold-rolled carbon steel flat products	Europe	Usinor/Arbed/Aceralia (Comp/ECSC.1351 21.11.2001)
Aluminium		Global	Alcan/Alusuisse (Comp/M.1663, 14.03.2000) Norsk Hydro/VAW (Comp/M. 2702, 04.03.2002) Elkem/Sapa (Comp/M.2404, 26.06.2001)

With the number of companies in the market established, these companies are then labelled as being either UK, (other) EU or global companies. This is decided on the basis of the share of supply that was gathered from published research.

The cost shocks of environmental policy are then introduced. Depending on the scenario being modelled, either fixed or marginal costs can change. UK companies are assumed to be affected by both UK and EU policies, while other EU companies are assumed to be affected only by the EU ETS. There is no attempt to address the financial impact of national environmental policies other than those introduced by the UK government. There is assumed to be no change in the costs of global companies, operating outside the EU.

With these amended costs, the revised prices, quantities and profits of the companies in the market can be calculated. In examining these short-term effects, it is assumed that there are no changes in the number of companies in the market and that companies cannot respond to the policy shocks by changing their costs, i.e. that no abatement takes place.

6. Data

The data required to run the model were substantial. They included financial data of individual companies, fuel use and CO_2 emissions per product, in addition to the price of an average product. Other data inputs included the own-price elasticity of demand, the total volume of product consumed, the number of firms manufacturing the product, and the proportion of total consumption supplied by imports.

These data were gathered for each of the following sectors: cement, newsprint, steel and petroleum. Numerous sources were used, including academic articles, competition inquiries, company accounts, company environmental reports and material gathered from trade associations, the UK Department of Trade and Industry, the UK Office of National Statistics, and The Carbon Trust. The market data is sourced from sector market reports; while the elasticity estimates are taken from the economic literature, although, in the case of aluminium smelting, no elasticity estimates could be found. The production cost data are concerned with the marginal cost of production (although the average variable cost of production is often used as a proxy); the fixed cost of production (including fixed operating costs, depreciation of capital assets and financing costs); and an abatement curve of the unit cost and potential for reducing electricity use and abating CO_2 emissions. The production cost data are taken from published sector studies and

Table 2. Data sources

Variable	Data sources
Industry elasticity	Academic articles and competition inquiries
Import penetration	Competition inquiries, analyst reports and national trade statistics
Energy intensity	The Carbon Trust and company environmental reports
Fixed and marginal costs	FAME database and competition inquiries
Price	Companies and competition inquiries
Quantity	Trade associations and competition inquiries

Table 3. Assumptions

Variable	Cement	Newsprint	Petroleum	Steel	Aluminium
Price elasticity of demand	−0.27	−0.5	−0.8	−0.62	−1.1
Marginal/average variable cost of production	£14/t	£195/t	£0.08/litre	£190/t	£786/t
Tonnes CO₂ emitted/marginal unit of output	1.09/t	0.63/t	0.0002/t	1.75/t	2.2/t
Electricity consumer/marginal unit of output (kWh/t)	136	648	0.1	330	15,351
Market share of non-EU suppliers (%)	5	15	11	20	70

were corroborated with company accounts from a sample of firms. Abatement cost data are taken from a database developed for the UK Department of the Environment, Food and Rural Affairs supplemented with material derived from industry discussions. Tables 2 and 3 detail some of the sources and assumptions.

UK costs were used for companies in the UK, Europe and the rest of the world, and no account was taken of existing differences in the terms of trade. Market shares for each location of company were achieved by attributing an appropriate number of companies to that location. Thus, for example, in a sector where the model was predicted to have 10 companies, if the UK market share was 40%, European 30% and rest of the world 30%, then four companies were labelled as UK, three European and three rest of the world.

7. Scenarios

The scenarios involved combinations of allowance prices of €7.5/tCO₂, €15/tCO₂ and €30/tCO₂, all with allowances fully grandfathered. Shortly before the EU ETS was introduced in 2005, allowance prices had been around €7/tCO₂. The scenario with a price of €7/tCO₂ reflects this initial situation. However, once participating countries had fixed their allocations and as gas prices rose, increasing demand for coal and increasing the demand for allowances, the price rose to around €25/tCO₂. The two higher-price scenarios are intended to reflect the recent range of actual allowance prices and to encompass some departure from this range to either higher or lower prices in the future while acknowledging that future prices could lie outside the range of these scenarios.

Table 4. Effect on marginal costs

Sector	Impact of carbon price on short-run marginal production cost (% increase)	
Allowance price	€15/tCO$_2$	€30/tCO$_2$
Cement	70	144
Newsprint	2.6	6.0
Petroleum	0.3	0.6
Steel	8.0	17
Aluminium	4.0	13

The scenarios also incorporate the UK's Climate Change Levy (a tax on the business use of energy) and Climate Change Agreements. The Agreements are sectoral targets for energy use or energy intensity which, if achieved, entitle the holder to an 80% reduction in the tax rate applicable under the Climate Change Levy. Within the model, their only effects are to modify the cost of electricity and to cause a minimum level of energy efficiency improvement to take place.

The impact of the opportunity cost of carbon allowances on the marginal cost of production has been estimated and is shown in Table 4. It ranges from 0.3% for petroleum refining with an allowance price of €15/tCO$_2$, to 17% for steel with an allowance price of €30/tCO$_2$. The cement sector is an exception, with the impact on its marginal production costs lying well outside this range, at up to 140%.

8. Results

The results, shown in Table 5, exhibit the following features.

The EU ETS delivers emissions reductions and has a positive (or at least non-negative) impact on earnings before interest, tax, depreciation and amortization (EBITDA). This is because companies respond to the increase in marginal cost brought about by the EU ETS by cutting back output and so increasing prices to cover the additional costs, and simultaneously benefiting from the free allocation of grandfathered allowances. The petroleum refining sector shows little reduction in

Table 5. Results, Effect of EU ETS and UK policy measures, percentage change

Sector	Emissions		Physical production output		EBITDA	
Allowance price scenario	Euro 15/tCO$_2$	Euro 30/tCO$_2$	Euro 15/tCO$_2$	Euro 30/tCO$_2$	Euro 15/tCO$_2$	Euro 30/tCO$_2$
Cement	−12	−14	−1.2	−4.4	13	25
Newsprint	−4	−4	−0.2	+0.68	9	15
Petroleum	−0.4	−0.7	−0.2	−0.7	0.4	0.6
Steel	−14	−21	−2.1	−10.6	12	18
Aluminium	−100	−100	−100	−100	−100	−100

Source: Oxera.

emissions because it has a low intensity of emissions and has relatively little opportunity for abatement.

UK aluminium smelters are assumed to be outside of the trading part of the scheme, but still exposed to the UK-specific electricity price increase that this would engender. In practice, some aluminium smelters may own and some may have contractual arrangements with fossil-fuel power stations, meaning that they do participate in the EU ETS, and the results described below will not apply to them.

There is a stark contrast between the results for the aluminium smelting sector and those for the other sectors. In short, because aluminium smelting is assumed to be a global market, even relatively small changes in cost are predicted to have significant impacts on the competitiveness of UK/EU companies relative to global companies (which are assumed not to have environmental policies applied to them).

Prior to the introduction of the policies, there is one representative UK aluminium smelting company, one representative EU company and four representative global companies in the model equilibrium. From this starting position, the model simulation produces an outcome that in any of the scenarios tested the UK (and EU) aluminium smelters exit the market and their place is taken by companies operating exclusively outside the UK or EU. There is a subtle difference between the scenarios concerning how this position is reached. On some occasions, the initial impact of the policy is sufficiently severe to cause both the UK and EU companies to exit the market immediately. In other situations, one of the two companies remains in the market initially (with the other one closing), but the impact of a new global company entering in order to take the place of the first closure is, in turn, sufficient to precipitate the exit of the second non-global company. While this discussion has been framed in terms of global companies entering the market and non-global companies leaving the market, it can also equally well be thought of as existing companies located in the UK/EU relocating to outside of these areas.

UK and EU aluminium smelters are much more exposed to adverse competitiveness implications from the introduction of environmental policies, due to the global nature of competition in this market, than participants in any of the other markets analysed. However, as previously noted, some aluminium smelters are protected via contracts or association with electricity generators who either participate in the EU ETS or generate power from renewable sources. Hence the impact of the trading scheme may be that instead of the aluminium smelting activity ceasing, the profitability of the power generation activity is made lower than that of comparable power generators, where power prices are under the contracts or between associated companies are not raised to the new levels in the electricity market at large.

For other sectors, the ostensibly toughest policy scenario, where the CO$_2$ price is €30/t, leads to the largest increase in profits. This is because, although the CO$_2$ price, and hence marginal cost rise, is significant, the grandfathered allowances are more valuable. As the proportion of allowances to be grandfathered remains high in these scenarios, the effect of receiving such a valuable allocation dominates the higher marginal costs. If the high CO$_2$ price were associated with a much lower proportion of allowances being grandfathered, the profit impact would be expected to be markedly different.

The pattern of impact between the sectors is that the steel and cement sectors are notably more affected, in terms of both profit and predicted emissions savings, than the newsprint sector. In contrast, the petroleum sector is only very marginally affected, due to its relatively low energy, and hence carbon, intensity.

Although emissions are cut while profits are boosted, the increase in costs, and in prices, invariably has a negative impact on output produced and sold, and prices to consumers rise. The impacts on output across the different sectors are reported in Table 5. The output changes drive a large proportion of the total UK emissions reduction in each sector, also reported in Table 5.

Again, a number of observations can be drawn.

In all the markets modelled other than aluminium, the impact of the introduction of the policies is to reduce the total amount of output produced and sold within the UK.

When the geographic market is wider than the UK, the impact of the output reduction within the market can be asymmetric across locations of companies. Most clearly, for the market in which there is non-EU production (steel), despite the overall fall in market output, the non-EU companies are predicted to see their output increase. In the case of newsprint in one scenario, the change in output is actually predicted to be positive, because there is an implied reduction in the marginal cost of production as a result of improved energy efficiency.

The composition of these effects on prices, output and profits is shown in Figures 1–5.

The figures show the cumulative change in EBITDA:

- from the increase in the marginal cost of production
- compensated by the allocation of allowances
- after adjusting for changed product prices
- accounting for change in demand
- noting the effect of abatement action.

This presentation shows the extent to which the impact of profit is a consequence of marginal cost increases, the extent to which this is compensated for by additional income from grandfathered

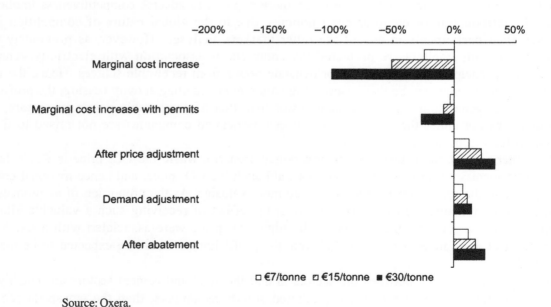

Source: Oxera.

Figure 1. Decomposition of effect on EBITDA for steel.

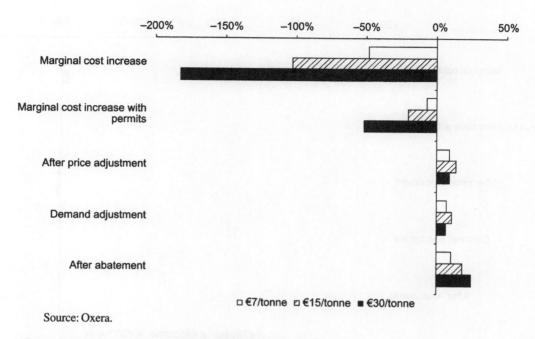

Source: Oxera.

Figure 2. Decomposition of effect on EBITDA for cement.

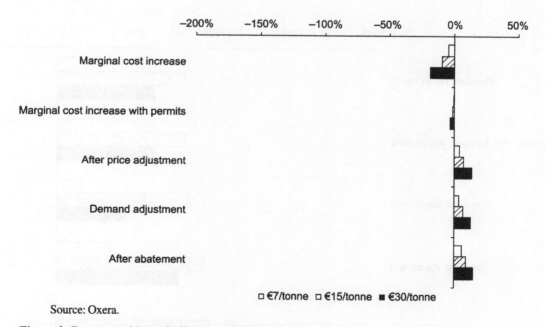

Source: Oxera.

Figure 3. Decomposition of effect on EBITDA for newsprint.

allowances or higher prices, and the relative offsetting of this position by demand changes and abatement cost savings.

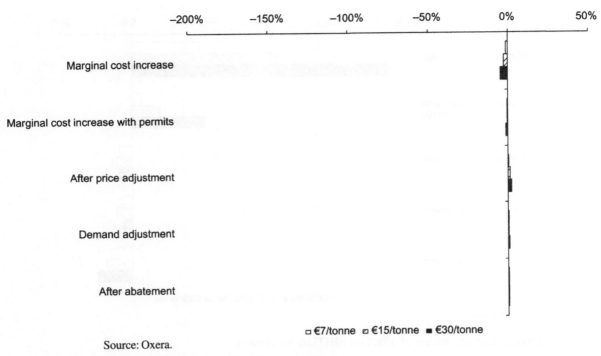

Source: Oxera.

Figure 4. Decomposition of effect on EBITDA for petroleum.

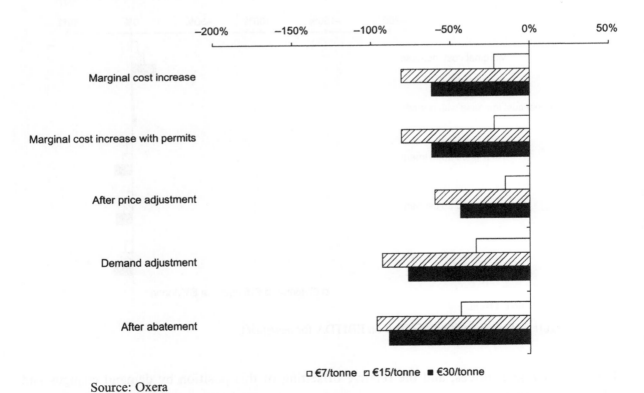

Source: Oxera

Figure 5. Decomposition of effect on EBITDA for aluminium.

9. Conclusions

9.1. The impacts on profits

The impacts of policies were most significant in the most energy-intensive sectors and those facing the greatest international competition. Even here, changes in EBITDA were commonly positive and large, being greater than 10%, and reaching as high as 25%. Prices rise in the cement sector, which is a UK market, because the EU ETS applies to 90–95% of the product supplied in the UK; and thus cement manufacturers are able to pass costs on to consumers. Prices rise in the steel sector, which is an EU market, because the EU ETS applies to 80% of the product supplied in Europe; as such, steel manufacturers are able to pass on a proportion, 65%, of their marginal cost increases to consumers.

At the same time, across all the sectors and policies, there was a reduction in volume of production, in most cases by much less than 1%. In two extreme cases – steel and cement – under the 'toughest' policy scenario, the output reductions were of 10% and 5%. This supports the suggestion, made for example by the CBI, that the EU ETS might cause a reduction in employment in some sectors.

The one exception to this picture is aluminium smelting, which, if not tied to electricity production, is exposed to large increases in marginal cost, with consequential migration of production outside the EU trading area. In all the scenarios, EU production of aluminium ceases.

9.2. The impact on emissions

The emissions reduction effects are caused in part by a reduction in UK output – a combination of a change in the share of the UK market held by UK producers and of weaker demand from consumers as a consequence of higher prices. They are also caused by investment in carbon-efficient technologies. Most of the emissions reduction is attributable to greater carbon efficiency, driven by the carbon abatement curves prepared for The Carbon Trust by Ecofys. Only in the steel and cement sectors does output reduction contribute to a significant carbon reduction.

It is notable that the abatement curves predict similar levels of emissions reduction across all policy scenarios. There is an initial level of abatement that is achieved under low allowance prices, according to the abatement curve method. This is presumably because the curve contains a volume of abatement that has been deemed beneficial or costless to the company. Thereafter, little additional abatement is stimulated by increasing incentives from tougher policies, which indicates that the abatement curve is quite steep, i.e. abatement costs rise steeply after the initial, virtually costless, actions are exhausted.

9.3. The impact on output

In the steel and cement sectors, there were reductions in output of 10% and 5% in the scenarios involving the highest penalties on carbon emissions, although, in both cases, these reductions were accompanied by greater increases in profits as prices rose. The increased profits combined with slightly reduced output result in a stronger financial position for the companies. In reaching the new equilibrium level of output, in none of the scenarios is capacity hit so hard that profits fall and companies exit the market, although there might be some shedding of labour and manufacturing capacity within companies.

In newsprint, a sector with medium energy intensity, impacts on output were small, at around 1% or less, but the effects on profits were still significant in some cases, being as large as +15%. These levels of output and profit change are unlikely to have a material effect on labour or investment.

Acknowledgements

We thank, at Oxera, Gareth Davies, and at The Carbon Trust, James Wilde, for comments on this article, and Amra Topcagic for her contribution to the Oxera research. We also thank the referees for their insightful questions and helpful suggestions.

Notes

1 The significance of this market structure is that firms pass less of a marginal cost increase through to their customers than firms in a perfectly competitive market would do.
2 See, for example, Ten Kate and Niels (2005).
3 Incomplete cost pass-through can be consistent with isoelastic demand if the cost increase is not industry-wide, which is relevant to industries subject to intense international competition.

References

Baker, G.P., Jensen, M.C., Murphy, K.J., 1988. Compensation and incentives: practice vs. theory. Journal of Finance 43, 593–616.

Baumol, W.J., 1958. On the theory of oligopoly. Economica 25(99), 187–198.

Baumol, W.J., 1959. Business Behavior, Value and Growth. Macmillan, New York.

Bovenberg, A.L., Goulder, L.H., 2000. Neutralising the Adverse Industry Impacts of CO_2 Abatement Policies: What Does it Cost? Resources for the Future Discussion Paper 00–27.

Bulow, J.I., Pfleiderer, P., 1983. A note on the effect of cost changes on prices. Journal of Political Economy 91, 182–185.

Commission of the European Communities, 2000. Green Paper on Greenhouse Gas Emissions Trading within the European Union.

Defra, 2004a. UK Announces Consultation on Draft National Allocation Plan for the EU Emissions Trading Scheme [available at www.defra.gov.uk].

Defra, 2004b. UK Draft National Allocation Plan for 2005–07 [available at www.defra.gov.uk].

Dutta, P.K., Radner, R., 1999. Profit maximization and the market selection hypothesis. Review of Economic Studies 66(4), 769–798.

Friedman, M., 1953. Essays in Positive Economics. University of Chicago Press, Chicago, USA.

Govindarajan, V., Anthony, R., 1983. How firms use cost data in pricing decisions. Management Accounting, July, 30–37.

Jensen, M.C., Murphy, K.J., 1988. Compensation and incentives: practice vs theory. Journal of Finance 43, 593–616.

Kreps, D., Sheinkman, J., 1983. Quantity precommitment and Bertrand competition yield Cournot outcomes. Bell Journal of Economics 14, 326–337.

Koplin, H.T., 1963. The profit maximisation assumption. Oxford Economic Papers 15(2), 130–139.

Koutsoyiannis, A., 1984. Goals of oligopolistic firms: an empirical test of competing hypotheses. Southern Economic Journal 51(2), 540–567.

Lucas, M.R., 2003. Pricing decisions and the neoclassical theory of the firm. Management Accounting Research 14, 201–217.

Martin, S., 1993. Advanced Industrial Economics. Blackwell.

Murphy, K.M., 1985. Corporate performance and managerial remuneration: an empirical analysis. Journal of Accounting and Economics 7, 11–42.

Nabil, A-N., Baliga, S., Besanko, D., 2004. The Sunk Cost Bias in Managerial Pricing decisions. Mimeo.

National Statistics, 2002. United Kingdom National Accounts Blue Book, and further information provided by National Statistics.

Oxera, 2004. CO_2 Emissions Trading: How Will it Affect UK Industry? Report prepared for The Carbon Trust [available at www.oxera.com].

Quirion, P., 2003. Allocation of CO_2 Allowances and Competitiveness: A Case Study on the European Iron and Steel Industry. Mimeo.

Shim, E., Sudit, E., 1995. How manufacturers price products. Management Accounting 76, 37–39.

Stiglitz, J.E., 1991. Symposium on Organizations and Economics. Journal of Economic Perspectives 5(2).

Ten Kate, A., Niels, G., 2005. To what extent are cost savings passed on to consumers? An oligopoly approach. European Journal of Law and Economics 20, 323–337.

Varian, H.R., 1992. Microeconomic Analysis. W.W. Norton, London.

Ventosa, M., Baillo, A., Ramos, A., River, M., 2005. Electricity market modelling trends. Energy Policy 33, 897–913.

Vollebergh, H.R.J., de Vries, J.L., Koutstaal, P.R., 1997. Hybrid carbon incentive mechanisms and political acceptability. Environmental and Resource Economics 9, 43–63.

www.climatepolicy.com

CO$_2$ cost pass-through and windfall profits in the power sector

Jos Sijm[1]*, Karsten Neuhoff[2], Yihsu Chen[3]

[1] *Energy Research Centre of The Netherlands (ECN), PO Box 37154, 1030 AD Amsterdam, The Netherlands*
[2] *Faculty of Economics, University of Cambridge, Sidgwick Avenue, Cambridge CB3 9DE, UK*
[3] *Department of Geography and Environmental Engineering, Johns Hopkins University, 3400 North Charles Street, Baltimore, MD 21218m, USA*

Abstract

In order to cover their CO$_2$ emissions, power companies receive most of the required EU ETS allowances for free. In line with economic theory, these companies pass on the costs of these allowances in the price of electricity. This article analyses the implications of the EU ETS for the power sector, notably the impact of free allocation of CO$_2$ emission allowances on the price of electricity and the profitability of power generation. As well as some theoretical reflections, the article presents empirical and model estimates of CO$_2$ cost pass-through for Germany and The Netherlands, indicating that pass-through rates vary between 60 and 100% of CO$_2$ costs, depending on the carbon intensity of the marginal production unit and various other market- or technology-specific factors. As a result, power companies realize substantial windfall profits, as indicated by the empirical and model estimates presented in the article.

Keywords: Emissions trading; Allocation; CO$_2$ cost pass-through; Windfall profits; Power sector

1. Introduction

A major characteristic of the present EU Emissions Trading Scheme (ETS) is that almost all the CO$_2$ allowances are allocated for free to the installations covered by the scheme. During the first phase of the EU ETS (2005–2007), more than 2.2 billion allowances of 1 tonne each are being allocated per year (EC, 2005). During the first phase of the EU ETS (2005–2007), more than 2.2 billion allowances of 1 tonne each are being allocated per year (EC, 2005), about 60% of which is allocated to the power sector.

Against this background, this article analyses the implications of the EU ETS for the power sector, notably the impact of free allocation of CO$_2$ emission allowances on the price of electricity and the profitability of power generation. In Section 2 we discuss the effect of different generation technologies being used to generate electricity. How does the internalization of CO$_2$ allowance prices by individual generators into their bids feed through to the power price and how does this in turn affect profitability? Sections 3–5 present empirical and model findings on passing through

* Corresponding author. Tel.: +31-224-56-8255
E-mail address: sijm@ecn.nl

the costs of CO_2 emission allowances to power prices in the countries of north-western Europe and implications for the profitability of power production in these countries at the national and company level. The article concludes with a brief summary of the major findings and policy implications.

2. Theory

The EU ETS is a cap-and-trade system based primarily on the free allocation of a fixed amount of emission allowances to a set of covered installations. Companies can either use these allowances to cover the emissions resulting from the production of these installations or sell them to other companies that need additional allowances (Reinaud, 2005). Hence, for a company using an emission allowance, this represents an opportunity cost, regardless of whether the allowances are allocated for free or purchased at an auction or market. Therefore, in principle and in line with economic theory, a company is expected to add the costs of CO_2 emission allowances to its other marginal (variable) costs when making (short-term) production or trading decisions, even if the allowances are granted for free (Burtraw et al., 2002, 2005; Reinaud, 2003).

Different generation technologies produce different levels of CO_2 emissions, and therefore the opportunity costs of CO_2 emissions per unit of power produced differ as well. For example, a combined-cycle gas turbine produces about 0.48 t of CO_2 per MWh of electricity, while a typical coal power station emits about 0.85 tCO_2/MWh. A CO_2 price of €20/tCO_2, therefore, increases the generation costs for the gas plant by €9.6/MWh and for the coal plant by €17/MWh.

During a certain load period, the competitive electricity price is only affected by the price increase of the marginal production unit. This can be illustrated by a marginal cost (price) duration curve, as presented in Figure 1. On the x-axis the 8760 hours of a year are depicted, sorted in descending order of the marginal system costs. The y-axis gives the marginal costs of the marginal generation unit. The competitive electricity price in any one hour is affected by the cap-and-trade system through the price increase of the marginal unit. Hence, the amount at which the power price increases due to the passing through of CO_2 costs may differ per hour or load period considered, depending on the marginal generation unit concerned. As a consequence, the CO_2 cost pass-

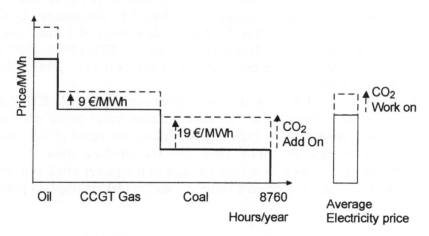

Figure 1. Pass-through of CO_2 opportunity costs for different load periods (at a price of €20/tCO_2).

through is defined as the average increase in power price over a certain period due to the increase in the CO$_2$ price of an emission allowance.

We represent the difference between the behaviour of individual generators and the impact on the system price by defining the 'add-on' and the 'work-on' rate. In a competitive environment, generators 'add-on' the opportunity costs of CO$_2$ allowances to the power price. The increase of the bid of the marginal unit will then determine how much of the CO$_2$ allowance prices are 'worked-on' the electricity price. However, in a liberalized market, prices are ultimately determined by a complex set of market forces. As a result, the work-on rate may be lower than the add-on rate.

One reason why the work-on rate may be lower than the add-on rate is from a market demand response. If higher power prices reduce electricity demand, then an expensive power station might not need to operate and a cheaper generator will set the marginal price. The change in power price is smaller than the change in marginal costs due to emissions trading. Hence, while the add-on rate will remain at 100%, the work-on rate will be lower than 100%. Although price responsiveness is typically rather low for households and other small-scale consumers of electricity, the effect may be more significant for major end-users such as the power-intensive industries. Power-intensive industry would substitute electricity purchases with the self-generation of electricity. This pathway is less attractive, as the EU ETS also covers large-scale self-generation by industry and, therefore, faces similar cost increases, thus reducing the demand response of power-intensive industry. Nevertheless, through self-generation, power-intensive industry would benefit from the economic rent due to the transfer of valuable, freely allocated assets.

The extent to which carbon costs are passed through to power prices also depends on changes in the merit order of the supply curve due to emissions trading. This is illustrated in Figure 2, where the supply curve is characterized by a step function with two types of technologies – A and B. The vertical dash line indicates the fixed demand. In Figure 2a, when there is no change in the merit order, the change in the power price (Δp_2) will always be equal to the marginal CO$_2$ allowance costs of the marginal generation technology B. The resulting pass-through rate will always be unity (in terms of both the add-on rate and the work-on rate). However, when there is a switch in the merit order – as displayed in Figure 2b – the situation changes. In this case, the marginal technology is A with CO$_2$ allowances costs equal to Δp_3 while the change in the power price is Δp_4. Therefore, while the add-on rate for the marginal production technology A is 100%, the work-on

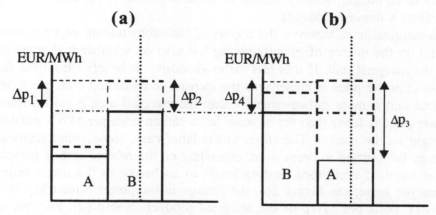

Figure 2. Pass-through rates under changes in the merit order.

rate, $\Delta p_4 / \Delta p_3$, will be less than 1 since $\Delta p_4 < \Delta p_3$.[1] In markets with surplus capacity, competitive pressures from excess generation capacity also impact on the merit order and, in turn, the work-on rate (Reinaud, 2003).

In addition, there may be several reasons why generators do not add on the full CO_2 costs to their power bid prices:[2]

- The expectation of power producers that their current emissions or output will be used as an input factor for the determination of the allocation of allowances in future periods, mainly after 2012 but possibly even 2008–2012. This creates an incentive to increase today's output and thus encourages generators not to add on the full allowance price to their energy bids.
- Voluntary agreements or the regulatory threat of governments to intervene in the market if generators make excessive windfall profits from the free allocation might induce generators to limit the add-on.
- Other reasons, such as the incidence of non-optimal behaviour among power producers, market imperfections, time lags or other constraints, including the incidence of risks, uncertainties, lack of information, and the immaturity or lack of transparency of the carbon market.

2.1. The impact on generators' profits

An important question is how the pass-through of CO_2 opportunity costs affects the profitability of power stations. A main purpose of the free allocation of emissions allowances under the US cap-and-trade programmes for SO_2 and NO_x, as well as under the EU ETS for CO_2, is to obtain the political support of large emitters. Thus, the free allocation aims to ensure that the introduction of the ETS does not reduce the profitability of the eligible companies.

The impact of emissions trading in general and free allocation of emission allowances in particular can be illustrated by means of Figure 2, which illustrates the implications of emissions trading for generators' profits where the supply curve consists of different types of technology. Where emissions trading does not lead to a change in the merit order of the supply curve (and in total demand; see Figure 2a), the change in the power price (Δp_2) is just about equal to the CO_2 costs per MWh of the marginal production unit (B). For this unit, this implies that profits do not change where all the allowances have to be bought, while it results in windfall profits in the case of full grandfathering (equal to Δp_2 times volume produced).

For the infra-marginal unit, however, the impact of emissions trading on operational profits does not only depend on the degree of grandfathering but also on whether it is more or less carbon-intensive than the marginal unit. If it is less carbon-intensive, it benefits from the fact that the ET-induced increase in power price is higher than the increase in its carbon costs per MWh. However, if the infra-marginal unit is more carbon-intensive than the marginal unit, it suffers from a loss, as the increase in power price is lower than the increase in its carbon costs per MWh; notably if allowances have to be bought on the market. Therefore, in the latter case, some grandfathering to this infra-marginal unit may be justified to break even, depending on the relative carbon intensity of this unit.

On the other hand, if emissions trading leads to a change in the merit order (while total demand remains the same; see Figure 2b), the change in the power price (Δp_4) is lower than the change in the CO_2 costs per MWh of the marginal production unit (A). For this unit, emissions trading results in a profit per MWh (equal to Δp_4) under free allocation, but in a loss (equal to

$\Delta p_3 - \Delta p_4$) if all the allowances have to be bought. Therefore, for this unit, some grandfathering may be justified in order to break even.[3] For the infra-marginal unit (B), the increase in power price is higher than the increase in CO_2 costs, regardless of whether allowances have to be bought or not. Therefore, even if this unit has to buy all its allowances, it will benefit from ET and, hence, there is no need for any grandfathering for this unit to break even.[4]

If the electricity demand response to ET-induced price increases is sufficiently large to stop the operation of a set of power generators with higher variable costs, and thus the market clearing price of electricity is reduced to the variable costs of a technology with lower variable costs, this will reduce the profits of all units operating during this period, as all of them will receive revenues corresponding to the lower market clearing price.

3. Empirical estimates of passing through CO₂ costs

This section presents some empirically estimated rates of passing through CO_2 opportunity costs of EU emissions trading to power prices in Germany and the Netherlands. We use two different approaches to estimate these rates. First, we look at the forward power market, particularly the year-ahead market where, for instance, electricity delivered in 2006 is traded during every day of the year 2005. In this approach, we assess the extent to which changes in forward power prices can be explained by changes in underlying forward prices for fuel and CO_2 allowances. Secondly, we study the spot market, notably the German power exchange (EEX), by comparing hourly spot electricity prices for the period from January 2005 to March 2006 with the corresponding hourly electricity prices in the year 2004. More specifically, we examine to what extent a change in the spot power price, for example at 9a.m. on the first Monday in January 2006 relative to the first Monday in January 2004, can be explained by a change in the price of a CO_2 allowance on the EUA market.

First of all, however, some background information will be provided on trends in prices for fuel and CO_2 allowances and dark and spark spreads in the power sectors of Germany and The Netherlands during the years 2004–2005.

3.1. Trends in forward prices and costs

For the years 2004–2005, Figures 3 and 4 present power prices versus fuel and CO_2 costs to generate one MWh of power (assuming a fuel efficiency of 40% for coal and 42% for gas, a related emission factor of 0.85 and 0.48 tCO_2/MWh for coal and gas, respectively, and full 'opportunity' costs for generating electricity by either coal or gas). While Figure 3 covers the case of coal-generated off-peak power in Germany, Figure 4 presents the case of gas-generated peak power in the Netherlands.[5]

The German case shows that the fuel (i.e. coal) costs to generate power have been more or less stable at a level of about €16/MWh during the years 2004–2005. In addition, the CO_2 costs of coal-generated power have been stable during the second part of 2004 but have approximately tripled during the first part of 2005 from about €6/MWh in January to about €18/MWh in July. This suggests that the increasing off-peak prices in Germany over this period may have been caused primarily by the rising CO_2 prices (and not by higher fuel prices). However, during the second part of 2005 (August–December 2005), CO_2 costs per coal-generated MWh have been generally stable while off-peak prices have continued to rise. This indicates that factors other than fuel and CO_2 costs influence power prices.

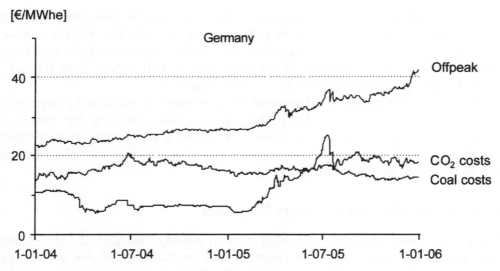

Figure 3. Off-peak power prices versus fuel/CO_2 costs in Germany (year-ahead, 2004–2005).

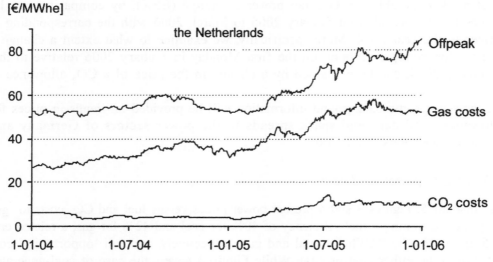

Figure 4. Peak power prices versus fuel/CO_2 costs in The Netherlands (year-ahead, 2004–2005).

The Dutch case illustrates that the fuel (i.e. gas) costs to produce electricity have risen substantially from around €33/MWh in early January 2005 to about €56/MWh in early September 2005. CO_2 costs of gas-generated power have also increased over this period, but less dramatically, i.e. from €4 to €11/MWh (partly due to the relatively low – but constant – emission factor of gas-generated electricity). This suggests that, besides the CO_2 cost pass-through, the rising peak load prices in The Netherlands over this period – from about €52 to €80/MWh – are largely due to other factors, especially the rising gas prices. However, comparable to the German case, where both gas and

CO_2 costs have been more or less stable during the last quarter of 2005 (or even declined slightly as far as gas costs are concerned), peak power prices continued to increase to €84/MWh in late December 2005.

3.2. Trends in dark and spark spreads on forward markets

Figures 5 and 6 present trends in dark/spark spreads and CO_2 costs per MWh over the years 2004–2005 in Germany and The Netherlands, based on forward (i.e. year-ahead) prices for power, fuels and CO_2 emission allowances. For the present analysis, a *dark* spread is simply defined as the difference between the power price and the cost of *coal* to generate 1 MWh of electricity, while a *spark* spread refers to the difference between the power price and the cost of *gas* to produce 1 MWh of electricity. If the costs of CO_2 are included, these indicators are called '*clean dark/spark spreads*' or '*carbon compensated dark/spark spreads*'.[6]

For Germany, Figure 5 depicts trends in dark spreads in both peak and off-peak hours, based on the assumption that a coal generator is the price-setting unit during these periods.[7] In addition, it

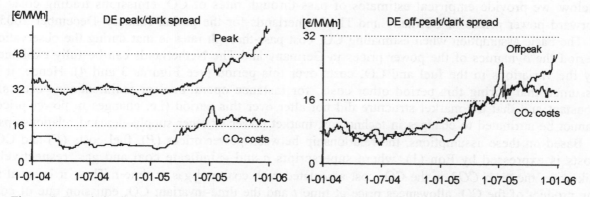

Figure 5. Trends in dark spreads and CO_2 costs per coal-generated MWh in Germany during peak and off-peak hours (year-ahead, 2004–2005).

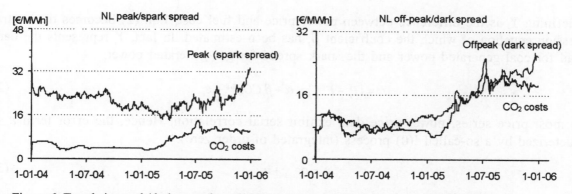

Figure 6. Trends in spark/dark spreads and CO_2 costs per gas/coal-generated MWh in The Netherlands during peak and off-peak hours (year-ahead, 2004–2005).

shows the costs of CO_2 allowances required to cover the emissions per MWh generated by a coal-fired power plant (with an emission factor of 0.85 tCO_2/MWh). The figure suggests that up to July 2005, changes in the dark spread can be largely explained by changes in the CO_2 costs per MWh. Since August 2005, however, this relationship is less clear, as the CO_2 costs have remained more or less stable, while the dark spreads have continued to increase rapidly.

For the Netherlands, Figure 6 depicts trends in the spark spread during the peak hours and the dark spread during the off-peak hours, based on the assumption that a gas- versus coal-fired installation is the price-setting unit during these periods, respectively. In addition, it presents the costs of CO_2 allowances to cover the emissions per MWh produced by a gas- and coal-fired power station, with an emission factor of 0.48 and 0.85 tCO_2/MWh, respectively. Similar to the German case, Figure 7 suggests that, during the period January–July 2005, changes in the dark/spark spreads in The Netherlands can be largely attributed to changes in the CO_2 costs per MWh, but that afterwards this relationship is less clear.

3.3. Statistical estimates of CO_2 cost pass-through rates on forward markets

Below, we provide empirical estimates of pass-through rates of CO_2 emissions trading costs to forward power prices in Germany and The Netherlands for the period January–December 2005.

The basic assumption when estimating CO_2 cost pass-through rates is that during the observation period the dynamics of the power prices in Germany and The Netherlands can be fully explained by the variations in the fuel and CO_2 costs over this period (see Figures 3 and 4). Hence, it is assumed that during this period other costs, for instance operational or maintenance costs, are constant and that the market structure did not alter over this period (i.e. changes in power prices cannot be attributed to changes in technology, market power or other supply–demand relationships).

Based on these assumptions, the relationship between power prices (P), fuel costs (F) and CO_2 costs is expressed by Eqn (1), where superscripts c and g indicate coal and gas, respectively. Likewise, the term $CO2_t$ is the CO_2 cost associated with coal and gas at time t. Thus, it is equal to the product of the CO_2 allowances price at time t and the time-invariant CO_2 emission rate of coal or gas generators. In our analysis, fuel costs are assumed to be fully passed on to power prices.[8] This is equivalent to fixing the coefficient β_2 at unity.

$$P_1 = \alpha + \beta_1 CO2_t^{c,g} + \beta_2 F_t^{c,g} + \varepsilon_t \tag{1}$$

By defining Y_t as the difference between power price and fuel cost, Eqn (2) becomes the central regression equation of which the coefficient β_1 has been estimated. In fact, Y_t represents the dark spread for coal-generated power and the spark spread for gas-generated power.

$$Y_t = \left(P_t - F_t^{c,g}\right) = \alpha + \beta_1 CO2_t^{c,g} + \varepsilon_t \tag{2}$$

Like most price series, power price data exhibit serial correlation. Hence, the error term ε_t is characterized by a so-called I(0) process (integrated of order zero).[9]

$$\varepsilon_t = \rho\varepsilon_{t-1} + u_t, \tag{3}$$

where u_t is a purely random variable with an expected value of zero, i.e. $E(u_t) = 0$, and a constant variance over time, i.e. $Var(u_t) = \sigma^2$.

In 2005, electricity forward contracts were traded at the German power exchange EEX for only a limited number of days. For the remaining days, a settlement price was reported based on the chief trader principle. This requires all chief traders to daily submit a spreadsheet with their evaluation of prices for more than 40 different contract types. It is unlikely that all contract types would be updated on a daily basis commensurate with CO$_2$ prices. Since the different protocols used by various companies for reporting power prices are proprietary information, we do not possess such information and are unable to consider it in the estimation procedure. Thus, to illustrate the effect, we assume in the Appendix that the reported prices are a weighted average over the prices during the previous days or weeks. Estimating Eqn (1) without considering this creates an error on the left-hand side of the equation that we are estimating. This error creates a bias in the estimation of β_1.

This bias exists if we estimate β_1 using an ordinary least-square estimation, but can increase significantly if we estimate a non-cointegrated process based on Eqn (3), using other approaches that iteratively determine both β_1 and p. The alternative approach we would usually apply in such a situation is an estimation based on the first differences. But once again we show in the Appendix that the error on the left-hand side of the equation can create a very strong bias in this estimation.

Hence, we conclude that the least affected alternative is a simple OLS estimator. We accept that we have an estimator that might slightly underestimate the CO$_2$ pass-through. We are somewhat concerned about the fact that price series are typically autocorrelated. In fact, both power prices and CO$_2$ costs series are I(1) processes. Thus, if CO$_2$ and electricity price series are not also cointegrated, then the error terms follow an I(1) process and will fail to converge to zero. However, since both forward electricity prices and CO$_2$ prices are bounded, this turns out to be less of an issue in our analyses. Finally, we know that the typical confidence intervals reported by our estimation will no longer accurately represent the uncertainty in the estimation. Therefore, we apply bootstrapping to illustrate the accuracy of our estimation. In particular, we estimate β_1 using the data from a restricted observation period; thus we can examine the robustness of the estimation. More specifically, we first construct a subset of data for bootstrapping (e.g. January–October). We repeat this process by sliding the 2-month window (e.g. January–February merged with May–December), resulting in a total of six regressions with bootstrapped data.

Table 1 summarizes the estimated CO$_2$ pass-through rates in Germany and The Netherlands and also gives the maximum and minimum values of the OLS estimator associated with various bootstrapping estimations. With a confidence of about 80%, we can say that these rates are within the interval of 60 and 117% in Germany, and between 64 and 81% in The Netherlands. In light of the aforementioned methodological difficulties, the results presented in Table 1 need to be interpreted with caution. In particular, we offer some explanations of possible complexities and discuss the potential direction of bias.

First, the very high pass-through rate for Germany might be partially explained by increasing gas prices during 2005. Given that gas generators (instead of coal generators) set the marginal price in German markets during some peak hours, this could contribute to power prices increasing in peak forward contracts. As coal generators benefit from this gas cost-induced increase in power prices, this leads to an overestimation of the pass-through rate of CO$_2$ costs for coal-generated power.

Finally, Sijm et al. (2005, 2006) present and discuss a wide variety of further estimations of CO$_2$ pass-through rates. In general, the estimations based on the period January–July 2005 result in lower pass-through rates than estimations based on the period 2005 as a whole. For instance, the pass-through rate for The Netherlands peak hours is estimated at 38% for the period January–July 2005, while it is estimated at 78% for 2005 as a whole. This difference in estimated pass-through

Table 1. Empirical estimates of CO_2 pass-through rates in Germany and The Netherlands for the period January–December 2005, based on year-ahead prices for 2006 (%)

Country	Load period	Fuel (efficiency)	OLS	Bootstrap (2 months)	
				Min	Max
Germany	Peak	Coal (40%)	117	97	117
	Off-peak	Coal (40%)	60	60	71
Netherlands	Peak	Gas (42%)	78	64	81
	Off-peak	Coal (40%)	80	69	80

rates between the period January–July and 2005 as a whole could possibly be caused by some delays in the market internalizing the CO_2 price (i.e. market learning), rapidly rising gas prices (notably during the first period of 2005), higher power prices due to increasing scarcity and/or market power (particularly during the latter part of 2005), or by various other factors affecting power prices in liberalized wholesale markets.

3.4. Empirical estimate using the hourly spot markets in Germany

Another approach to assessing the impact of the CO_2 allowance costs on the wholesale power price is to compare the day-ahead electricity prices per hour on the German power exchange (EEX for every day in 2005 with the corresponding prices in 2004). The implicit assumption is that factors other than CO_2 and fuel costs remained unchanged during these two years. According to Eqn (4), the difference in the electricity price during a particular hour after the introduction of the ETS and the corresponding hour in 2004 is explained by the difference in coal prices during the hours concerned, the impact of the CO_2 price on the EUA market, and by an error term:

$$P_{2005,t} - P_{2004,t} = p^{coal}_{2004,t} - p^{coal}_{2004,5} + \beta p^{co2}_{2005,t} + \varepsilon_t \qquad (4)$$

We set $p^{co2}_{.t}$ to reflect the costs of CO_2 emissions at the daily allowance price for a coal-fired power station with an emission rate of 0.9 tCO_2/MWh. As coal is at the margin during most of the day, this can then also be interpreted as the work-on rate for coal power stations.

Figure 7 depicts β for different hours of the day. We have split the observation period into three sections, mainly to examine whether the daily pattern is consistent over time. While this pattern did not change during the day, the level of work-on rate increased for each subsequent period considered.

Figure 7 invites three observations. First, during off-peak periods the work-on rate seems to be less than 1. This could be partly explained by intertemporal constraints of power stations – they prefer to operate during off-peak periods if this saves start-up costs. As CO_2 costs increase the start-up costs, they also create additional incentives to lower prices during off-peak periods to keep the station running (Muesgens and Neuhoff, 2006). Second, if coal generators set the price during peak periods, then these are usually vintage stations with higher heat rates and therefore higher emission costs. Finally, the increase in gas prices during the year 2005–2006 is likely to also explain some of the price increase during peak periods. As open-cycle gas turbines might be called upon during some peak periods, their increased costs with higher gas prices can further push up the power price.

Therefore we now focus on the hour 3–4 p.m., for which intertemporal effects and the gas-price impact from peaking units running at maximum a few hours a day is least prevalent, as indicated

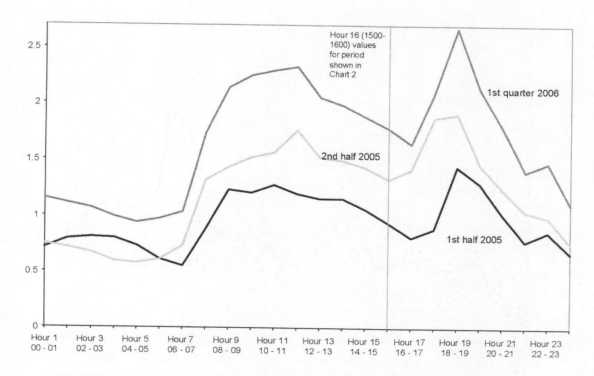

Figure 7. Work-on rate of CO_2 costs on the German spot power market for different time periods, assuming coal generators are at the margin.

by the lower value for this hour relative to other peak hours in Figure 7. Figure 8 depicts for each day the price increase of electricity in the hour 3–4 p.m. relative to the pre-ETS year 2004. The curves are again corrected for coal prices and therefore *de facto* depict:

$$P_{2005,t} - P_{2004,t} - \left(p^{coal}_{2005,t} - p^{coal}_{2004,5} \right) \qquad (5)$$

As can be seen from Figure 8, during January the entire CO_2 price was not passed through, but subsequently a close link seems to exist between the increase in the CO_2 cost and the increase in the electricity price relative to 2004. In September the public debate in Germany revolved about whether the inclusion of CO_2 opportunity costs into the electricity price is appropriate, and induced generation companies to proceed with some caution. It seems that eventually the power firms' management took the position that any other behaviour than pass-through is inappropriate, and publicly acknowledged such behaviour, thus allowing traders to return to the habit of fully internalizing the CO_2 opportunity costs.

By the end of the year 2005, the German electricity prices further increased. We did not analyse the reasons for this development. The price increase could be attributed to one of the following three factors: (i) scarcity of generation capacity, (ii) higher gas prices than in previous winters, thus higher prices when gas is at the margin, and (iii) the exercise of market power.

Looking at the overall picture suggests that market participants in Germany have fully passed through the opportunity costs of CO_2 allowances in the spot market.

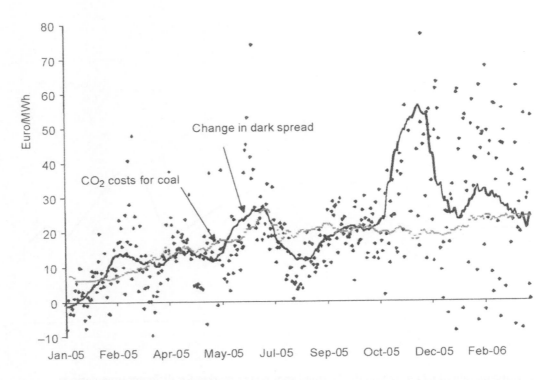

Figure 8. Coal-price-corrected price increase for electricity (3–4 p.m.) depicted as dots and their 40-day moving average (dark line) and the evolution of the CO_2 price (grey line).

4. Model estimates of CO_2 cost pass-through

In addition to the empirical estimates, CO_2 cost pass-through rates have been estimated for some EU countries by means of the COMPETES model.[10] COMPETES can simulate and analyse the impact of the strategic behaviour of large producers on the wholesale market under different market structure scenarios (varying from perfect competition to oligopolistic and monopolistic market conditions). The model has been used to analyse the implications of CO_2 emissions trading for power prices, company profits and other issues related to the wholesale power market in four countries of continental north-western Europe (Belgium, France, Germany and The Netherlands).

The major findings of the COMPETES model with regard to CO_2 cost pass-through are summarized in Table 2. They are compared to model results from the Integrated Planning Model (IPM), which are described in more detail by Neuhoff et al. (this issue). As results are very sensitive to the gas/coal shift, small differences in the assumptions about gas prices, available gas generation capacity and interconnection capacity can explain the differences between the results of both models for The Netherlands.

Table 2. Model estimates of electricity price increases (in €/MWh) due to CO_2 costs at €20/t

	Belgium	France	Germany	Netherlands	United Kingdom
COMPETES	2–14	1–5	13–19	9–11	
IPM			17	15	13–14

Under all scenarios considered, power prices turn out to increase significantly due to CO_2 emissions trading. In case of a CO_2 price of €20/tonne, these increases are generally highest in Germany (€13–19/MWh) with an intermediate position for Belgium (€2–14/MWh) and The Netherlands (€9–11/MWh). The model predicts very low price increases for France (€1–5/MWh), which reflects the predominant nuclear generation basis of this country.

Differences in absolute amounts of CO_2 cost pass-through between the individual countries considered can be mainly attributed to differences in fuel mix between these countries. For instance, during most of the load hours, power prices in Germany are set by a coal-fired generator (with a high CO_2 emission factor). On the other hand, in France they are often determined by a nuclear plant (with zero CO_2 emissions), while The Netherlands take an intermediate position – in terms of average CO_2 emissions and absolute cost pass-through – due to the fact that Dutch power prices are set by a gas-fired installation during a major part of the load duration curve.

In relative terms (i.e. as a percentage of the full opportunity costs of EU emissions trading), COMPETES has generated a wide variety of pass-through rates for various scenarios and load periods analysed. While some of these rates are low (or even zero where the power price is set by a nuclear plant), most of them vary between 60 and 80%, depending on the country, market structure, demand elasticity, load period and CO_2 price considered.

In addition, Table 2 provides the results of simulation runs by the IPM, a detailed power sector model for the EU developed by ICF Consulting. At a price of €20/tCO_2, the average amount of CO_2 cost pass-through in the UK is estimated at €13–14/MWh, while for Germany and The Netherlands this amount is estimated at €17 and €15/MWh, respectively.[11]

5. Estimates of windfall profits

As COMPETES includes detailed information at the operational level for all (major) power companies in the countries covered by the model, it can also be used to estimate the impact of emissions trading on firms' profits at the aggregated level as well as at the level of major individual companies. Such quantitative results are helpful in order to understand the qualitative impact, but the numbers should only be taken as an indication of the order of magnitude involved. We discuss this aspect in more detail at the end of the section.

Table 3 presents a summary of the changes in total companies' profits due to emissions trading under two scenarios: perfect competition (PC) and oligopolistic competition, i.e. strategic behaviour by the major power producers (ST). These ET-induced profit changes can be divided into the following two categories.

1. *Changes in profits due to ET-induced changes in production costs and power prices*. This category of profit changes is independent of the allocation method. In fact, the estimation of this category of profit changes is based on the assumption that all companies have to buy their allowances and, hence, that CO_2 costs are 'real' costs.

2. *Changes in profits due to the free allocation of emission allowances*. This category of profit changes is an addition or correction to the first category for the extent to which allowances are grandfathered – rather than sold – to eligible companies.

We start with the analysis of the impact in a perfectly competitive environment. In the fourth column of Table 3 it is assumed that all companies have to buy all their emissions allowances on

Table 3. Changes in aggregated power firms' profits due to CO_2 emissions trading in Belgium, France, Germany and The Netherlands, based on COMPETES model scenarios

Scenario[a] (1)	Price elasticity (2)	Total profits [M€] (3)	Change in profits due to: Price effects [M€] (4)	Change in profits due to: Free allocation [M€] (5)	Total change in profits due to emissions trading [M€] (6)	Total change in profits due to emissions trading [%] (7)
PC0-ze	0.0	13919				
PC20-ze	0.0	27487	5902	7666	13567	98
PC0	0.2	13919				
PC20	0.2	21904	1712	6272	7984	57
ST0-le	0.1	53656				
ST20-le	0.1	59570	−82	5996	5914	11
ST0	0.2	32015				
ST20	0.2	36782	−542	5308	4767	15

[a] PC and ST refer to two different model scenarios, i.e. perfect competition (PC) and oligopolistic (or strategic) competition (ST). Numbers attached to these abbreviations, such as PC0 or PC20, indicate a scenario without emissions trading (CO_2 price is 0) versus a scenario with emissions trading (at a price of €20/tCO_2). The additions 'ze' and 'le' refer to a zero price elasticity and low price elasticity (0.1), respectively, compared with the baseline scenario with a price elasticity of 0.2.

the market, i.e. there are no windfall profits due to grandfathering. Even under this condition, total company profits increase in the perfect competition scenarios. This results from the fact that, on average, power prices are set by marginal units with relatively high carbon intensities that pass their relatively high carbon costs through to these prices. Infra-marginal units with relatively low carbon intensities are not faced by these high carbon costs but benefit from the higher power prices on the market. Profits increase by €6 billion if we assume no demand response, and by €2 billion if we assume a very strong demand response of 0.2.[12] Thus, the high demand elasticity scenarios (i.e. 0.1 and 0.2) provide a lower bound estimation of windfall profits. Note that in the long-term investment equilibrium we expect a fixed ratio between demand and the number of power stations, and hence a reduction of demand will not affect profitability of individual power stations. The total profits of power generators are obviously further increased if we consider the impact of the free allocation (column 5), as illustrated in column 6.

The model provides additional insights into the impact of the strategic behaviour of power generators. If we assume that power generators act strategically, they will push up prices and, hence, their profits will double in the reference case that ignores emissions trading. Further empirical work would be needed to assess to what extent this level of profits corresponds to the situation before the introduction of emissions trading. If we now introduce emissions trading into the model scenarios, then profitability in the absence of free allocation is slightly reduced (by less than 1%). While all generators profit from the higher prices, the effect of a smaller market dominates this effect and therefore slightly reduces their revenues.

COMPETES is based on the assumption of a linear demand function, which implies a lower rate of passing through under oligopolistic competition than that in competitive markets. If constant elasticity of demand supply were assumed in the model, then higher pass-through rates than for competitive markets would result. These lower pass-through rates in the case of oligopolistic competition explain why profits due to emissions trading (excluding free allocation) are slightly reduced in the ST scenarios. Note, however, that due to strategic behaviour, profits in the reference ST scenario are significantly higher than in the CP scenario. Free allocation (column 5) once again makes all scenarios very profitable for power industry (column 6).

Under the present EU ETS, however, companies do not have to buy their emission allowances on the market but receive them largely for free. This implies that they are able to realize windfall profits due to grandfathering, as they still pass on the carbon costs of grandfathered emission allowances. The fifth column of Table 3 shows estimates of these profits, based on estimates of total firms' CO$_2$ emissions and the assumption that power companies receive, on average, 90% of the allowances to cover their emissions for free. At a price of an emission allowance of €20/tCO$_2$, these windfall profits vary between €5.3 and 7.7 billion, depending on the scenario considered. As total production and total emissions are generally higher under the competitive scenarios (because companies do not exercise their market power to withdraw output), total windfall profits due to grandfathering are also higher under these scenarios (compared to the oligopolistic scenarios based on strategic behaviour).

There are major differences, however, in profit performance due to emissions trading at the individual firm level, as can be seen from Table 4. This table presents changes in profits due to emissions trading under two scenarios – PC20-ze and ST20 – for the major power companies covered by COMPETES, including the so-called 'competitive fringe' of these countries.[13] Even if they have to buy their allowances, companies such as E.ON and EdF seem to benefit most from emissions trading, especially from the increase in power prices due to the pass-through of carbon costs (i.e. type 1 windfall profits). This is not surprising, given the high share of nuclear production in total generation by these companies.

On the other hand, some companies make a loss due to emissions trading when they have to buy their emissions allowances. In both scenarios, these companies are, in particular, ESSENT, NUON, STEAG AG and Vattenfall Europe. The losses for ESSENT and NUON are mainly due to the fact that these Dutch companies lose market shares in favour of foreign, less carbon-intensive companies, while they tend not to make profits from ET-induced price increases in the Dutch market, as marginal gas generators push up the price in line with cost increases of inframarginal units. The losses for STEAG AG and Vattenfall Europe are predominantly due to their portfolio mix. For STEAG AG, this portfolio is purely based on coal, while a large component of Vattenfall's portfolio is based on brown coal. Brown coal is more carbon-intensive than Germany's electricity-price-setting coal. This unbalanced portfolio is reflected in profit losses in the absence of free allowance allocation.

Once the additional profits due to grandfathering are accounted for, however, all companies benefit from emissions trading under both scenarios presented in Table 4. As coal- and other carbon-intensive companies (such as RWE, STEAG AG and Vattenfall Europe) receive relatively large amounts of CO$_2$ emission allowances for free, they benefit relatively more from this effect of emissions trading on firms' profits.

Although the above-mentioned quantitative estimates of changes in profits are helpful in order to understand the qualitative impact of the EU ETS on the profitability of power generation at the firm level, they have to be judged in light of the restrictions of the modelling approach:

First, it is a static model, which therefore does not capture the impact on investment decisions or, alternatively, the restraint of the potential threat of entrants or regulatory intervention put on power generators to keep prices down. In the long run, new investment is required, and therefore the best estimate for long-term power prices is the cost of the entry of a new generator. This

Table 4. Changes in profits of individual power companies operating in Belgium, France, Germany and The Netherlands, based on two COMPETES model scenarios (in M€)

| | Total profits | | Change in profits due to: | | |
Perfect competition (PC)	PC0	PC20-ze	Price effects	Free allocation	Total change in profits
Comp Nationale du Rhone	127	154	28	0	28
Comp Belgium	204	340	84	51	135
Comp France	200	326	7	119	126
Comp Germany	743	2119	147	1230	1376
Comp Netherlands	128	172	−22	66	44
A	2007	4575	1517	1051	2568
B	1722	2883	625	536	1161
C	4405	6807	2178	225	2402
D	768	1890	748	373	1122
E	319	535	−42	257	216
F	204	261	−90	148	57
G	1861	4565	802	1902	2704
H	52	92	13	27	41
I	217	438	−25	245	220
J	962	2329	−69	1436	1367
Total	13919	27487	5902	7666	13567

| | Total profits | | Change in profits due to: | | |
Oligopolistic competition (ST)	ST0	ST20	Price effects	Free allocation	Total change in profits
Comp Nationale du Rhone	425	433	8	0	8
Comp Belgium	250	269	−60	80	20
Comp France	1576	1422	−472	317	−155
Comp Germany	1972	2997	−319	1344	1025
Comp Netherlands	392	469	−59	136	77
A	3269	4226	757	199	956
B	2775	3220	245	199	445
C	12287	12709	323	98	422
D	1646	2182	330	205	536
E	775	923	−99	247	147
F	650	620	−195	166	−29
G	2896	3245	−119	468	349
H	339	348	−51	60	9
I	658	1001	−196	539	343
J	2103	2718	−636	1251	615
Total	32015	36782	−542	5308	4767

PC and ST refer to two different model scenarios, i.e. perfect competition (PC) and oligopolistic (or strategic) competition (ST). Numbers attached to these abbreviations, such as PC0 or PC20, indicate a scenario without emissions trading (CO$_2$ price is 0) versus a scenario with emissions trading (at a price of €20/tCO$_2$). The additions 'ze' and 'le' refer to a zero price elasticity and low price elasticity (0.1), respectively, compared with the baseline scenario with a price elasticity of 0.2.

model therefore provides insights into profitability during the transition period when emissions trading is implemented, but the structure of generation assets has not adjusted to reflect the new optimal investment mix. Thus we see this analysis as a guide towards understanding the type of compensation that power generators can expect in the transition period before we shift towards a new equilibrium.

Second, modelling of strategic behaviour tends to capture qualitative effects, but the quantification typically requires stronger assumptions. For example, market design of transmission or balancing markets can have a significant impact on opportunities to exercise market power by strategic players.

Third, in the strategic model scenarios we assume a linear demand function. With linear demand functions, strategic firms reduce the CO$_2$ cost pass-through relative to the competitive model scenarios. Analytical research shows that this result is inverted if we instead assume a constant elasticity of demand function. In this case, strategic firms increase the CO$_2$ pass-through rate relative to a competitive scenario. However, we believe that the empirical demand curves would be somewhere between two extreme cases: constant elasticity and linear demand (i.e. zero elasticity). Furthermore, given the fact that all the economic rent from introducing EU ETS goes to producers (at the expense of consumers) under fixed demand scenarios, the profitability of firms under constant elasticity cases would be less than that under liner demand cases in general.

5.1. Estimates of windfall profits at national level

Recently, Frontier Economics (2006) has estimated windfall profits due to the EU ETS for the four largest power companies operating in The Netherlands (ESSENT, NUON, E.ON and Electrabel). For the year 2005, these profits are estimated at €19 million for the four companies as a whole. This estimate is rather low, as it is based on some stringent, specific assumptions and conditions for the year 2005. On the one hand, it is assumed that 90% of the power produced during 2005 was already sold in 2003 and 2004, when CO$_2$ prices and (assumed) pass-through rates were low, resulting in additional revenues of power sales in 2005 of €69 million. On the other hand, it is assumed that the 'allocation deficit' of the four companies (i.e. the difference between the allowances grandfathered and the allowances needed to cover their emissions) was met by market purchases in 2005 only, when CO$_2$ prices were high, resulting in a total cost of €50 million.[14]

Although the estimate by Frontier Economics of the windfall profits in The Netherlands (and the underlying assumptions and conditions) can, to some extent, be justified for the year 2005, it does not provide an adequate, 'representative' estimate of the windfall profits due to the EU ETS in the years thereafter. A more representative estimate of these windfall profits can be based on one of the following three approaches.

Firstly, based on the COMPETES methodology outlined above, changes in profits due to CO$_2$ emissions trading have been estimated for the operations of the four largest power companies in the Netherlands in an 'average' year. Table 5 shows that, at a price of €20/tCO$_2$, these changes vary between €250 and 600 million for the four companies as a whole, depending on the scenario considered. As explained, these changes are the result of two different effects of emissions trading, called the price and grandfathering effects. As can be observed from Table 5, the price effect – based on the assumption that power companies have to buy all their emission allowances – leads to losses in three out of four scenarios. This is due to the fact that (i) power demand is assumed to respond significantly to higher prices (i.e. we assume demand elasticities of 0.1 and 0.2 in the scenarios with losses due to the price effect), (ii) the share of non-carbon power generation in The Netherlands is relatively low (and, hence, the benefits of ET-induced price increases for non-carbon generators are low), and (iii) the share of gas-fired power-generation – setting the power price – is relatively high in The Netherlands

Table 5. Changes in aggregated profits due to CO_2 emissions trading for the four largest power firms in The Netherlands (E.ON, Electrabel, ESSENT and NUON), based on COMPETES model scenarios

Scenario[a]	Price elasticity	Total profits [M€]	Change in profits due to:		Total change in profits due to emissions trading	
			Price effects [M€]	Free allocation [M€]	[M€]	[%]
PC0		995				
PC20	0.2	1394	−78	477	399	40
PC20-ze	0.0	1580	109	477	585	59
ST0		2151				
ST20	0.2	2408	−179	436	257	12
ST20-le	0.1	3359				
ST20-le	0.1	3610	−185	436	251	7

[a] PC and ST refer to two different model scenarios, i.e. perfect competition (PC) and oligopolistic (or strategic) competition (ST). Numbers attached to these abbreviations, such as PC0 or PC20, indicate a scenario without emissions trading (CO_2 price is 0) versus a scenario with emissions trading (at a price of €20/tCO_2). The additions 'ze' and ' le' refer to a zero price elasticity and low price elasticity (0.1), respectively, compared to the baseline scenario with a price elasticity of 0.2.

(and, hence, high-carbon generators such as coal-fired installations are faced by high carbon costs that are not matched by equally higher power prices).

On the other hand, when assuming that the power companies in The Netherlands receive 90% of their needed emission allowances for free, the grandfathering effect far outweights the price effect, resulting in major total windfall profits due to emissions trading based largely on free allocation.

Secondly, following the methodology used by Frontier Economics for an average, 'representative' year, it may – for instance – be assumed that (i) total CO_2 emissions of the four major power companies in The Netherlands is about 37.5 $MtCO_2$ per year, while the amount of allowances grandfathered to these companies is 35 $MtCO_2$ per annum (hence, the allocation deficit is 2.5 $MtCO_2$ per year; i.e. about 7% of total emissions), (ii) the price of a CO_2 allowance bought is, on average, equal to the price of a CO_2 allowance passed through to power prices, and amounts to €20/tCO_2, and (iii) the average pass-through rate is 50%. In that case, the total windfall profits of the four major power companies in The Netherlands amounts to €325 million.

Finally, the third approach to estimating windfall profits is based on ET-induced price increases of domestically produced power sales in The Netherlands. These sales amount to around 100 TWh per year. Assuming that (i) 75% of this volume is sold during peak hours and the remaining part during the off-peak period, (ii) during peak hours, power prices are set by a gas-fired installation with an emission factor of 0.4 tCO_2/MWh and during the off-peak period by a coal-fired plant with an emission factor of 0.8 tCO_2/MWh, (iii) the CO_2 price is, on average, €20/t, (iv) the average pass-through rate is 40% during the peak and 50% during the off-peak, and (v) the allocation deficit for the power sector as a whole is equivalent to 4 million tCO_2 per year. In that case, the total windfall profits amount to €360 million per year.[15]

To conclude, at a price of €20/tCO_2, estimates of windfall profits due to the EU ETS in the power sector of The Netherlands for an average, 'representative' year vary between €300 and 600 million. This compares to about half the value of the emission allowances grandfathered to the power sector or some €3–5/MWh produced in The Netherlands.[16] It should be emphasized, however, that these estimates ignore the impact of ETS-induced profit changes on new investments in generation capacity and, hence, on production costs, power prices and company profits in the long run towards a new equilibrium.

UK power sector profits from the EU ETS were estimated at £800m/yr in a report to the DTI (IPA Energy Consulting, 2005). Such profits occur even though power sector emissions (157 MtCO$_2$) exceeded free allocation (134 MtCO$_2$), making the UK power sector by far the largest buyer on the EU ETS market. In the IPA model, the UK power sector in aggregate would break even if free allocation were cut back to 45 MtCO$_2$/yr. At this point the earnings from higher power prices, after accounting for impact on demand, would fund the purchase of emission allowances from auctions, other sectors or internationally. The profit impact is sensitive to the CO$_2$ price (assumed to be €15/t) and can increase if with lower gas prices the electricity price is set by more CO$_2$ intensive coal plants. Profits are also highly unequally distributed between individual companies, as the previous section illustrated for The Netherlands. In the first year of the ETS, utilities might not have realised all the modelled profits, as some production was covered by longer-term contracts and because changes in wholesale prices take time to feed through to retail price changes.

6. Summary of major findings and policy implications

In theory, power producers pass on the opportunity costs of freely allocated emission allowances to the price of electricity. For a variety of reasons, however, the increase in power prices on the market may be less than the increase in CO$_2$ costs per MWh generated by the marginal production unit. This is confirmed by empirical and model findings, showing estimates of CO$_2$ cost pass-through rates varying between 60 and 100% for wholesale power markets in Germany and The Netherlands. Using numerical models we find that, at a CO$_2$ price of €20/t, ET-induced increases in power prices range between €3 and 18/MWh, depending on the carbon intensity of the price-setting installation. As most of the emission allowances needed are allocated for free, the profitability of power generation increases accordingly. Model and empirical estimates of additional profits due to the EU ETS show that these 'windfall profits' may be very significant, depending on the price of CO$_2$ and the assumptions made. For instance, at a CO$_2$ price of €20/t, ETS-induced windfall profits in the power sector of The Netherlands are estimated at €300–600 million per year, i.e. about €3–5 per MWh produced and sold in The Netherlands.

Acknowledgements

We thank Prof. Benjamin F. Hobbs of the Johns Hopkins University (Baltimore, USA) as well as those ECN staff members who contributed to the 'CO$_2$ Price Dynamics' project, notably Stefan Bakker, Michael ten Donkelaar, Henk Harmsen, Sebastiaan Hers, Wietze Lise and Martin Scheepers (for details, see Sijm et al., 2005, 2006). We also thank Alessio Sancetta for guidance on the econometric analysis, Jim Cust for research assistance, and the UK research council project TSEC and Climate Strategies for financial support.

Notes

1 Model analyses show that when CO$_2$ costs exceeds €20/t, emissions trading would induce substantial changes in the production merit order (Sijm et al., 2005).

2 For a full discussion and illustration of these reasons, see Chapter 4 of Sijm et al. (2005).

3 It should be observed, however, that the change in the merit order might occur only during a certain load period. This has to be accounted for when analysing the impact of emissions trading on firms' profits and the implications for assessing the extent of grandfathering to break even.

4 Similar findings can be derived by means of Figure 1, showing different types of technology along the load duration curve. By comparing the revenues (price/MWh × hours loaded) and the corresponding real/opportunity costs with and without emissions trading, changes in profits can be derived for different types of technology, including a change in the merit order of these technologies.

5 In this section, unless otherwise stated, coal refers to the internationally traded commodity classified as coal ARA CIF AP#2, while gas refers to the high caloric gas (with a conversion factor 35, 17 GJ/m³) from the Dutch Gas Union Trade & Supply (GUTS). Moreover, prices for power, fuels and CO_2 refer to forward markets (i.e. year-ahead prices).

6 These spreads are indicators for the coverage of other (non-fuel/CO_2) costs of generating electricity, including profits. For the present analysis, however, these other costs – for instance capital costs, maintenance or operating costs – are ignored as, for each specific case, they are assumed to be constant for the (short-term) period considered – although they may vary per case considered – and, hence, they do not affect the estimated pass-through rates.

7 It is acknowledged, however, that during certain periods of the peak hours – the 'super peak' – a gas generator is the marginal (price-setting) unit but, due to lack of data, it is not possible to analyse the super-peak period in Germany separately.

8 In Sijm et al. (2006), this assumption was dropped, but it turned out that the estimated pass-through rates for fuel and CO_2 costs were unreliable due to the observation that fuel and CO_2 costs are highly correlated.

9 An I(0) (integrated of order zero) is an autoregressive process with one period of lag, i.e. AR(1) and with a propensity factor $|\rho|<1$ (see Eqn (3)) (Stewart and Wallis, 1981). This indicates a process of correlation frequently experienced in everyday life. For instance, if the ambient temperature was high yesterday and there are no major changes in the weather conditions, the temperature today should be more or less similar. In this case, the temperature today provides a prior belief from which tomorrow's temperature can be inferred. Statistically, when assuming that ε_t is characterized by an I(0) process (i.e. $|\rho|<1$) in Eqn (3), the series is at least weakly independent. Therefore, both PW and OLS will be adequate to estimate pass-through rates given the correct specification. However, we are aware of the possibility of a non-cointegration process since three series – power prices, fuel costs and CO_2 costs – follow an I(1) process based on the Dickey–Fuller test. Thus, in this article, we intend to provide a preliminary assessment of the empirical CO_2 pass-through rates.

10 COMPETES stands for Comprehensive Market Power in Electricity Transmission and Energy Simulator. This model has been developed by ECN in cooperation with Benjamin F. Hobbs, Professor in the Whiting School of Engineering of The Johns Hopkins University (Department of Geography and Environmental Engineering, Baltimore, MD, USA). For more details on this model, see Sijm et al. (2005) and references cited therein, as well as the website http://www.electricitymarkets.info.

11 The high estimate for The Netherlands (compared to a similar estimate by the COMPETES model) might be caused by the older nature of the IPM model, with coal having a stronger influence on power prices.

12 This implies an increase in the wholesale price level from €20 to €30/MWh, and hence of the retail price level (including transmission, distribution and marketing costs) from let's say €70 to €90/MWh, would result in a reduction of demand by 10%.

13 The competitive fringe of a country – denoted as Comp Belgium, Comp France, etc. – refers to the collections of (smaller) producers in a country that lack the ability to influence power prices due to their small market share and, therefore, they were modelled behaving competitively (i.e. as price takers).

14 However, in May 2006, when the verified emissions of the four companies were published, it turned out that these companies did not have an allocation deficit but rather a small surplus. This implies that the estimate of the windfall profits by Frontier Economics was indeed quite conservative, as actually it is at least €50 million higher.

15 This figure includes not only the windfall profits of the four largest power companies in The Netherlands but also of all other Dutch power producers benefiting from ET-induced increases in the price of electricity.

16 Note that in The Netherlands the share of non-carbon fuels in total power production is low and that power prices are usually set by carbon-fuelled installations, notably gas-fired plants. In countries where the share of non-carbon fuels is much higher or where power prices are set by either high carbon-fuelled (i.e. coal) installations or by a non-carbon fuelled generator, the windfall profit per MWh or allowance grandfathered may be substantially different than in The Netherlands.

References

Burtraw, D., Palmer, K., Bharvirkar, R., Paul, A., 2002. The effect on asset values of the allocation of carbon dioxide emission allowances. Electricity Journal 15(5), 51–62.

Burtraw, D., Palmer, K., Kahn, D., 2005. Allocation of CO_2 Emissions Allowances in the Regional Greenhouse Gas Cap-and-Trade Program. RFF Discussion Papers 05–25.

EC, 2005. Further Guidance on Allocation Plans for the 2008 to 2012 Trading Period of the EU Emission Trading Scheme. European Commission, Brussels.

Frontier Economics, 2006. CO$_2$ Trading and its Influence on Electricity Markets. Final report to DTe, Frontier Economics Ltd, London.

IPA Energy Consulting, 2005, Implications of the EU Emissions Trading Scheme for the UK Power Generation Sector, report to UK Department of Trade and Industry.

Muesgens F., Neuhoff, K., 2006. Modelling Dynamic Constraints in Electricity Markets and the Costs of Uncertain Wind Output. EPRG WP 05/14.

Neuhoff K., Keats Martinez, K., Sato, M., 2006. Allocation, incentives and distortions: the impact of EU ETS emissions allowance allocations to the electricity sector. Climate Policy 6(1), 73–91.

Reinaud, J., 2003. Emissions Trading and its Possible Impacts on Investment Decisions in the Power Sector. IEA Information Paper, Paris.

Reinaud, J., 2005. Industrial Competitiveness under the European Union Emissions Trading Scheme. IEA Information Paper, Paris.

Sijm, J., Bakker, S., Chen, Y., Harmsen, H., Lise, W., 2005. CO$_2$ Price Dynamics: The Implications of EU Emissions Trading for the Price of Electricity. ECN-C–05-081, Energy Research Centre of the Netherlands, Petten, The Netherlands.

Sijm, J., Chen, Y., ten Donkelaar, M., Hers, S., Scheepers, M., 2006. CO$_2$ Price Dynamics: A Follow-up Analysis of the Implications of EU Emissions Trading for the Price of Electricity, ECN-C–06-015, Energy Research Centre of the Netherlands, Petten, The Netherlands.

Stewart, M., Wallis, K., 1981. Introductory Econometrics, 2nd edition. Basil Blackwell, Oxford.

Appendix 1

Biased estimation of pass-through rate if frequency of estimation is higher than frequency of observation of forward electricity prices

While EEX offers daily clearing prices for the forward prices, these are typically not based on trades but on averages of the survey results among various traders. Given that chief traders are expected to submit daily an updated price prediction on 40 contract types, it is unlikely that they will update this prediction daily, and hence the daily prices overstate the information content of the data.

This note attempts to understand why a delay in observing the forward electricity price p_t results in a bias in the estimation b of the pass-through rate r. Let us assume that electricity prices are formed according to:

$$p_t = rc_t + e_t \quad \text{with } e_t \text{ independent and identical distributed} \tag{A1}$$

but we can only observe q_t with

$$q_t = \frac{p_t + p_{t-1}}{2} \tag{A2}$$

This reflects that trading volume is limited, with trades only on a few days. In the absence of trades, the power exchange asks traders to report their best guess of trades and uses the average reported prices. However, traders only infrequently update their reports; hence the reported price is an average of the real price over various periods. How does this effect the estimation b of the pass though rate? We estimate that

$$q_t = bc_t + \eta_t \tag{A3}$$

1. OLS estimation

First, assume we use OLS, and therefore chose b to minimize $\sum_t \eta_t^2$

$$\hat{b} = \frac{\sum c_t q_t}{\sum c_t^2} \quad \text{(using def of } q_t\text{)}$$

$$= \frac{\sum c_t \dfrac{p_t + p_{t-1}}{2}}{\sum c_t^2} \quad (\text{using def of } p_t)$$

$$= r\frac{\sum c_t (c_t + c_{t-1})/2}{\sum c_t^2} + \text{error term (assume independence of } c \text{ and } e)$$

$$= r - \frac{r}{2}\frac{\sum c_t (c_t - c_{t-1})}{\sum c_t^2} = \begin{cases} <r & \text{if} \quad c_0 < c_T \\ >r & \text{if} \quad c_0 > c_T \end{cases} + \text{error}$$

2. AR(1) estimation

Second, assume we estimate using an AR(1) process with $\eta_t = p\eta_{t-1} + \gamma_t$ with γ_t independent and identical distributed.
We minimize

$$\sum \gamma_t^2 = \sum (\eta - p\eta_{t-1})^2$$

$$= \sum (q_t - bc_t - \rho(q_{t-1} - bc_{t-1}))^2$$

$$= ..[without \quad b]... - 2b\sum (c_t - \rho c_{t-1})(q_t - \rho q_{t-1}) + b^2 \sum (c_t - \rho c_{t-1})^2$$

Using the first-order condition

$$\hat{b} = \frac{\sum (c_t - \rho c_{t-1})(q_t - \rho q_{t-1})}{\sum (c_t - \rho c_{t-1})^2} \left(\text{using def of } q_t\right)$$

$$= \frac{\sum (c_t - \rho c_{t-1})\dfrac{p_t - \rho p_{t-1} + p_{t-1} - \rho p_{t-2}}{2}}{\sum (c_t - \rho c_{t-1})^2} \left(\text{using def of } p_t\right).$$

(assume independence of c and e)

$$= r\frac{\sum (c_t - \rho c_{t-1})\dfrac{c_t - \rho c_{t-1} + c_{t-1} - \rho c_{t-2}}{2}}{\sum (c_t - \rho c_{t-1})^2} + \text{error term}$$

$$= \frac{r}{2} + \frac{r}{2}\frac{\sum (c_t - \rho c_{t-1})(c_{t-1} - \rho c_{t-2})}{\sum (c_t - \rho c_{t-1})^2} + \text{error}$$

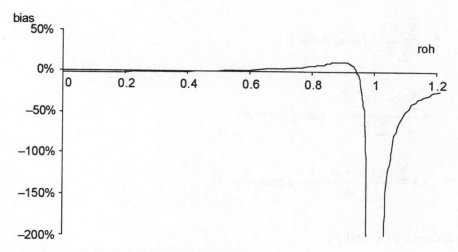

Figure A1. Bias in estimated pass-through rate.

3. Quantification of bias

We use the CO$_2$ prices from January–December 2005 as input for c_t and calculate the bias in the estimated pass-through rate at the example of a time lag of 20 days. This reflects the delays in updating under the chief trade principle applied to determine the contract settlement prices. The OLS creates a bias of 2%. Figure A1 presents the bias that results if the AR(1) process is assumed, depicted for different values of ρ.

An AR(1) process is usually estimated in an iterative two-stage procedure. In this case the biased estimator for b will result in a wrong estimation of the error term, thus influencing the estimation of ρ, which in turn feeds back to the next estimation of b. Hence the effect might be further distorted. This analysis suggests that the OLS estimator will provide a less biased estimation of the pass-through rate b than AR estimation. This is caused because rather than p, the underlying forward price, only a time averaged q is available for the estimation.

4. Cointegration

We note that both approaches fail to address an aspect that is typically present in commodity price data: they are autocorrelated. If forward prices and CO$_2$ prices are not cointegrated, then error terms under both estimations might not converge. The typical response is to run an estimation using the first differences. This is typically a successful approach in the case of non-cointegrated AR(1) processes (but does not have the quick convergence properties that otherwise characterize estimations using levels).

However, once again the price formation process precludes such attempt for the daily forward prices. Let us define $dc_t = c_t - c_{t-1}$ and likewise for dq_t and dp_t. As above, we would estimate:

$$\hat{b} = \frac{\sum dc_t dq_t}{\sum dc_t^2} \left(\text{using def of } q_t \right)$$

$$= \frac{\sum dc_t \dfrac{dp_t + dp_{t-1}}{2}}{\sum dc_t^2} \left(\text{using def of } p_t \right)$$

$$= r\frac{\sum dc_t \left(dc_t + dc_{t-1}\right)/2}{\sum dc_t^2} + \text{error term}$$

(assume independence of c and e)

$$= \frac{r}{2} - \frac{r}{2}\frac{\sum dc_t \left(dc_{t-1}\right)}{\sum dc_t^2} \sim \frac{r}{2}$$

This suggests that, given the price formation, a first difference estimation using daily price data will bias the estimation of b significantly downward. One possible alternative approach would be to use monthly average prices, but then the number of observation points is reduced.

Allocation, incentives and distortions: the impact of EU ETS emissions allowance allocations to the electricity sector

Karsten Neuhoff[1]*, Kim Keats Martinez[2], Misato Sato[1]

[1] *Faculty of Economics, University of Cambridge, Sidgwick Avenue, Cambridge, CB3 9DE, UK*
[2] *ICF International, Egmont House, 25–31 Tavistock Place, London WC1H 9SU, UK*

Abstract

The allowance allocation under the European emission trading schemes differs fundamentally from earlier cap-and-trade programmes, such as SO_2 and NO_x in the USA. Because of the sequential nature of negotiations of the overall budget, the allocation also has to follow a sequential process. If power generators anticipate that their current behaviour will affect future allowance allocation, then this can distort today's decisions. Furthermore, the national allocation plans (NAPs) contain multiple provisions dealing with existing installations, what happens to their allocation when they close, and allocations to new entrants. We provide a framework to assess the economic incentives and distortions that provisions in NAPs can have on market prices, operation and investment decisions. To this end, we use both analytic models to illustrate the effects of the incentives, and results from numerical simulation runs that estimate the magnitude of impacts from different allocation rules.

Keywords: Allowance allocation; Emission trading; Power sector; Economic incentives

1. Introduction

The 25 national allocation plans (NAPs) established autonomously by the EU Member States (MSs) are central to the EU emissions trading scheme (ETS). According to Articles 9–11 and Annex III of the ETS Directive (2003/87/EC), NAPs must state how the total quantity of emissions allowances will be distributed to installations within their jurisdiction for each trading phase. The process of deciding the second phase allocation is currently under way. Each MS must submit their NAPs for 2008–2012 to the EU Commission by 30 June 2006. Over the subsequent 3-month period, these will be assessed by the Commission according to criteria outlined in the Directive.

How to initially allocate allowances has long been a central issue in the debate on market-based instrument design. Since Montgomery put forward some 30 years ago that market efficiency would be independent of the initial allocation 'modes' used to distribute tradable permits (Montgomery, 1972), considerable advances have been made to further understanding of the implications of

* Corresponding author. Tel.: +44-1223-335290; fax: +44-1223-335299
E-mail address: karsten.neuhoff@econ.cam.ac.uk

allocation to the functioning of an allowance market. Recent literature, primarily discussing allocation in the context of the USA's SO_2 and NO_x programmes, evaluates different allocation modes using analytical, empirical and comparative approaches (e.g. Ellerman et al., 2000). This literature gives support for the argument that allocation indeed matters: the choice of allocation mode has distributional effects, but also consequences for efficiency and hence the overall costs of emissions abatement (Burtraw et al., 2001, 2002).

However, the EU ETS is a unique undertaking compared with the US programmes on several grounds. Addressing these differences is crucial when applying insights from the existing literature to allocation issues in the EU ETS. Three key differences in particular increase the complexity with the EU ETS. Firstly, the EU emissions trading scheme is by far the largest of its sort. Distributional considerations carry significant weight when giving away assets of such value to private sector agents. At CO_2 prices of €20/tCO_2, the annual value of emissions allowances reaches approximately €44 billion.[1] By law, the level of auctioning is likely to remain low.[2] Certain modes of free allowance allocation can create incentives of some significance for rational firms in a competitive market to adjust decisions on operation, investment and closure in order to influence future allocations.

Secondly, in most US programmes, allowances have been allocated at the beginning of the programme, with a clear understanding that no subsequent allocation will take place. In sharp contrast to this 'one-off' allocation, the EU ETS adopts a sequential approach. Allocation plans are decided for one commitment period at a time, with repeated negotiations about the allocation for the following period. Although consistent with the iterative nature of international emission reduction negotiations, this allocation approach can have significant implications for the efficiency of the market compared with a one-off allocation. For example, it creates perverse incentives for CO_2-intensive plants to remain in operation in order to receive free allocations, even if closure or replacement is socially more efficient. In addition, firms might invest in and operate more carbon-intensive technologies if they anticipate that future allocations of allowances will be proportional to today's emissions, output or fuel choice. This implies higher overall abatement costs to meet the cap.

Thirdly, further complications are introduced due to the decentralization of allocation (Åhman et al., 2005). Under the current system, where some discretion over NAPs is retained by each MS, we expect that allocation rules will reflect national interests. For example, where the actions of a single MS is expected to have a small impact on the European CO_2 price, national policies may be pursued with the objective of reducing impacts on domestic electricity prices. Pursuing the national objective can, however, have an adverse impact on CO_2 emissions. If many countries set out to minimize electricity prices, increased demand for allowances pushes up prices in the EU ETS, increasing the overall costs of abatement for Europe. High CO_2 prices, moreover, are likely to trigger some emission reductions among other market participants and increase the use of international mechanisms (e.g. CDMs and JI).

The potential complexity of allocation plans has thus reached new heights with the EU ETS. The objective of this article is to draw a clear set of messages to guide future allocations from our detailed analysis of the financial incentives resulting from the allocation process for power generators in liberalized electricity markets. The electricity sector plays a key role in determining the CO_2 price and ultimately in the success of the overall scheme (electricity represents around 60% of overall emissions regulated under the EU ETS). Insights from this sectoral study also have a useful bearing on other carbon-intensive sectors covered by the scheme.

In this study, we use both analytic models to illustrate the effects of incentives, and results from numerical simulation runs that estimate the magnitude and the relative impacts of different allocation rules. We do not assess strategic behaviour of generators in the electricity, gas or CO_2 market (e.g. Newbery, 2005) but assume a competitive market. First, power dispatch simulations of Great Britain (England, Wales and Scotland) and all of Europe are solved for the reference baseline – using one-off grandfathering and auctioning allocation methods.[3] The base-case results are compared with results from simulations of alternative allocation scenarios, to demonstrate numerically the extent to which allocation can distort operation, investment, electricity prices and CO_2 emissions.

We do advise caution, because there is some debate as to whether dominant generation companies in some European countries are restrained not by the competition from existing companies or new entrants, but by the threat of triggering regulatory intervention. Such companies can develop prices that mimic the prices of competitive markets. However, the threat of windfall profit taxes, the anticipation of the impact of their current behaviour on the ongoing negotiations about allowance allocation for future periods, or the link to developments in other sectors of energy policy might induce such companies to refrain from adding the opportunity costs of CO_2 prices to the wholesale price level of electricity.

The remainder of this article is structured as follows. In Section 2 we describe the reference case, which mimics the results of an efficient cap-and-trade programme, and then discuss the distortions that result due to allocation to existing power stations. Section 3 deals with new entrants. Section 4 sets out some conclusions.

2. Allocation to incumbents

For the phase I trading period, incumbent firms received allowances based on their historic emissions. Most Member States took some average over a 3–5-year period between 1990 and 2002. For future trading periods, the Member States have to again define NAPs for the ETS.[4] The Commission and various Member States initially announced that current behaviour will not be the basis for future allocations. It is, however, difficult for governments to commit to not redefining allocation methods and base periods in future. It is likely that the base period will be adjusted over time to reflect changes in the distribution of plants over time. It is, for example, difficult to envisage that in phase II a government will decide to allocate allowances to a power plant that closed down in phase I. This suggests that some element of 'updating' of allocation plans cannot be avoided if such plans are made sequentially.

A consistent methodology of allocating allowances is therefore likely to make allocation contingent on the past activities of a plant. We show that such contingent allocation has detrimental impacts on the efficiency of emissions trading, which vary with the specific allocation methodology. The incentives that the allocation methodology creates for the separation of power plants has been extensively discussed (Bernard et al., 2001; Palmer and Burtraw, 2003, 2004; Entec and NERA, 2005; Keats and Neuhoff, 2005). This section extends this discussion by addressing issues specific to the EU ETS.

2.1. The 'updating dilemma'

We begin by presenting a theoretical framework for evaluating the impact of updating before moving on to quantify its impacts. To illustrate the effect of updating, consider a generation system with various technologies. In our auction base case, as the CO_2 price increases, the generation

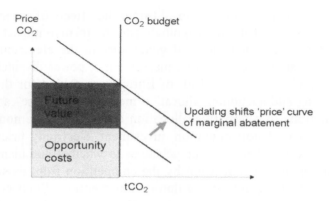

Figure 1. Impact of updating on marginal abatement cost curve.

portfolio will shift towards less carbon-intensive power generation. The track of the relationship between CO_2 price and resulting CO_2 emissions is referred to as the marginal abatement cost curve (MACC), as shown in Figure 1. With updating, the emitter receives some future allowances with today's emissions. The value of this future allocation will drive a wedge (indicated by the area labelled 'future value') between the market price of CO_2 allowances and the polluter's internal opportunity cost. This can be represented as an upward shift of the MACC. The CO_2 market price must therefore rise to ensure that the CO_2 budget is not violated (see Boeringer and Lange, 2005).

From the perspective of one country, using policies that promise updating is a tempting option. Emissions from the country will have little effect on the ETS price. Yet, by adding future value, updating essentially provides an output subsidy that reduces the variable cost of the economic activity. Thus national efforts to reduce economic activity, and hence CO_2 emissions, are reduced. Updating can therefore have adverse effects on emission levels, for example, by biasing investments in carbon-intensive technologies (e.g. coal). Moreover, if the demand for electricity is price-elastic, any resulting drop in electricity prices (Harrison and Radov, 2002) could trigger higher electricity consumption that induces additional production, with additional CO_2 emissions.

This approach will also have consequences on neighbouring jurisdictions. Figure 2 illustrates a case with two countries. Each country is characterized by a marginal abatement cost curve and emission budget. The right-hand side of Figure 2 illustrates that with international trade the individual marginal abatement cost curves and the budgets are added, and obviously the same equilibrium price X results.

If one country, say Country B, employs updating, then a wedge is created between CO_2 price and opportunity costs of CO_2 emissions. As companies' opportunity costs of reducing CO_2 emissions are not affected, the MACC has to shift upwards. When we allow trading of allowances between the two countries, the joint MACC also shifts upwards. The market now clears at the new equilibrium Y with higher CO_2 prices. How this joint equilibrium is reflected in national output choices can be seen by moving along the dashed line from point Y to the left. The resulting CO_2 price in Country A is higher and the country will implement additional CO_2 emission reductions equal to $E_A^1 - E_A^2$. The CO_2 prices will also be higher in Country B, but as the MACC has been shifted up even further, the country increases its emissions of CO_2 by $E_B^2 - E_B^1$. The global budget ensures that the

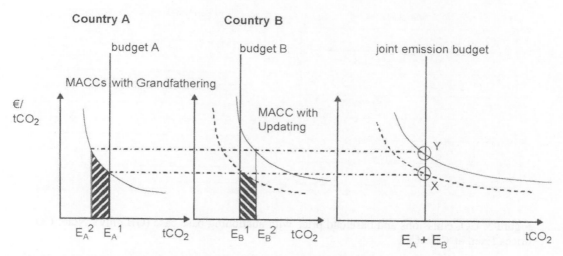

Figure 2. Impact of updating in a two-country emission trading system.

total emission reductions are not affected. Comparing the shaded areas under the MACCs, it is clear that savings made in Country B are outweighed by the additional abatement costs incurred by Country A.

One might argue that Country B or its companies 'pay' for these additional abatement efforts of Country A. However, in the process, Country B introduces a wedge, reducing the marginal opportunity costs for its industry and consumers at the expense of a higher 'international' CO_2 price and thus higher marginal opportunity costs for industry and consumers in other countries covered by the ETS. This might be referred to as 'free-riding' on others' emissions reductions.

Åhman et al. (2005) recognize that individual Member States' decisions on NAPs affect the overall efficiency of the system, and also that a strong EU approval process of NAPs is required to limit distortions from heterogeneity of NAPs. In addition, the application of updating is not limited to cross-border distortions. Similar arguments can be made about allocation procedures that differ across sectors (see Keats Martinez and Neuhoff, 2005).

Acknowledging the problems associated with defining future allocations as a function of output levels in the past, some governments have declared that they will not allow the use of updating. Such an announcement's credibility can be enhanced if accompanied by a clear outline of the allocations approach in future trading periods.

2.2. Quantifying impacts

2.2.1. Base case: auctioning or one-off grandfathering

Various studies have modelled the impact of CO_2 allowances on the European power sector (see, for example, Sijm et al., this issue). To quantify the impact of CO_2 allowances on both the GB and the EU power sector, we use ICF International's Integrated Planning Model® (IPM). This is a linear programming model that selects generating and investment options to meet overall electricity demand today and on an ongoing and forward looking basis over the chosen planning horizon at minimum cost. For the GB simulations, England, Wales and Scotland are treated as an island with no electrical interconnection to its neighbours. In the European simulations, IPM is designed to

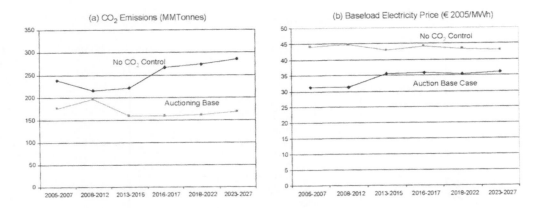

Figure 3. CO_2 emissions and baseload price with auctioning base case (GB only). Note: CO_2 prices fixed at €20/tCO_2.

replicate the operations of the interconnected European power system, using an accurate engineering representation of power plants, transmission links and fuel supply options.

In order to calculate the distortions induced by the NAPs, we have to define a reference or base case. In our base case we assume that all allowances are auctioned. This base case creates the same investment, operation and closure decisions as a one-off allocation of free allowances.[5] The 'only' difference between auctioning and one-off allocation allowances are the rents transferred from government to historic emitters. In this article we do not discuss the mix of auctioning and free allocation required to compensate power companies for the effect of the CO_2 emission trading scheme (see Keats Martinez and Neuhoff, 2005). This does not apply to companies in regulated market environments or in situations where companies are exposed to regulatory threats, e.g. windfall profit taxes. In the extreme case of pure auctions, companies will face the full costs and can pass these on. With complete free allocation there is little impact on their average costs and thus on prices (Burtraw et al., 2005). Results for the auctioning case and the no-CO_2 case are shown in Figure 3.

2.2.2. Updating with an output-based uniform benchmark

To update allocation, governments may consider using benchmarks. How does the choice of benchmark impact electricity prices and CO_2 emissions? We start by quantifying the impacts of the simplest form of updating: using an output-based uniform benchmark (OB UB). In this case, the allocation in the following compliance period is equal to the product of the benchmark and electricity production in the preceding compliance period (Palmer and Burtraw, 2004). To avoid distortions between any sources of power generation, the uniform benchmark also envisages the allocation of CO_2 allowances to low-carbon technologies such as wind, hydro, solar or nuclear.

The simulation results for GB presented in this section assume that all power stations receive, for free, an allowance of 0.35 tCO_2 per MWh electricity produced in the preceding compliance period. This benchmark is phased out linearly so that by 2023 no further allocation is received. In the model it is also assumed that GB is small relative to the European market, such that even with changing GB emissions, the CO_2 price stays at €20/tCO_2. The simulation results in Figure 4 show that the electricity price increases, but by far less than in the auction case.

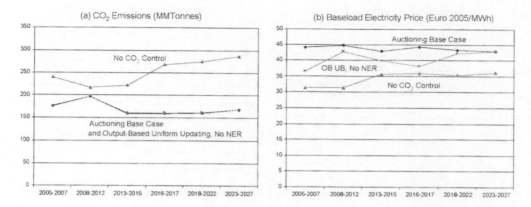

Figure 4. CO_2 emissions and baseload price with updating using an output-based uniform benchmark (GB only, €20/tCO_2).

Figure 4 also shows that the impact on CO_2 emissions was very small when compared to the auction case. While lowering electricity prices, updating using an output-based uniform benchmark does not result in any significant increase in CO_2 emissions. The benefits of future allocation reduced the production costs of operation, resulting in a reduction in prices without affecting the dispatch order. Output-based updating therefore acts as a production subsidy (Fisher, 2001).

This, however, may not be the whole story. For modelling purposes we assumed that demand is exogenous. In reality electricity demand is price-elastic in the mid- and long term, when higher prices induce more energy-efficient investment. Hence we expect electricity demand to increase with the output-based updating. To meet this additional demand, more generation is required, resulting in higher CO_2 emissions.

For modelling purposes we also assumed that a fixed CO_2 price does not constrain CO_2 emissions. However, if updating increases CO_2 emissions on a European scale, then allowance prices will appreciate, and this in turn will compensate for (some) of the previous electricity price reductions.

2.2.3. Updating with an output-based fuel-specific benchmark
As basing phase II allocation on activities in phase I was discouraged by the EU Directive, some Member States update allocations using output-based fuel-specific benchmarks (FSB), where the benchmark is set higher for coal-fired plants than for gas-fired plants. Here, we assess the impact of this alternative updating method and compare with the output-based uniform benchmark approach.

In our model, gas-fired plants receive 0.35 tCO_2 and the coal-fired power stations receive 0.75 tCO_2 per MWh generated in the preceding compliance period.[6] The results for our GB simulation are shown in Figure 5. The fuel-specific updating scenario leads to higher CO_2 emissions, and electricity prices are lower because of the output subsidy, but CO_2 emissions are significantly above the auctioning case.

2.2.4. Updating in an international context
To test the net impact that updating can have on the efficiency of the EU ETS as a whole, we simulate four scenarios for all countries in Europe. The IPM treats the electricity dispatch system

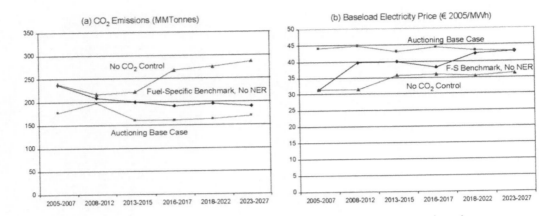

Figure 5. CO_2 emissions and baseload price with updating using an output-based fuel-specific benchmark (GB only, 20€/tCO_2).

as a system of integrated and interconnected markets. It assumes that the competitive market allows for the optimal operation decisions of power stations across multiple jurisdictions. The first scenario defines the business-as-usual case ('No-CO_2 control'), and the second simulates a situation where all European countries use allocation by auctioning and a price of €20/tCO_2. For the final two cases, we apply different allocation methodologies to the UK, Germany and The Netherlands: first an output-based uniform benchmark, and then a fuel-specific benchmark. All other European countries continue to auction allowances. The impact of updating in these three countries on CO_2 emissions is reported for 2008–2012 in Figure 6.

On an overall European scale, the results show that updating using an output-based uniform benchmark in the UK, Germany and The Netherlands has a smaller impact on emissions than

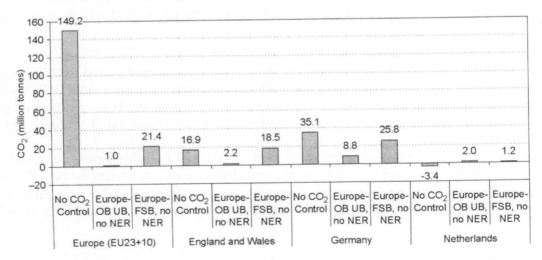

Figure 6. CO_2 Emissions with base case, updating using output-based uniform benchmark and output-based fuel-specific benchmark for Europe (EU23+10), England and Wales, Germany and The Netherlands (20€/tCO_2, 2008–2012 only).

using an output-based fuel-specific benchmark in the same three countries. The No-CO_2 control case results in the highest emissions. Emissions were lowest with all countries adopting the auctioning approach.

Comparing the impact of different allocation procedures for the three individual countries, we observe a similar behaviour in Germany and England & Wales. Distortions in the allocation process mean that CO_2 emissions increase from the auction to the output-based uniform benchmark case and then again to the output-based fuel-specific benchmark case. Emissions are highest in the No-CO_2 control case. The Netherlands proved a special case, with emissions in the BAU case lying below the auction case. Two explanations underlie these results: first, the large proportion of gas-fired plants makes The Netherlands a preferred country for electricity generation under emissions trading; second, the high level of interconnection with neighbouring countries allows trade to utilize this opportunity.

These numerical simulations provide a useful insight into the magnitude of distortions induced by allocation to the power sector. Since the CO_2 emissions cap for Europe is fixed, high CO_2 emissions projections imply increased scarcity and allowance prices. This could induce an increased flow of allowances through the flexible mechanisms of the Kyoto Protocol, including the clean development mechanism (CDM) and joint implementation (JI). The extent to which CO_2 prices would have to adjust to achieve the same level of European-wide emissions is a question requiring further research.

2.3. Closure rules: the impact of 'contingent allocation'

With a one-off allocation, the ownership of the allowances remains unaffected by closure of the power station. If the continued operation of a plant is no longer profitable, then owners can sell the allowances and close the plant.

Closure decisions are distorted if the allocation of allowances is contingent on the activity level of a plant. Plant owners will retain plants on the system and continue operation at minimum-run conditions in order to receive allowances in the next trading period.[7]

In addition, most countries, with the exception of Sweden and The Netherlands, explicitly include closure rules within their NAPs. For example, in Germany, entities that close down operations (defined as emitting less than 10% of its average annual baseline emissions) will not receive allowances from the following year. Such formal closure rules further discourage the closure of inefficient plants within a trading period, as allocation essentially becomes a subsidy for continued production (Åhman et al., 2005).

These closure rules have two consequences for the power system. First, with more plants staying on the system, there is more electricity supply and therefore prices can initially be reduced. Secondly, as inefficient old plants are artificially retained on the system, investment in more efficient new plants is delayed. This increases power prices and CO_2 emissions.

We quantify the impact of the implicit closure rules for the Great Britain electricity system: if a power plant closes, it does not receive any allocation in the following compliance period. Table 1 lists the initial annual allocation of allowances to the different technologies. We assume that this is the allowance allocation for the period 2005–2008 and will be linearly phased out until 2028. We again fix the CO_2 price at €20/tCO_2.

Comparing results for the cases where allocation of allowances is contingent on plant existence during the 3–5-year allocation period with the base case (auction or one-off grandfathering), the

Table 1. Assumed initial allocation to incumbents for period 2005–2007

	Initial allocation (tCO$_2$/MW/year)
CCGT (combined-cycle gas turbine)	1893
OCGT (open-cycle gas turbine)	473
Hydro (pumped storage or pondage hydro)	0
Diesel generator	947
Nuclear	0
Renewables	0
Conventional coal boiler	2840
Conventional steam turbine (burning fossil fuel other than coal)	1420

number of retirements of plants falls. With no CO$_2$ constraint, only 0.4 GW of capacity was retired for economic reasons. In the auction case, 7.1 GW of capacity is retired by 2015 and 14.2 GW by 2022. In contrast, free allocation to existing plants reduces cumulative retirements to 2.5 GW and 7.2 GW over the same periods. This reduces the investment in new lower-carbon plant. For our parameter choice, we did not observe strong effects of contingent allocation on CO$_2$ emissions. Power prices are slightly lower in the contingent allocation case. As the scenario analysis for new entrant allocation in Section 3 illustrates, such results can drastically change with small changes to the choices of parameter.

2.5. Summary of allocation to existing facilities

The allocation procedures applied by NAPs combine various aspects discussed in this section. Table 2 illustrates and summarizes the transition from an efficient allocation based on auction (or one-off grandfathering) to the various dimensions of distortions that are created by the iterative grandfathering approach using a moving baseline in current NAPs.

The economically efficient allocation methods are auctions or a one-off free allocation of allowances. The first set of impacts will result if allowances are only allocated in the future, if the power stations are operational today. The value of future allocations delays closure of plants beyond their socially efficient lifespan. This effect is reinforced if the amount of allocation increases with the CO$_2$ intensity of the technology. With such technology-specific allocation, more CO$_2$-intensive technologies receive additional encouragement to stay operational, further delaying the shift towards less CO$_2$-intensive power stations.

The second set of impacts follows, if the amount of future allocations is related to current electricity production. A uniform benchmark would not create distortions between the operation of different technologies. In our model, the output-based uniform updating resulted in lower electricity prices. We did not look at the impact on electricity demand and implied changes in CO$_2$ emissions. Output-based updating also implements a closure condition – only power stations that produce will receive allowances in the future. Thus it creates some distortions as discussed above. Many of the discussions about output-based benchmarks assumed that these benchmarks are fuel- or technology-specific. Updating based on such benchmarks does create strong distortions in the operation and can create significant increases in CO$_2$ emissions.

Reality can offer even more distortions. The allocation of CO$_2$ allowances in phase I of the EU ETS was based on baseline CO$_2$ emissions, and the current discussions surrounding phase II

Allocation, incentives and distortions: the impact of EU ETS emissions allowance allocations to the electricity sector

Table 2. Effect of allocation methods to power sector incumbents

	Impacts	More expenditure on extending plant life relative to new build		Increase plant operation		Less energy efficiency investments
	Distortions	Discourage plant closure	Distortion biased towards higher emitting plant	Shields output (and consumption) from average carbon cost	Distortion biased towards higher emitting plant	Reduce incentives for energy efficiency investments
Allowance allocation method						
Auction						
Benchmarking	capacity only	X				
	capacity by fuel/plant type*	X	X			
Updating from previous periods'	output only	Y		X		
	output by fuel/plant type*	X	X	X		
	emissions	X	X	X	X	X

Note: X indicates a direct distortion arising from the allocation rule. Y indicates indirect distortions if allocation is not purely proportional to output/emissions.

* Differentiating by plant type adds additional distortions compared to purely fuel-based distinctions.

indicate that this will remain the dominant metric. Among our model runs, the output-based fuel-specific benchmark using a moving baseline best reflects the distortions created by the emission-based NAPs, assuming that they also use a moving baseline. The emission-based updating creates additional distortions not captured by our model run. First, it reduces the incentive to operate the more efficient power stations of the same fuel type. This may not be a large problem, as generators typically prefer to run more fuel-efficient power stations. Second, the emission-based allocation reduces the incentives to invest in efficiency improvements of existing and new power stations.

As the European budget for CO_2 emissions is capped, if many Member States implement this allocation methodology, increases in national emissions are likely to push up the European price of CO_2 allowances. They, in turn, increase the electricity prices across all states, and thus the subsidy-effect of free allocation that lowers electricity prices is partly offset.

3. Allocation to new entrants

We assess the economic incentives and their impacts resulting from allocation to new projects of power generators. All Member States have made provisions that guarantee a certain volume of free allowances to new entrants for a defined period. Section 3.1 uses a simple analytic model to illustrate the impact of a uniform allocation of CO_2 allowances to all new projects, Section 3.2

discusses how increased allocation to coal affects the equilibrium. In Section 3.3 we then use a numerical model to calculate the impacts of different allocation schemes in the UK and European system, taking into consideration the existing assets and investment pathways. Finally, Section 3.4 summarizes the results of all model runs.

NE provisions are often viewed as a 'general' or 'synthetic' compensation mechanism in the EU ETS. For example, by encouraging firms to establish new sources rather than to expand the operation of existing facilities, it aims in part to compensate for distortions created by closure conditions, including delaying the shift towards new efficient investment. Also it is sometimes argued that NE provisions create 'fairness' among incumbents and new entities; if existing facilities receive allowances, so should new facilities. Barriers to entry for new firms due to inadequate liquidity in the market may be a more appropriate, but also more difficult, justification for NE allocations (Baron and Bygrave, 2002). Free NE allocations compensate for the direct additional costs incurred by new entrants to the market. By improving their access to capital, free allowances can facilitate entry by new firms; hence NE reserves address the wider issues of market power (Åhman et al., 2005) and thus increase competition within rather concentrated national European electricity markets (Åhman and Zetterberg, 2003; Pedersen, 2002, cited in Baron and Bygrave, 2002). As most new projects are initiated by existing utilities, the expression 'new entrant allocation' seems a bit misleading and could perhaps be replaced by 'new project allocation' in future discussions.

Most phase I NAPs provide for NE allocations based on a general emission rate and predicted activity level. For example in The Netherlands (NL), new entrants are allocated allowances based on projected output or fixed cap factor multiplied by uniform emission rate in line with that of a combined-cycle gas turbine (CCGT). In France, Germany and Poland, CO_2-intensive power generators, such as coal-fired installations, receive the highest number of allowances per kW installed. The literature highlights the risk that NE provisions can create distortions (Harrison and Radov, 2002). In order to illustrate how these rules can impact electricity prices and CO_2 emissions in our GB simulations, we focus on two approaches: one based on a uniform benchmark and one based on a fuel-specific benchmark. In both cases the forecast capacity factor of new entrants is fixed at 60%.

3.1. New entrant allocation with a uniform benchmark

To illustrate the impact of new entrant allocation, we calculate the long-term investment equilibrium for a competitive electricity market. Section 3.3 will subsequently assess the impact in real electricity markets, where existing generation assets do affect the generation and price structure.

In our simplified model we assume that the highest prices are set by demand side response or open cycle gas turbines, followed by combined-cycle gas turbines with high variable and low fixed costs, and coal-fired power stations with low variable and high fixed costs. We compare two cases. First, the system is small relative to the EU emission-trading scheme and the EU CO_2 price is not affected by changes in national emissions of CO_2. Second, the model represents the entire EU ETS, and we set a fixed CO_2 budget and endogenously determined CO_2 price.

The results with uniform NE allocation are shown in Figure 7. With a fixed allowance price, as the value of the NE allocations increases, additional gas power stations replace peaking generation, usually provided by open-cycle gas turbines, or demand side response as the value of the allocation increases. The electricity price falls and CO_2 emissions fall. Nevertheless, at a certain value of total NE allowances (between €40 and €50/KWh), the option for CCGT to replace peakers is exhausted and it becomes viable to invest in new coal-fired power stations. From this point onwards,

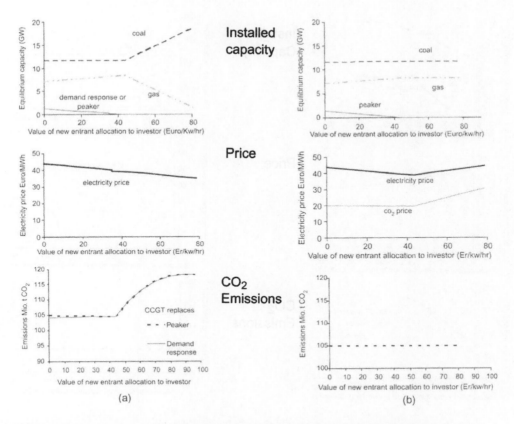

Figure 7. Long-term equilibrium effect of increasing levels of uniform new entrant allocation.

coal-fired power stations are built in preference to CCGT. This results in significant increases in CO_2 emissions, even as electricity prices continue to fall.

The right-hand side of Figure 7 shows what happens if same uniform new entrant allocation provision is applied at the European level, i.e. when the CO_2 budget is fixed. When the value of the new entrant allocation is sufficiently high that construction of new coal-fired power stations is made viable, with a fixed CO_2 cap, however, the equilibrium price of CO_2 will increase and the higher exposure of coal power stations to CO_2 prices reduces the expected benefit of operating the coal power station. This prevents the additional construction of coal-powered stations. Higher CO_2 prices, however, feed through to higher electricity prices.

3.2. New entrant allocation with a fuel-specific benchmark

Figure 8 illustrates the effect of a fuel-specific new entrant allocation in the long-run equilibrium. With a fixed CO_2 price, the additional support for coal-powered stations implies that even small values of new entrant allocation result in incentives to build additional coal-powered stations. This increases national CO_2 emissions and lowers electricity prices. With a fixed CO_2 budget, the cap on total emissions implies that CO_2 prices must rise. The higher CO_2 prices again feed through to higher electricity prices.

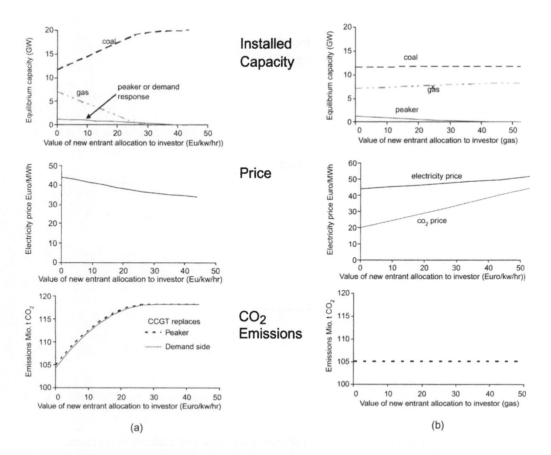

Figure 8. Long-term equilibrium effect of increasing levels of fuel-specific new entrant allocation.

This analysis highlights the dangers of a fuel-specific new entrant allocation at the European level. In equilibrium, fuel-specific benchmarking increases the social costs of complying with the CO_2 cap.

3.3. Aggregate impact on CO_2 emission and electricity prices for Europe

We also used the IPM to assess how updating and new entrant allocation can affect the evolution of the power system in England and Wales for a series of cases with a fixed CO_2 price. For 2005–2007, NE allocation based on a uniform benchmark assumes a benchmark rate of 0.35 tCO_2 per MWh for all power plants together with an annual load factor of 60% for both technologies. The fuel-specific NE allocation assumes 0.75 tCO_2 per MWh for new coal-fired plants. The allocation drops linearly over time so that by 2028 NE would have to purchase all their allowances from the market. Figure 9 summarizes the results, which are taken from our European simulation. In these, Germany, The Netherlands and the UK were subject to the alternative allocation method, whilst all other countries applied auctioning or one-off grandfathering.

Starting with a base case assuming no updating or NE allocation, CO_2 emissions decrease when a NE allocation is used. The allocation results in accelerated construction and operation of combined-

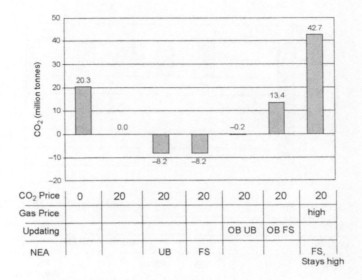

Figure 9. Effect of various allocation methods on England & Wales CO_2 emissions in period 2008–2012 (assuming fixed CO_2 price on CO_2 emissions). NEA = new entrant allocation, UB = uniform benchmark, FS = fuel-specific benchmark, OB = output-based.

cycle gas turbines and thus lower CO_2 emissions. For our given set of input parameters, the results for uniform-benchmark or fuel-specific benchmark were the same. This result was caused because, with the first set of parameters, the subsidy to coal was not large enough to justify any construction of new coal power stations. The resulting reduction in CO_2 emissions, however, could be dramatically reversed. When we increased the price of natural gas above €4.9/MMBTu and assumed that there would be no fall in the allocation over time, coal became the preferred new-build option. Emissions of CO_2 increase above the No-CO_2 and fuel-specific updating cases. The implementation of uniform updating did not affect emissions. If, however, updating is fuel-specific (e.g. producers with coal power stations expect higher future allocations than producers with gas power stations), then dispatch decisions are distorted and emissions increase.

Figure 10 illustrates the impact on electricity prices of the different allocation methods for the same England & Wales cases. The simulations are run on the assumption that European CO_2 prices are not affected by the changes of CO_2 emissions in the UK. If various EU countries implement allocation plans that would increase national CO_2 emissions, then this assumption is no longer valid, and CO_2 prices will rise and feed through to higher electricity prices.

3.4. Summary of the numerical results

Table 3 summarizes the impact of different allocation methods examined for our GB simulation which are based on the assumption that the UK emission pattern will have limited impact on the European allowance price, which is therefore set as fixed.

Uniform allocation of allowances creates the fewest distortions for both incumbents and new entrants. For a fixed CO_2 price, the uniform benchmarks for allocation to existing and new facilities resulted in a reduction in electricity prices, with limited impact on CO_2 emissions. We caution that

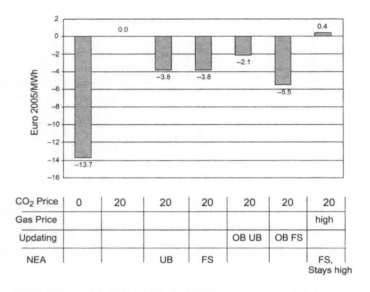

Figure 10. Effect of various allocation methods on England & Wales prices in period 2008–2012 on electricity price (assuming fixed CO_2 price).

this 'optimistic' result is based on price-independent electricity demand and our assumptions on available technologies and fuel prices. Furthermore, as we assume forward-looking investors, we did not model the time delay of 3–5 years between the implementation of new entrant allocation rules and new investment decisions that affect electricity prices. Finally, the reduction in electricity prices is typically far lower than the value of the free allowances, as investors and operators discount CO_2 price and regulatory uncertainty. Thus uniform allocation of allowances can be interpreted as an inefficient capacity payment scheme.

Table 3. Impact from allocations for period 2005–2017 (GB simulation only)

	Average CO_2 emissions (million tCO_2)	Average baseload prices (€/MWh)	Cumulative retirements (MW)	Average gas use (TBTU)	Average coal use (TBTU)
No closure rules, high FS NER, high gas price	241	45.26	12,977	359	1,623
No CO_2 control	226	32.79	556	1,221	1,628
FS updating, no NER	215	37.01	5,118	1,325	1,440
Closure rules, no NER	187	43.28	3,318	1,694	946
Closure rules, uniform NER	180	41.86	3,678	1,766	829
Closure rules, FS NER	180	41.86	3,678	1,766	829
Uni updating, no NER	178	39.72	10,640	1,804	776
Auctioning base case	178	43.96	10,629	1,798	780
No closure rules, uniform NER	170	41.81	20,597	1,863	670
No closure rules, FS NER	170	41.81	20,597	1,863	670

Fuel-specific benchmarks applied to existing power stations create incentives to shift production towards more CO_2-intensive generators. Whether we refer to fuel-specific updating or NE allocation, for any given price of CO_2, these allocation methods will result in CO_2 emissions in excess of the auctioning case. If operators and investors expect that future NAPs are similar to current NAPs, then they anticipate receiving fuel-specific allocation in the future. If the CO_2 budget were fixed, this would imply that CO_2 prices, and hence electricity prices, would have to rise.

4. Conclusions

This article illustrates the set of distortions that can result from allocation of CO_2 allowances to existing facilities and new entrants in the form of *closure rules* where allocation is lost once the facility shuts down, *updating* where allocation in forthcoming compliance periods is a function of generation or emissions levels today, and *allocations to new entrants* based on different benchmarks.

We illustrated the set of distortions that can result from allocation of CO_2 allowances to existing facilities and new entrants.

The first set of distortions is introduced with uniform updating (e.g. based on past power output). From a national perspective, assuming fixed CO_2 prices, free allowances reduce the opportunity costs (updating) or scarcity prices (new entrant allocation) and thus feed through to somewhat lower electricity prices. The regulatory uncertainty involved in the future benefit might imply that the decrease in electricity prices might be far lower than the value of allowances handed out. The failure to internalize the CO_2 externality into the electricity prices limits investment in energy efficiency and results in higher electricity consumption. Thus electricity production and national CO_2 emissions increase. If all European countries implement such policies, the suggested higher CO_2 emissions would translate into higher CO_2 prices and feed through to higher electricity prices.

Overall, an allocation based on a purely uniform benchmark creates the fewest distortions for both incumbents and new entrants. A similar approach for both facilities would increase transparency and avoid difficulties in defining what a new entrant is, relative to an existing facility (Entec and NERA, 2005). However, this does not suggest that it is desirable from an equity perspective, as power generators might receive free allowances above the level they require to cover any additional costs from the emission trading scheme.

A justification for the free allocation of allowances is that they are used to compensate emitters for otherwise reduced profitability due to the introduction of ETS. This provides a rationale for output-based fuel- and technology-specific allocation, whereby CO_2-intensive generators receive more compensation than CO_2-efficient generators. Relative to the distortions created by uniform benchmarking, this has the following impacts. Fuel-specific benchmarks applied to existing power stations create incentives to shift production towards more CO_2-intensive generators. If applied on a European scale, the overall increase in CO_2 emissions inflate CO_2 prices. These feed through to higher electricity prices.

Fuel-specific allocation to new entrants creates additional incentives to invest in CO_2-intensive power stations. The fixed EU allowance budget prevents additional CO_2 emissions and would thus push up CO_2 prices to a level at which investment in CO_2 power stations is unprofitable. Thus fuel-specific new entrant allocation increases CO_2 emissions and electricity prices.

Allocation relative to past emissions is prevalent in current NAPs. If such direct updating continues, then the incentives that ETS could offer existing power stations to increase fuel and CO_2 efficiency are severely reduced. Any improvement will reduce the future allowance allocation.

We note that NAPs were designed in anticipation of some of these distortions. The NAPs aimed to counter some of these distortions, e.g. by transfer provisions between power stations. However, it seems impossible to comprehensively address the complex set of interactions of incentives from various provisions in NAPs. Any such assessment tends to be valid for only one scenario and not robust to changes of fuel and technology prices.

Nevertheless, despite the complex interactions, we have shown that it is possible with the aid of simulation tools to make an assessment of the distortionary impact of allocation procedures both at the national and international level. These tools provide useful insights to policy makers as they assess the impacts of forthcoming NAPs. Our numerical calculations for the UK assuming a fixed CO_2 price illustrate how quantitative results can invert with a change in the assumption of gas prices and investors' expectations. This suggests that it is rather tricky to micro-manage NAPs with the well-intended objective of correcting for inappropriate incentives following from individual provisions.

Acknowledgements

Financial support from the UK Research Council Project TSEC, and from the Carbon Trust and Climate Strategies is gratefully acknowledged.

Notes

1   2.2 billion tonnes of annual CO_2 emissions in phase I (EC, 2005).
2   A maximum of 5% and 10% of allowances may be auctioned in phases I and II, respectively, under Articles 9–11 and Annex III of the ETS Directive. This gradual incorporation of auctioning is inconsistent with the fact that private and equity ownership are considerably lower in the EU, and hence EU citizens are more likely than US citizens to object to free allocation.
3   In terms of their incentive effects, one-off grandfathering and auctioning are equivalent and efficient. Thus, both represent the zero-distortions reference case here.
4   Defined by the Kyoto process (e.g. 2005–2007, 2008–2012).
5   Most of the US cap-and-trade programmes for SO_2 and NO_x used such a one-off allocation. Given the larger value of CO_2 allowances, the novel experience with a CO_2 trading scheme and the iterative nature of the definition of national or regional targets, such a one-off allocation was not viable under the ETS.
6   Although technology-specific benchmarks may be intended as incentives for clean technologies, at the same time, they also provide channels to make 'concessions' for technologies and sites that cannot achieve lower emission targets (Entec and NERA, 2005).
7   To address such distortions, Åhman et al. (2005) propose 'the 10-year rule', which they argue can parallel the incentives of one-off grandfathering, hence eliminating the trade-off between updating and one-off allocation.

References

Åhman, M., Zetterberg, L., 2003. Options for Emissions Allowance Allocation under the EU Emissions Trading Directive. IVL Discussion Paper.
Åhman, M., Burtraw, D., Kruger, J.A., Zetterberg, L., 2005. The Ten-year Rule: Allocation of Emission Allowances in the EU Emissions Trading System. RFF Discussion Paper 05–30.
Baron, R., Bygrave, S., 2002. Towards International Emissions Trading: Design Implications for Linkages. OECD/IEA Information Paper.
Bernard, A.L., Fischer, C., Vielle, M., 2001. Is There a Rationale for Rebating Environmental Levies? RFF Discussion Papers 1–31.
Boeringer, C., Lange, A., 2005. On the design of optimal grandfathering schemes for emission allowances. European Economic Review 49, 2041–2055.

Burtraw, D., Palmer, K., Bharvirkar, R., Paul, A., 2001. The Effect of Allowance Allocation on the Cost of Carbon Emissions Trading. RFF Discussion Papers 01–30.

Burtraw, D., Palmer, K., Bharvirkar, R., Paul, A., 2002. The effect on asset values of the allocation of carbon dioxide emissions allowance. Electricity Journal 15(5), 51–62.

Burtraw, D., Palmer, K., Kahn, D., 2005. Allocation of CO_2 Emissions Allowances in the Regional Greenhouse Gas Cap-and-Trade Program. RFF Discussion Papers 05–25.

Ellerman, A.D., Joskow, P.L., Schmalensee, R., Montero, J.P., Bailey, E.M., 2000. Markets for Clean Air: The U.S. Acid Rain Program, Cambridge University Press, Cambridge, UK.

Entec and NERA, 2005. EU Emissions Trading Scheme Benchmark Research for Phase 2. DTI.

Fisher, C., 2001. Rebating Environmental Policy Revenues: Output-Based Allocations and Tradable Performance Standards. Discussion Paper 01–22.

Harrison, D.J., Radov, D.B., 2002. Evaluation of Alternative Initial Allocation Mechanisms in a European Union Greenhouse Gas Emissions Allowance Trading Schemes. NERA Report to DG Environment, European Commission, NERA.

Keats Martinez, K., Neuhoff, K., 2005. Allocation of carbon emission certificates in the power sector: how generators profit from grandfathered rights. Climate Policy 5, 61–78.

Montgomery, W.D., 1972. Markets in licenses and efficient control programs. Journal of Economic Theory 5(3), 395–418.

Newbery, D.M.G., 2005. Climate Change Policy and its Effect on Market Power in the Gas Market. EPRG Working Paper Series 05/10.

Palmer, K., Burtraw, D., 2003. Distribution and Efficiency Consequences of Different Approaches to Allocating Tradable Emission Allowances for Sulphur Dioxide, Nitrogen Oxides and Mercury. Mimeo.

Palmer, K., Burtraw, D., 2004. Electricity, Renewables, and Climate Change: Searching for a Cost-effective Policy. RFF Report.

Sijm, J., Neuhoff, K., Chen, Y., 2006. CO_2 cost pass-through and windfall profits in the power sector. Climate Policy 6(1), 49–72.

www.climatepolicy.com

CO$_2$ abatement, competitiveness and leakage in the European cement industry under the EU ETS: grandfathering versus output-based allocation

Damien Demailly*, Philippe Quirion

CIRED (International Research Centre on Environment and Development) CNRS/EHESS, 45 bis avenue de la Belle Gabrielle, 94736 Nogent/Marne, France

Abstract

A recurring concern raised by the European GHG Emissions Trading Scheme (ETS) is the fear of losses to EU industry through competition: both loss in domestic production and loss in profits. This article analyses how production and profits in the European cement industry may be affected by different approaches to the allocation of emissions allowances. We analyse two contrasting methods for the allocation of free allowances. With 'grandfathering', the number of allowances a firm gets is independent of its current behaviour. With 'output-based allocation', the number of allowances is proportional to the firm's current production level. Whereas almost all the quantitative assessments of the EU ETS assume grandfathering, the real allocation methods used by Member States, notably because of the updating every 5 years and of the special provisions for new plants and plant closings, stand somewhere between these two polar extremes. We study the impacts of these two contrasting allocation methods by linking a detailed trade model of homogeneous products with high transportation costs (GEO) with a bottom-up model of the cement industry (CEMSIM). The two allocation approaches have very different impacts on competitiveness and emissions abatements. Grandfathering 50% of past emissions to cement producers is enough to maintain aggregate profitability (EBITDA) at its business-as-usual level, but with significant production losses and CO$_2$ leakage. For an output-based allocation over 75% of historic unitary (tCO$_2$/tonne-cement) emissions, the impact on production levels and EBITDA is insignificant, abatement in the EU is much lower, but there is almost no leakage. Policy makers need to recognize to what extent different allocation approaches may change the impacts of emissions trading, and adopt approaches accordingly.

Keywords: Grandfathering; Output-based allocation; Competitiveness; Leakage

1. Introduction

The European GHG Emissions Trading Scheme (ETS) is the most important ETS worldwide and arguably the most important European climate change mitigation policy currently in place.

* Corresponding author. Tel.: +33-1-43-94-73-65; fax: +33-1-43-94-73-70
E-mail address: demailly@centre-cired.fr

Assessing the environmental effectiveness and economic efficiency of the EU ETS is therefore of the utmost importance. Furthermore, many other countries, including the USA, have not implemented similar policies to date, so the EU ETS may impact the competitiveness of European CO_2-intensive industries.

However, the debate is blurred because terminology such as 'competitive disadvantage', 'competitive distortion' and 'competitiveness' can have very different meanings. Following Krugman (1994), one can even argue that at the macroeconomic level, the very notion of competitiveness is meaningless. However, for an industrial sector, the situation is different and these terms can basically be reduced to two interpretations:

1. a loss in domestic production, which in turn may induce leakage to imports from production in other parts of the world ('pollution havens')
2. a loss in profits, hence in stock value, of domestic firms.

It is essential to disentangle these two effects since, as we shall see, different allocation criteria would impact them in completely different – and often opposite – ways. Hence, in the present article, we analyse two contrasting allocation methods. In the former, labelled 'grandfathering' (GF), the number of free allowances a firm gets is independent of its current behaviour. As we demonstrate later, this assumption applies well to the US SO_2 trading system, but much less to the EU ETS.

In the latter, labelled 'output-based allocation' (OB), firms receive allowances *proportional to their current production level* – sometimes known as *intensity-based allocation*. In its pure form, this allocation method is currently excluded by the Commission, because it amounts to an '*ex-post*' adjustment (allocation dependent upon behaviour during the same trading period), but it does incorporate some features of the real-word allocation method. Notably, repeated allocation over sequential periods gives the potential for 'updating' based on output or emissions in the previous period, which offers a weaker (deferred) form of output-based allocation, as detailed in Section 2. The allocation methods used by Member States in phase 1 thus stand somewhere in between our two polar cases, and so are the methods allowed by the directive for phase 2.

Almost all the quantitative assessments of the EU ETS that have been recently published assume grandfathering, as defined above (Bernard et al., 2006; Criqui and Kitous, 2003; Klepper and Peterson, 2004, 2005; Reilly and Paltsev, 2005). An exception is IEA (2004). As we shall see in our simulations, this assumption has a critical influence not only on competitiveness but also on the environmental impact of the ETS (emissions reductions in the EU and abroad).

We studied the impacts of these allocation methods on the EU-27 cement industry, which represents around 10% of world emissions from the cement industry, through the CEMSIM-GEO model. GEO is a trade model we developed to deal with homogeneous products with high transportation costs (Demailly and Quirion, 2005a, 2005b). The world is divided into more than 7,000 areas, which allows us to compute transportation costs. In the new version of GEO we use here, we assume that a Cournot oligopoly competition takes place in every area among all the producers of the world, where demand is assumed to be linear.[1] This setting is inspired by Brander (1981) and Brander and Krugman (1983). Moreover, producers are subject to a capacity constraint.[2]

CEMSIM is a bottom-up model of the cement industry, developed by the IPTS (Szabo et al., 2003, 2006). It pays particular attention to fuel and technology dynamics. Seven technologies are included, characterized by energy, material and labour consumptions, an investment cost, and a set of retrofitting options.

We apply GEO to cement for three reasons. Firstly, GEO is particularly suited to the cement sector because transportation costs and capacity constraints are central to explaining international trade patterns of this homogeneous product. Secondly, cement is an important greenhouse gas emitter, due to growth in cement consumption over the last decades and the very high carbon emissions per tonne, both from fuel combustion and from the process itself. The sector's emissions from fuel combustion represented 2.4% of global carbon emissions in 1994 (IEA, 1999). Adding process emissions, the sector accounts for around 5% of global anthropogenic CO$_2$ emissions. Thirdly, the cement sector is potentially one of the most seriously impacted by a climate policy: among twelve EU-15 industry sectors, non-metallic minerals – mostly cement – have the second highest direct CO$_2$ emission/turnover ratio, just after power production (Quirion and Hourcade, 2004).

In Section 2, we briefly describe how allowances are allocated in the EU ETS. Section 3 presents a simple theoretical model in order to explain the main differences between grandfathering and output-based allocation. Section 4 describes the applied model and Section 5 describes the scenarios and provides the results of the simulations. Section 6 concludes.

2. Allowance allocation in the EU ETS

The most straightforward way of modelling an emission trading scheme (ETS) is to assume that firms covered by an ETS behave as if they were covered by an emission tax or auctioned emission allowances, i.e. that they factor the value of allowances into their marginal production decisions, irrespective of how many allowances they get for free. Such a behaviour is consistent with profit maximization as long as the number of free allowances the firm gets is independent of its current behaviour (especially of its production level): freely allocated allowances have an opportunity cost, so it is rational to add them to the marginal production cost as though the firm had to buy them through an auction or on the market. Throughout the article, we shall label as 'grandfathering' any allocation method in which the number of free allowances the firm gets is independent of its behaviour.

Under such an allocation, combined with profit maximization, whether the allowances are auctioned or freely distributed does not impact production nor emissions, but only profits and stock value. Tietenberg (2002, p. 3) makes this case as follows:

> Whatever the initial allocation, the transferability of the permits allows them to ultimately flow to their highest-valued uses. Since those uses do not depend on the initial allocation, all initial allocations result in the same outcome and that outcome is cost-effective.

These assumptions have been used in most assessments of the EU ETS (e.g. Bernard et al., 2006; Klepper and Peterson, 2004, 2005; Reilly and Paltsev, 2005).[3]

However, the assumption that the number of free allowances a firm gets is independent of its current behaviour applies well to the US SO$_2$ trading system, but much less to the EU ETS, for at least three reasons (Åhman et al., 2005; Schleich and Betz, 2005):[4]

• Allowances are first allocated for a 3-year period (2005–2007), and then every 5 years, taking into account new information. In particular, if a firm reduces its production, it may well receive fewer allowances in the subsequent periods. In the extreme case of a plant closure, no allowance will be allocated in the following periods;

- In all national allocation plans (NAPs), allowances are allocated for free to new entrants, although according to different formulae (Åhman et al., 2005). Furthermore, new entrants are defined extensively, including installations increasing their permitted production capacity;
- All national allocation plans but two (Sweden and the Netherlands, cf. Åhman et al., 2005) state that if an installation is closed, it will stop receiving allowances, from the next year and thereafter.[5]

Compared to auctioning or grandfathering, all these features constitute an incentive for firms to increase their production level. Unfortunately, modelling the precise features of all 25 NAPs would be very difficult: the allocation methods differ across Member States, and the NAPs for 2008–2012 are not yet decided. Instead we shall model two extreme cases, knowing that the actual allocation method in the EU ETS stands somewhere in between them:

- Pure grandfathering (GF), as described above
- Output-based allocation (OB), under which firms receive an amount of allowances, proportional to their current production.

These two scenarios are identical to those tested in other policy contexts by Haites (2003) and Edwards and Hutton (2001).

3. Grandfathering vs. output-based allocation: the basic theory

A simple theoretical model will help us understand how the two allocation methods differ. Let us take a set of N homogeneous firms competing under Cournot competition with a linear demand curve on the goods market. These firms choose an output and an abatement level in order to maximize their profit:

$$\underset{q,ua}{Max}\ \pi = P(Q)q - q.c(ua) - P_{CO2}(e - gf - q.ob) \tag{1}$$

with

$$e \equiv q(ue_0 - ua) \tag{2}$$

$$Q = \sum_N q \tag{3}$$

$$P(Q) = a - b.Q \tag{4}$$

where $P(Q)$ is the inverse demand, decreasing; Q the aggregate output; q a firm's output, c the marginal production cost, assumed constant with respect to production and increasing with ua (for unitary abatement), which is the abatement level per unit of output; P_{CO2} the allowance price, assumed exogenous;[6] e the level of emissions per firm; gf the amount of allowances grandfathered (if any) to a firm; ob (for output-based) the amount of allowances distributed for each unit of output (if any); ue_0 the baseline unitary emission; and $a > 0$ and $b > 0$ are the parameters of the demand curve.

The case of pure auctioning can be studied by setting both *gf* and *ob* to zero; grandfathering, by setting *ob* to zero; and output-based allocation, by setting *gf* to zero.

Profit maximization leads to the following first-order conditions:

$$\frac{\partial \pi}{\partial ua} = 0 \Leftrightarrow c'(ua) = P_{CO2} \tag{5}$$

Equation 5 is the usual condition of equalization of the marginal abatement cost to the price of CO$_2$, which is unaffected by the allocation method. This result is consistent with (and is indeed the basis of) Tietenberg's conclusion above.

$$\frac{\partial \pi}{\partial q} = 0 \Leftrightarrow P(Q) = c(ua) + b.q + P_{CO2}(ue_0 - ua - ob) \tag{6}$$

Summing Eqn 6 over the *N* firms and solving using Eqn 4 yields:

$$P = \frac{a + N.ec}{N+1} \tag{7}$$

$$Q = \frac{a - P}{b} \tag{8}$$

where *ec*, the extended variable production cost, is defined as:

$$ec \equiv c(ua) + P_{CO2}(ue_0 - ua - ob) \tag{9}$$

From Eqns 6, 7 and 8, we can see that:

- Under auctioning or grandfathering (i.e. if *ob* = 0), firms add the value of emissions per unit of output ($ue_0 - ua$) to their marginal production cost. Furthermore, the marginal production cost increases with abatement, which raises the output price further. To what extent these extra costs are passed on to consumers depends on the number of firms *N*.
- *gf* does not influence either the output price or the output level. This is because grandfathered allowances have an opportunity cost. This is consistent with Tietenberg's quotation above. However, from Eqn 1, compared with auctioning, grandfathering increases the profit level.
- Compared with auctioning or grandfathering, output-based allowances (a higher *ob*) reduce the price level and increase the output. If the sector considered is neither a net buyer nor a net seller on the allowance market ($ue_0 - ua = ob$), then *P* rises above its business-as-usual level only in so far as the marginal production cost increases with abatement. If the sector considered is a net buyer of allowances ($ue_0 - ua > ob$), then firms add to their marginal production cost the value of the allowances they must buy ($ue_0 - ua - ob$), as seen in IEA (2004). If, conversely, the sector is a net allowance seller ($ue_0 - ua < ob$), output may rise compared with business-as-usual. Finally, when *ob* tends to zero, the impact on *P* and *Q* tends to that of grandfathering or auctioning.

These conclusions are consistent with the theoretical models of Sterner and Höglund (2000), Fischer (2001) and Gielen et al. (2002), except that we take the allowance price as exogenous, which is justified by the fact that the sector we studied represents only a small share of the ETS (less than 12% of total allowances[7]). Otherwise, for a given overall level of emissions, output-based allocation implies a higher allowance price than grandfathering or auctioning: since unitary abatement is identical for a given allowance price (Eqn 5) and output is higher under OB (Eqns 7, 8 and 9), unitary abatement, and thus allowance price, must be higher under OB to obtain the same level of total abatement.

Because in these early models there is neither imperfect competition nor CO_2 leakage, OB leads to a higher cost, for a given abatement, than grandfathering. The inclusion of these two features may yield a different conclusion, as demonstrated by Fischer and Fox (2004) and Edwards and Hutton (2001), with general equilibrium models.

4. Presentation of CEMSIM-GEO

Cement is a product which is quite homogeneous throughout the world. The existence of different prices is mainly justified by the importance of transportation costs. Whereas a tonne of cement is sold around €80 when it leaves a plant in France, it costs €10 to transport it by road over 100 km. The cost is much lower by sea: transporting cement from a harbour in eastern Asia to Marseille is the same as from Marseille to Lyon. Such a characteristic must be taken into account when assessing the impact of an asymmetric climate policy on the cement industry: whereas coastal regions could be severely impacted, inland ones seem to be relatively protected.

In GEO, the trade model we developed (Demailly and Quirion, 2005a, 2005b), cement is a homogeneous product: the firms in the 47 producing countries are assumed to manufacture perfectly substitutable products. The world is divided into more than 7,000 areas, as displayed in Figure 1,

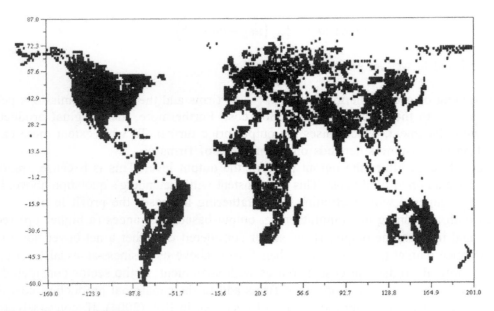

Figure 1. Areas of GEO.

and up to 1,600 real sea harbours and more 'land harbours' are represented, which allow us to compute realistic transportation costs.

In the new version of GEO we use here, we assume that a Cournot oligopoly competition takes place in every area among all the producers of the world. Producers compete on the market of an area given their extended variable production costs and their transportation cost from their plants to the market. Demand is assumed to be linear. This modelling is inspired by Brander (1981) and Brander and Krugman (1983). Moreover, producers are subject to a capacity constraint. When its capacity constraint is binding, a producer gives the priority to its domestic areas and sells its production in the most profitable areas. A cement firm may extend its available capacity to export by using plants located more deeply inside its territory, and consequently by increasing production cost through higher transportation costs. However, its exports are capped by its total capacity.

The use of the Cournot model instead of other competition representations (Bertrand, Stackelberg, limit price, etc.) is not only justified by the support of the literature or its tractability, but also by the fact that it is compatible with the following quotations from cement manufacturers and analysts (Oxera, 2004):

> Cement is a local commodity market … haulage costs are significant … therefore [we] expect significant cost pass-through.
>
> Cement travels on water, not well on land … imports set the price anywhere close to water with a decent port facility.
>
> As import prices often cap selling prices, margins will be squeezed as costs rise … we expect no change in current cement prices.

Indeed, let us take the example of a French inland area protected by transportation costs where no foreign firm is cost-competitive enough to be part of the equilibrium in this area. Demand is linear: $P = a - b \cdot Q$. The N identical French firms, with an extended variable production cost ec, equally share the market where the price P is given by: $P = \dfrac{a + N \cdot ec}{N + 1}$ (see Section 3). A rise in ec leads to a $N/(N + 1)$ cost pass-through.

Let us now assume that N' firms in a given foreign country, with a variable production cost c' and a transportation cost tc, are cost-competitive enough to be part of the equilibrium on the market of a French coastal area. Price is given by $P = \dfrac{a + N \cdot ec + N' \cdot \left(c' + tc\right)}{N + N' + 1}$. A rise in ec leads to a $N/(N + N' + 1)$ cost pass-through. The profit margin of French firms in this area is much more impacted than in the previous case.

The inland case corresponds to the first quotation above, and the coastal case to the second and third ones.

CEMSIM is a bottom-up model of the cement industry, developed by the IPTS (Szabo et al., 2003, 2006). It pays particular attention to fuel and technology dynamics. Seven technologies are included, characterized by energy, material and labour consumptions, an investment cost, and a set of retrofitting options. The technologies considered in CEMSIM are already used on a large scale. Assuming no large-scale commercial application in the near future, the model does not take into account emerging technologies such as mineral polymers, which could lead to radical emissions abatements (Prebay et al., 2006). We modified the original CEMSIM model to introduce more flexibility in the content of clinker – the carbon-intensive intermediary product – in cement and in the choice of non-primary fuels, following discussions with French cement industrials.

We used the CEMSIM database on consumption, production capacity and energy demand, energy prices from the POLES model developed by the LEPII-EPE as well as cement bilateral trade data from OECD, to calibrate the CEMSIM-GEO model, which is then recursively run with a yearly step.

Given the trade and technological details of CEMSIM-GEO, it is – for tractability's sake – a partial equilibrium model. Therefore we ignore the macroeconomic feedbacks, such as possible changes in GDP or exchange rates, although these impacts are expected to be very soft – see, for example, IPCC (2001) for GDP impacts. Furthermore, we do not explicitly model the substitutions between cement and other building materials, but since all the CO_2-intensive industries are covered by the EU ETS, substitutions should be limited. As a consequence, it does not seem unreasonable to work in partial equilibrium.

We highlight the fact that, in GEO, cement is assumed to be homogeneous throughout the world: we discount product quality or differentiation as a trade determinant. We calibrate non-transport barriers to match real bilateral trade data, assuming that, as soon as an exporter is competitive enough to export 1 kg of cement to the harbour of a country, the only barrier to trade it faces to export more and penetrate more deeply inside this country is road transportation costs. However, many more barriers seem to exist in the real-world cement trade. Foreign exporters cannot build up supply networks overnight. EU firms have the ability to keep the production of 'aggressive' foreign producers out of home markets, for example by restricting their access to port facilities by occupying them. EU firms, which are highly concentrated and have developed their activities in non-EU countries, have the ability to keep imports out of home markets through collusive behaviours (EC, 2000). These features lead to overestimation of the trade impacts of climate policies. Moreover, if the one-stage Cournot model is of interest notably for addressing the cost pass-through issue, its ability to provide quantitative results is more controversial. We also stress that the quantification of some technical flexibility in CEMSIM (clinker ratio, retrofitting and fuel choice) is very difficult. As a consequence, whereas our qualitative results are robust, our quantitative results should be considered very cautiously.

5. Simulations and results

In the following sections we present, for various scenarios, the results for 2008–2012 of some model outputs:[8] cement production cost, prices, consumption, production, EBITDA and CO_2 emissions in EU-27.

In the first set of scenarios, an EU-27 ETS is implemented with allowances grandfathered. These scenarios are the 'GF' scenarios. The scenario with firms being grandfathered 90% of their emissions in 2004 is the GF-90% scenario. This is our central GF scenario. Most of the model outputs under GF-90% do not depend on the amount of allowances allocated. When presenting such an output, to highlight this fact, we label this scenario 'GF' instead of 'GF-90%'.

In the second set of scenarios, a firm's allocation is assumed to be proportional to its current cement production. These scenarios are the 'OB' scenarios. In our central OB scenario, the output-based allocation of allowances is assumed to represent, for every firm, 90% of its 2004 emissions per tonne of cement (unitary emissions). This is the 'OB-90%' scenario.

For the 2005–2007 period, the CO_2 price is modelled at an average of €20/tCO_2, close to the average value observed in 2005. We then make different assumptions for the CO_2 price between 2008 and 2012: from €10 to €50/tCO_2.

According to the latest observations on the EU electricity market and to the emerging windfall profits debate in the EU, we assume that power generators have the ability to pass on to electricity customers 100% of their extended cost rise. For the sake of convenience, this rise in a given country equals the CO$_2$ price multiplied by the national unitary emission of the power sector, whatever the allocation method for the cement industry may be – as if the allowances in the electricity sector were always grandfathered.

For simplicity, we assume that non-EU-27 countries do not implement any climate policy, which leads to an overestimation of trade impacts and CO$_2$ leakage.

Some of the insights, especially under OB-90%, do not depend only on the CO$_2$ price but also on the amount of allowances allocated, so we performed some sensitivity tests. However, we will present them only for the model outputs that we judge the most important when studying the impacts on competitiveness of climate policies: production and EBITDA.

Under the 'business-as-usual' scenario (BaU), no climate policy is implemented.

We stress that the comparison between the two central scenarios, OB-90% and GF-90%, should be made cautiously, because there is no guarantee that they lead to the same environmental improvement. It is even more delicate to compare the OB and GF scenarios with the same CO$_2$ price assumption, because these systems, if also implemented for other sectors in the EU ETS, would lead to different prices (see Section 3).

5.1. Cost-competitiveness

We label as 'extended variable production cost', or simply 'extended cost', the cost with which firms compete on world cement markets, minus transportation costs, expressed in euros per tonne of cement. This determines the cost-competitiveness of firms.

(a) Grandfathering (GF)

As already explained, under GF the extended cost of EU cement manufacturers is defined by:

$$\text{Extended cost} = \text{variable production cost} + \text{CO}_2 \text{ opportunity cost}$$

$$\text{CO}_2 \text{ opportunity cost} = \text{CO}_2 \text{ price} * \text{emission per tonne of cement (unitary emission)}$$

Figure 2 shows how the opportunity cost increases with the CO$_2$ price. The rise is less than proportional. When the CO$_2$ price increases, cement producers are pushed to reduce their unitary emission by (1) diminishing the clinker content of cement – clinker being the CO$_2$-intensive intermediary product in cement production, (2) switching from high to low carbon-intensive fuels, and (3) using more energy-efficient technologies. In 2008–2012, however, the reduction in unitary emission is mostly due to the decrease in the clinker rate in cement (–10% for €20/tCO$_2$). This decrease is provoked not only by the rise in the extended cost of clinker – due to the opportunity cost of emission, the increase in electricity prices and the use of more expensive low-carbon fuels – but also to the drop in the consumption and price of added materials, the non-clinker materials in cement, due to significant cement production losses, as we will see below.[9] Decompositions of the extended cost under BaU and GF-20 (grandfathering with €20/tCO$_2$) are provided in Figure 3, mixing the different technologies and fuel sources.

For €20/tCO$_2$, the extended cost rises by €14 per tonne of cement. This rise not only leads EU firms to reduce their output but also impacts their cost-competitiveness compared with that of

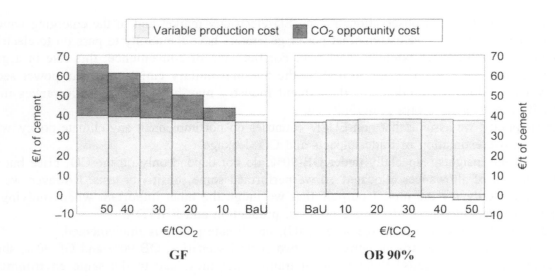

Figure 2. GF/OB-90% – EU-27 extended cost.

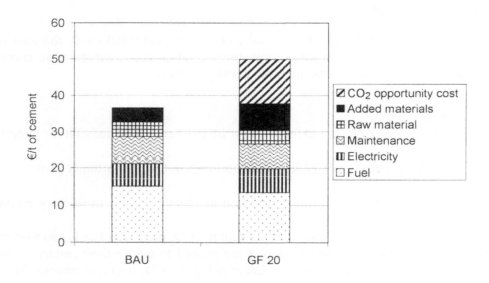

Figure 3. GF – structure of the EU-27 extended cost.

foreign firms. In GEO, where transportation cost is the only barrier to trade for exporters, this rise considerably facilitates the penetration of foreign cement into EU markets. Indeed, in the EU, €14/t allows an increase in the transport of cement by road by around 200 km.

These results, as well as the following (except EBITDA), are independent of the amount of GF allowances allocated.

(b) Output-based (OB) allocation

Under OB, the extended cost is defined by:

$$\text{Extended cost} = \text{variable production cost} + CO_2 \text{ price}*(\text{unitary emission} - \text{OB allowance})$$

We observe in Figure 2 that, according to CEMSIM-GEO, technical flexibility allows EU producers to decrease their unitary emission to 90% of their 2004 unitary emission for €20/tCO₂. It guarantees that the amount of output-based allowances allocated covers their emissions: they are neither buyers nor sellers on the CO₂ market, and their extended cost simply equals their variable production cost.

Whereas firms buy some emission allowances for lower CO₂ prices, from €30/tCO₂, the average unitary emission in the EU is lower than the amount of allowances allocated per tonne of cement. Cement manufacturers become sellers on the CO₂ market, which supposes that there are buyers such as the power suppliers. Therefore, although the EU variable production cost rises, its extended cost slightly decreases.

Obviously, this result depends on the allocation per tonne of cement: for a decreasing allocation, results tend to get closer to the GF case. However, according to the sensitivity test we made, we may consider that the extended cost of EU producers is not highly impacted under OB for amounts of output-based allowances over 75% of the 2004 unitary emission: the expected rise[10] remains below 10%.

To underline this point, whereas the extended cost, and therefore the cost-competitiveness of EU firms, is highly impacted under GF allocation, it is not under OB for an output-based allocation, provided that the allocation factor is over 75% of 2004 unitary emissions.

5.2. Prices

(a) Grandfathering (GF)

The results presented in Figure 4 show that, under GF, the average price applied by EU firms in their countries of origin increases significantly, following the rise of their extended cost. The cost

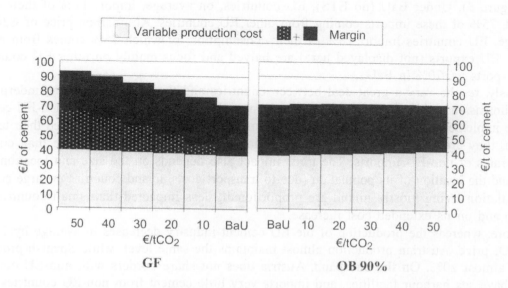

Figure 4. GF/OB-90% – EU-27 price and margin.

pass-through is limited by oligopolistic competition and by international pressure: on average 75% of the extended cost rise is passed on to consumers. Around half of this limitation is due to oligopolistic competition, the other half to international pressure.

However, if the margin over the extended cost tends to decrease, the margin over the variable production cost increases.

(b) Output-based (OB) allocation

As shown previously, the extended cost of EU firms under OB-90% is not significantly impacted. Figure 4 shows, unsurprisingly, that the EU domestic price demonstrates the same evolution. However, if the margin over the extended cost remains quasi-constant, the margin over the variable production cost decreases slightly because the latter increases.

Obviously, these results depend on the amount of allowances allocated per tonne of cement. But, according to sensitivity tests, cement prices are not highly impacted as long as the amount of allowances per tonne of cement is over 75% of the 2004 unitary emission: the expected rise of cement prices remains below 5%.

To sum up, the EU domestic price and the margin over the variable production cost increase very significantly under GF. Under OB, for output-based allocation over 75% of 2004 unitary emission, they are weakly impacted.

5.3. Consumption, production and trade

(a) Grandfathering (GF)

As we have seen, the impact of GF on the cement price in the EU is very significant. However, because of the low elasticity price of demand (0.2), consumption is not highly affected: it drops by 3% for €20/tCO$_2$. Should the elasticity be higher – and it could be, especially in the mid-to-long term – so would be the impact on consumption.

However, the cost-competitiveness drop of EU producers heavily impacts EU cement trade flows (Figure 5). Under BaU (no ETS), EU countries, on average, import 11% of their cement consumed, 75% of these imports coming from other EU countries. At a carbon price of €20/tCO$_2$, on average, EU countries import 18% of their consumption, of which 75% comes from non-EU countries. EU exports (not displayed here) are halved and focus mainly on other EU countries – 90% of exports vs. 70% in BaU.

Obviously, results vary a great deal between countries and the aggregate results underplay the regional dimension within Europe. In the countries with high rates of import from non-EU countries before the implementation of a climate policy, imports have already deeply penetrated their territory. Therefore, they are less protected by transportation costs and are more sensitive than countries with low rates of non-EU imports. The trade impact also depends on the size and location of the country, and the location of its population (due to transport costs, inland countries or large countries with population living mostly inland are proportionally less impacted than small countries near the coast) and on its extended cost increase.

Therefore, whereas the production of the EU cement industry decreases in average by 15% for a €20/tCO$_2$ price, Austrian production almost maintains the same level, while Spanish production drops by almost 20%. On the one hand, Austria does not share borders with non-EU countries, does not have sea harbour facilities, and imports very little cement from non-EU countries before the implementation of the ETS. On the other hand, Spain is a relatively large country but has a

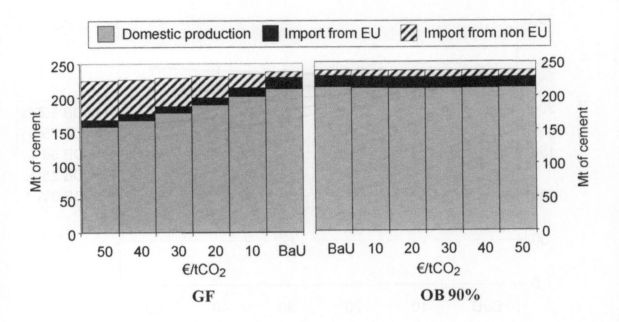

Figure 5. GF/OB-90% – EU-27 consumption and trade.

large number of sea harbours and imported in 2004 almost 20% of its cement consumption, mainly from non-EU countries.

We again emphasize some caveats of our trade modelling which lead to an overestimation of trade impact of climate policies: we ignore product quality or differentiation as a trade determinant, and non-transport barriers to trade which prevents foreign producers from increasing their exports, such as the difficulties in building a commercial network or the ability of EU firms to keep imports away out of home markets. Moreover, if the one-stage Cournot model is of interest notably for addressing the cost pass-through issue, its ability to provide quantitative results is more controversial. Finally, cement firms tend to be multinational firms, a characteristic that GEO is not perfectly designed to cope with. Hence, cement imported from non-EU countries does not necessarily come from non-EU firms.

In conclusion, whereas the qualitative results are robust and allow comparisons between the different scenarios, our quantitative results should be considered very cautiously.

(b) Output-based (OB) allocation

In sharp contrast, under OB-90%, EU consumption and imports are insignificantly impacted (Figure 5). This conclusion also holds for exports (not displayed here). However this does not hold for much tighter OB allocations (Figure 6). For allocation below 75% of 2004 unitary emission, the expected drop in production becomes significant (above 5%).

To sum up, whereas the impact on consumption is small because of the very low elasticity price of demand (and insignificant under OB), the impact on net import and production is great under GF, and the protection afforded by OB allocation declines if the allocation is under 75% of 2004 unitary emissions.

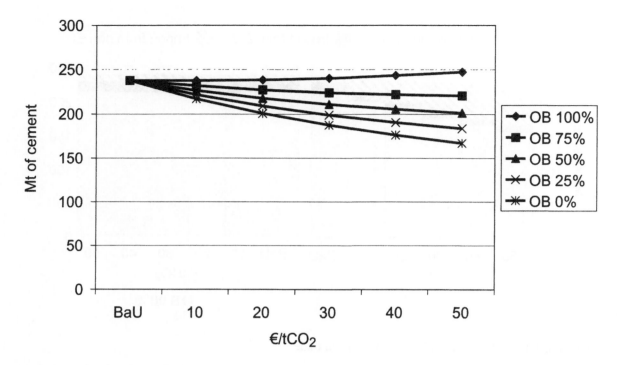

Figure 6. OB – EU-27 production.

5.4. Operating profitability (EBITDA)[11]

(a) Grandfathering (GF)
Under GF, EU firms see their production decreasing and their margin over variable production costs increasing with CO_2 prices. These facts have opposite effects on their EBITDA from cement sales, the EBITDA on cement.

$$\text{EBITDA on cement} = \sum_{\text{World areas}} (\text{Price} - \text{Variable cost} - \text{Transportation cost}) * \text{Production}$$

As we see in Figure 7, the EBITDA on cement increases with low CO_2 prices and then decreases. The net profit realized on the emission market, or simply the 'profit on emission', is given by:

$$\text{Profit on emission} = (\text{GF allocation} - CO_2 \text{ emission}) * CO_2 \text{ price}$$

Note that this is the only output of the model presented here which depends on the volume of GF allocation. For a GF allocation equal to 90% of historic emissions, cement manufacturers emit less than their allocation, because their production and their unitary emission drop enough for all the CO_2 prices tested. They are thus sellers on the CO_2 market, so their profit on emission is positive. Their emissions decrease and their profit on emission increases with rising CO_2 prices. As a result, the total EBITDA increases significantly with CO_2 prices, as does the share of profit arising from emission sales.

Obviously, this depends strongly on the amount of GF allowance allocated (Figures 8 and 9). If granted allowances equal to 50% of 2004 emissions, EU cement producers are significant buyers

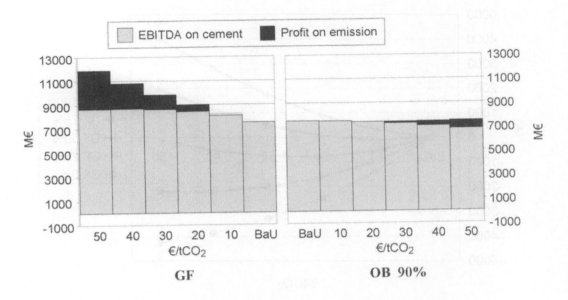

Figure 7. GF-90%/OB-90% – EU-27 EBITDA.

of CO$_2$ emission allowances but this remains more than offset by the value of the higher prices, and their EBITDA still rises; however, at allocations below this, they lose.

Once again, we stress that these aggregate results underplay the regional dimension within Europe. Whereas the EU EBITDA increases by 20% under GF-90% for a €20/tCO$_2$ price, Austrian EBITDA increases by around 30% and makes no profit on emissions – because its production is hardly impacted at all – while the Spanish cement industry – whose production is greatly impacted – does increase its EBITDA by around 10%, thanks to allowances sales. For an allocation of 50% of 2004 emissions, Austrian cement producers keep on benefiting from the system, whereas the Spanish lose.

(b) Output-based (OB) allocation

As already observed, the margin over variable production cost decreases under OB. As displayed in Figure 7, there is little impact on EBITDA at low CO$_2$ prices, but for high prices, in spite of the slight production rise we have observed, EBITDA on cement decreases. As we have already seen, EU-27 cement manufacturers turn out to be neither sellers nor buyers of allowances for €20/tCO$_2$, but for higher CO$_2$ prices, they become sellers and profit on emissions sales:

$$\text{Profit on emissions} = (\text{OB allocation} - \text{unitary emission})*\text{production}*\text{CO}_2 \text{ price}$$

This is positive and increases with price because they sell more and at a higher value. The aggregate impact on EBITDA is weak under OB-90%, even for high CO$_2$ prices.

Obviously, this conclusion about EBITDA depends on the amount of OB allowances allocated, which impacts both the profit on emissions and the EBITDA on cement.[12] Figure 10 indicates that, for allocation over 75% of 2004 unitary emission, our qualitative conclusion remains valid: the expected EBITDA drop is less than 5%.

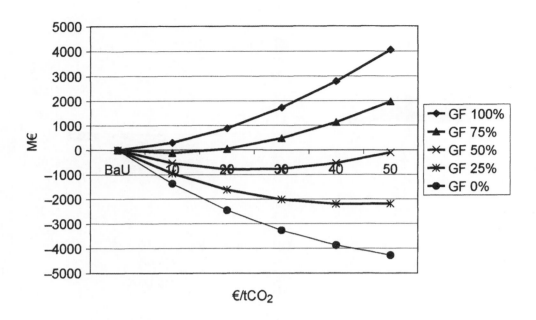

Figure 8. GF – EU-27 profit on emission.

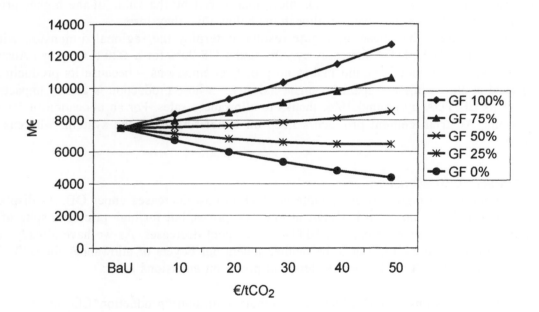

Figure 9. GF – EU-27 EBITDA.

To sum up, under GF and for allocations over 50% of past emissions, the EU EBITDA increases. Under 50%, it decreases. It is not highly impacted under OB as long as the amount of output-based allowances allocated is over 75% of 2004 unitary emission.

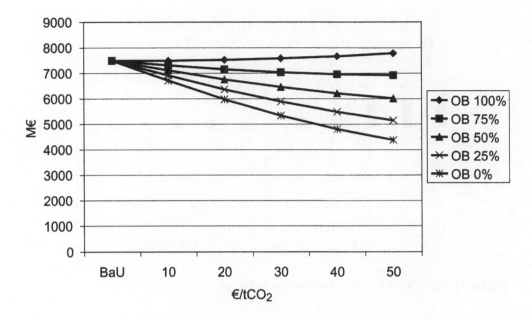

Figure 10. OB – EU-27 EBITDA.

5.5. CO$_2$ emissions

(a) Grandfathering (GF)

Under GF, the drop in EU CO$_2$ emissions by the cement industry is very important: −25% for €20/tCO$_2$. Half of this drop is due to the decrease in unitary emission, the other half to the production drop (mostly the rise of net imports). This explains the very important carbon leakage rate[13] observed in Figure 11: around 50%. It means that half of the emissions reduction made inside the EU is offset by an emissions rise outside.

We stress that not only is our trade representation (i.e. no product differentiation, focus on transport, no inertia in trade) responsible for this important leakage around 2010, but so also is the technical inertia: leakage decreases as time goes by with the introduction of more carbon-efficient techniques. Furthermore, the reader should bear in mind that we assume no climate policy outside the EU which explains a part of this high leakage rate.

(b) Output-based (OB) allocation

Under OB-90%, there is no significant production drop. The emissions reduction is only due to the improvement of the carbon efficiency of the EU cement industry. Therefore, for €20/tCO$_2$, it is halved compared with GF, but the leakage rate is much smaller, around 9%, and decreases with high prices (Figure 11). Finally, for a given CO$_2$ price, world emissions reductions are almost identical under GF and OB-90% – but slightly higher under GF.

Again we stress that some results depend on the OB allocation: the tighter the allocation, the closer are the EU emissions reductions and carbon leakage to the GF scenarios.

To sum up, under GF, the huge emissions drop is partially offset by an important carbon leakage. Under OB, for generous allocations, the drop is much weaker and so is the leakage. The tighter the

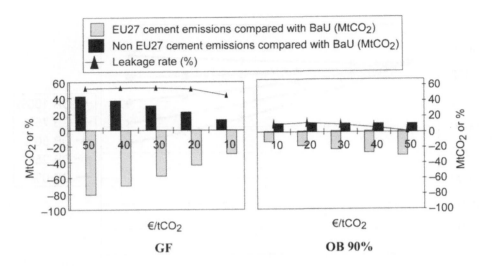

Figure 11. GF/OB-90% – EU-27 emissions reduction.

allocation, the closer are the EU emissions reductions and carbon leakage to GF. For every GF or OB scenario, world emissions reductions turn out to be very similar.

6. Conclusions

We have seen that the allowance allocation system of the EU ETS is neither grandfathering nor output-based allocation. But is it – and will it be in phase 2 – closer to the former or to the latter? This issue turns out to be a crucial one.

If the allowance allocation system is similar to grandfathering, EU cement producers (and many other firms also) will, in aggregate, benefit from a significant rise in their EBITDA, but lose market share to imports. Indeed, our simulations indicate that, whatever the allowance price, grandfathering 50% of past emissions to cement producers is enough to maintain their EBITDA to the business-as-usual level. Given that the Directive prevents Member States from auctioning more than 10% of the allowances for 2008–2012, and that the analyses of National Allocation Plans for 2005–2007 show that industry has benefited from an allocation level close to BaU (Reilly and Paltsev, 2005; Schleich and Betz, 2005), cement producers will certainly receive more than 50% of their past emissions in the next generation of NAPs. However, our simulations also indicate a significant production loss and CO_2 leakage rate under grandfathering. As a consequence, although CO_2 emissions reductions are high under grandfathering in EU-27 (around –25% for €20 per tonne of CO_2), about one-half of this drop is compensated for by a rise in emissions elsewhere.

If, conversely, the allowance allocation system is similar to output-based allocation for an allowance allocation ratio of 90% of historic unitary emissions, neither the production level nor the EBITDA is significantly impacted, even for a very high CO_2 price (€50 per tonne). Only if the allocation ratio were to drop below 75% of historic unitary emissions (a very unlikely policy choice) would competitiveness impacts (on production and EBITDA) be severe (above 5%). For any allocation ratio, abatement is reduced compared with auctioning or grandfathering, but so is leakage, and finally world emissions are almost the same.

Finally the allocation method – notably the updating criteria, the treatment of new entrants and the closure rules – turns out to be a variable of importance to determine the competitiveness impacts and the CO$_2$ emissions reduction achieved at the world level under the EU ETS.

Three important caveats are in order:

- First, despite the high level of regional disaggregation and incorporation of transport costs and port facilities in the GEO model, modelling trade impacts – and therefore the carbon leakage of climate policies – is still difficult, particularly over a relatively short period such as 2008–2012. Notably because the explicit representation of some non-transport barriers to trade (such as the ability of EU firms to keep imports out of 'home' markets through collusive behaviours or anti-competitive practices) is very difficult. Thus, although the *qualitative* results are robust, the *quantitative* ones should be considered very cautiously.
- Second, the allowance price depends on the allocation method, not only in the cement sector, but in the whole set of sectors covered by the EU ETS, especially power production. For a given emissions cap (or amount of allowances allocated), the allowance price would be higher under output-based allocation than under grandfathering.
- Third, implementing output-based allocation in the cement sector raises a difficult dilemma, due to the fact that 90% of cement emissions occur during the production of cement's main input, clinker, and that lowering the proportion of clinker in cement is one of the main means of cutting CO$_2$ emissions. If allowances are allocated in proportion to cement production, a producer may import clinker to make cement in Europe in order to receive free allowances and sell them. Leakage would then not be addressed. Alternatively, if allowances are allocated in proportion to clinker production, the incentive to reduce the clinker rate in cement vanishes, and so does a large part of CO$_2$ abatement. This problem is not taken into account in our simulations, since we model only trade in cement, not in clinker.

Ultimately, there exists at least one other means to address the competitiveness problem, other than free allocation of allowances. A tax or auctioned allowances with a border-tax adjustment as assessed in Demailly and Quirion (2005a, 2005b) offers the best of both worlds: compared with grandfathering, it prevents leakage; and compared with output-based allocation, it induces consumers to take into account the CO$_2$-intensity of the different building materials in their decisions, and does not suffer from the above-mentioned clinker dilemma.

Acknowledgements

The analysis presented in this article has benefited greatly from a close collaboration with the Institute for Prospective Technological Studies (IPTS, Joint Research Centre, European Commission). Our analysis is partly based on the world cement model CEMSIM developed by L. Szabo, I. Hidalgo, J. C. Ciscar, A. Soria and P. Russ, all of the IPTS. We thank them and the IPTS for their explanations about the model, for giving us free access to a world cement industry database compatible with the model structure, and for having hosted one of us at the IPTS for 2 months. We also thank Michael Grubb, Karsten Neuhoff, Neil Walker, Peter Zapfel, an anonymous referee and participants at two meetings organized by Climate Strategies in Oxford and London for their comments, as well as Françoise Le Gallo for providing data on the international cement trade.

Notes

1 See Smale et al. (this issue) for further explanation and discussion.
2 In this article, the capacity constraint is fixed: since we do not run the model beyond 2012, endogenizing investment, as in Demailly and Quirion (2005a, 2005b), would not make a significant difference.
3 The authors are aware of this limitation and write (Reilly and Paltsev, 2005, p. 11) 'We also cannot estimate the potential distortionary effects of non-lump sum distribution of some of the permits (those that under some countries' NAPs are retained for new entrants).'
4 Furthermore, the assumption of profit maximization may also be challenged: some managers may be reluctant to reduce production in order to sell allowances and increase the profit level, and use their information advantage over shareholders to maintain production above the profit-maximizing level (see Baumol, 1962).
5 Apart from the situation where, if a firm closes an installation and opens a new one in the same Member State, it may retain these allowances, but then will not get allowances for the new installation.
6 In this model and in the rest of the present article, we assume that the considered sector is too small to influence the allowance price. Indeed, 'minerals' (including cement, glass and lime sectors) represent around 12% of total allowances allocated in the EU ETS (Caisse des Dépôts, 2006).
7 12% corresponds to the cement, glass and lime sectors (Caisse des Dépôts, 2006).
8 More precisely, the figure presented for a given output variable in a given scenario is the average value of the output variable between 2008 and 2012.
9 For further details on technological evolutions, see Demailly and Quirion (2005a), where the decreases in added materials prices due to production losses are not taken into account.
10 To calculate the expected impact of a policy with an uncertain CO_2 price, we give a probability (a weight) to every price tested. We assume that probabilities are distributed according to a Gaussian curve centred at €25/tCO_2 – the average price of 2008 forwards from the beginning of 2006 – and that the probability that price is between €15 and €35 equals 50%.
11 Earnings Before Interest, Tax, Debt and Amortization.
12 The lower it is, the lower is the production and the higher is the margin on production cost, so that the effect on the EBITDA cement is not trivial, as under GF. Conversely, the lower the OB allocation, the lower is the profit on emission.
13 Leakage rate = increase in non EU-27 emissions / decrease in EU-27 emissions.

References

Åhman, M., Burtraw, D., Kruger, J.A., Zetterberg, L., 2005. The Ten-year Rule: Allocation of Emissions Allowances in the EU Emissions Trading System. RFF Discussion Paper 05–30.
Baumol, W.J., 1962. On the theory of expansion of the firm. American Economic Review 52(5), 1078–1087.
Bernard, A., Vielle, M., Viguier, L., 2006. Premières simulations de la directive européenne sur les quotas d'émissions avec le modèle GEMINI-E3 [available at http://ecolu-info.unige.ch/~nccrwp4/GEMINI-E3/GEMINIquotasfinal1.pdf].
Brander, J., 1981. Intra-industry trade in identical commodities. Journal of International Economics 11, 1–14.
Brander, J., Krugman, P., 1983. A 'reciprocal dumping' model of international trade. Journal of International Economics 15, 313–321.
Caisse des Dépôts, 2006. Panorama des Plans nationaux d'allocation des quotas en Europe, April 2006. [available at http://www.caissedesdepots.fr/FR/espace_presse/publications_doc/note8_panorama_PNAQ_europeens.pdf].
Criqui, P., Kitous, A., 2003. Impact of Linking JI and CDM Credits to the European Emissions Allowance Trading Scheme (KPI-ETS). Report for the European Commission.
Demailly, D., Quirion, P., 2005a. The Competitiveness Impacts of CO_2 Emissions Reductions in the Cement Sector. Report for the OECD, SMASH/CIRED.
Demailly, D., Quirion, P., 2005b. Leakage from climate policies and border tax adjustment: lessons from a geographic model of the cement industry. CESifo Venice Summer Institute, July.
EC [European Commission], 2000. The Court of First Instance reduces the fines imposed on the cement cartel by almost €140 million. Press release No 16/00 [available at http://curia.eu.int/en/actu/communiques/cp00/aff/cp0016en.htm].
Edwards, T.H., Hutton, J.P., 2001. Allocation of carbon permits within a country: a general equilibrium analysis of the United Kingdom. Energy Economics 23(4), 371–386.
Fischer, C., 2001. Rebating Environmental Policy Revenues: Output-based Allocations and Tradable Performance Standards. RFF Discussion Paper 01–22.

Fischer, C., Fox, A., 2004. Output-Based Allocations of Emissions Permits: Efficiency and Distributional Effects in a General Equilibrium Setting with Taxes and Trade. RFF Discussion Paper 04–37.

Gielen, A., Koutstaal, P., Vollebergh, H.R.J., 2002. Comparing emission trading with absolute and relative targets. Paper presented to the second CATEP Workshop, 25–26 March, London.

Haites, E., 2003. Output-based allocation as a form of protection for internationally competitive industries. Climate Policy 3(Supplement 2), S29–S41.

IEA [International Energy Agency], 1999. The Reduction of Greenhouse Gas Emission from the Cement Industry. IEA, Greenhouse Gas R&D Programme.

IEA [International Energy Agency], 2004. Industrial Competitiveness under the European Union Emissions Trading Scheme. IEA Information Paper.

IPCC, 2001. Climate Change 2001: Mitigation. Contribution of Working Group III to the Third Assessment Report of the Intergovernmental Panel on Climate Change (IPCC). Cambridge University Press, Cambridge, UK.

Klepper, G., Peterson, S., 2004. The EU Emissions Trading Scheme: Allowance Prices, Trade Flows, Competitiveness Effects. FEEM Working Paper 49.2004.

Klepper, G., Peterson, S., 2005. Emissions Trading, CDM, JI, and More: The Climate Strategy of the EU. FEEM Working Paper 55.2005.

Krugman, P., 1994. Competitiveness: a dangerous obsession. Foreign Affairs 73(2), 28–44.

Oxera, 2004. The European Emissions Trading Scheme: Implications for Industrial Competitiveness. Report for the Carbon Trust.

Prebay, Y., Ando, S., Desarnaud, E., Desbarbieux, T., 2006. Les enjeux du développement durable au sein de l'Industrie du Ciment: réduction des émissions de CO$_2$. Atelier Changement Climatique de l'Ecole des Ponts [available at http://www.enpc.fr/fr/formations/ecole_virt/trav-eleves/cc/cc0506/ciment.pdf].

Quirion, P., Hourcade, J.-C., 2004. Does the CO$_2$ emission trading directive threaten the competitiveness of European industry? Quantification and comparison to exchange rates fluctuations. EAERE, Annual Conference, Budapest.

Reilly, J.M., Paltsev, S., 2005. An Analysis of the European Emission Trading Scheme. MIT, Joint Program on the Science and Policy of Global Change Report No. 127.

Schleich, J., Betz, R., 2005. Incentives for energy efficiency and innovation in the European Emission Trading System. In: Proceedings of the ECEEE Summer Study, Mandelieu, 2005 [available at http://www.eceee.org/library_links/proceedings/2005/abstract/7124schleich.lasso].

Smale, R., Hartley, M., Hepburn, C., Ward, J., Grubb, M., 2006. The impact of CO$_2$ emissions trading on firm profits and market prices. Climate Policy 6(1), 31–48.

Sterner, T., Höglund, L., 2000. Output-based Refunding of Emission Payments: Theory, Distribution of Costs, and International Experience. RFF Discussion Paper 00–29.

Szabo, L., Hidalgo, I., Ciscar, J.C., Soria, A., Russ, P., 2003. Energy Consumption and CO$_2$ Emissions from the World Cement Industry. DG JRC-IPTS Report, Technical Report Series, EUR 20769 EN.

Szabo, L., Hidalgo I., Ciscar, J.C., Soria, A., 2006. CO$_2$ emission trading within the European Union and Annex B countries: the cement industry case. Energy Policy 34(1), 72–87.

Tietenberg, T., 2002. The Tradable Permits Approach to Protecting the Commons: What Have we Learned? FEEM Working Paper 36.2002.

www.climatepolicy.com

Free allocation of allowances under the EU emissions trading scheme: legal issues

Angus Johnston*

Trinity Hall, Cambridge University, Cambridge CB2 1TJ, UK

Abstract

This article provides a legal analysis of some of the key issues that arise in examining the system for allocating emissions allowances under the EU's emissions trading scheme directive (EU ETS). There is a strong series of arguments in support of the view that the free allocation of allowances under the various national allocation plans (NAPs) involves an element of State aid, which has neither been formally notified to, nor cleared by, the Commission under the EC Treaty. Even if it is found properly to have been notified, there are serious doubts as to whether the extent of aid granted satisfies the proportionality principle. As a result, the operation of the EU ETS may be subject to some legal uncertainty with regard to possible legal challenges to the current allocation of allowances. Going forward, proposals to amend the operation of the EU ETS must take into account similar State aid considerations (particularly proportionality) and the experience gained from the working of the EU ETS in phase I. The structural outline of a possible legislative package has been suggested, which could achieve the safeguarding of commercial and legal certainty under the current allocation regime, while at the same time providing a basis for amendment of the allocation mechanism under the EU ETS for phase II and beyond.

Keywords: Emissions trading; European Union; Law; Competition; State aid; EC law

1. Introduction

The introduction of the EU's emissions trading scheme (EU ETS) was a highly significant development in EU and international environmental law. The Council and the European Parliament adopted the EU ETS Directive[1] on 13 October 2003 and Member States were required to implement its provisions by 31 December 2003 (although the implementation process has in fact proved a rather more sedate affair than this short time-frame might have suggested).

This article is concerned with one aspect of the operation of the EU ETS, which has emerged in the early practice under the scheme. This is the extent to which the free allocation of allowances to operators (for those installations covered by the Directive) amounts to the grant of State aid in

* Corresponding author. Tel.: +44-1223-332551; fax: +44-1223-332537
E-mail address: acj29@cam.ac.uk

contravention of the provisions of the EC Treaty. This has become a pressing issue due to recent analysis (see Sijm et al., 2005, 2006 and this issue) which suggests that the opportunity cost associated with holding such an allowance (prior to submitting it in fulfilment of the requirements of the Directive at the end of the relevant accounting period) has been passed through to consumers in the electricity sector, in the form of increases in power prices. Assuming that such a pass-through has occurred, this article considers whether or not the free allocation of allowances thus amounts to State aid, and then goes on to assess the consequences of such a conclusion for the operation of the current system and for proposals for possible reforms to the EU ETS in the future. It will be argued that some degree of State aid is indeed present in the current regime, that it would be difficult to justify certain elements of that aid on the basis of the current EC legal provisions, and that great care must be taken to ensure that any future amended EU ETS complies with the State aid rules while at the same time achieving the intended environmental benefits.

2. Free allocation and State aid

Does the free allocation of allowances under the EU ETS conflict with State aid considerations under EC law?

2.1. The basic prohibition on the grant of State aid in the EC Treaty

The scheme of the EC Treaty assumes that aid granted by a Member State is prohibited unless some exception or exemption is provided for in or under the Treaty.[2] The general prohibition against such aid is laid down in Article 87(1) EC:

> Save as otherwise provided in this Treaty, any aid granted by a member State or through State resources in any form whatsoever which distorts or threatens to distort competition by favouring certain undertakings or the production of certain goods shall, in so far as it affects trade between Member States, be incompatible with the common market.

From this provision, and from the case law and decisional practice of the Commission, certain criteria must be met to show that something amounts to 'State aid' for these purposes. It must be established that:

- an 'advantage' has been conferred[3]
- which was granted by the State or through State resources[4]
- which distorts or threatens to distort competition[5]
- by favouring certain undertakings or the production of certain goods or services (i.e. a 'selectivity' criterion)[6]
- and which affects or may affect trade between EC Member States.[7]

In the EU ETS Directive, there are consistent references to the need for the national allocation plans (NAPs) (under which allowances are allocated to operators of relevant installations) to respect the EC State aid rules – see, in particular, Article 11(3).[8] This means that the Directive and its mechanisms do not operate, in and of themselves, as some kind of exception from the State aid rules. In turn, this means that the analysis of such NAPs in the light of the State aid rules is vital in coming to any conclusion about the compatibility of the allocation of allowances with EC law.

It is important to appreciate, however, that even if a particular action by a Member State does amount to aid under the EC Treaty, it may still be possible for that aid to be granted an exemption under specific Treaty provisions or under legislation adopted under the auspices of the Treaty. This point will be considered later (see Section 3), with particular concentration upon justifications relating to environmental matters and to 'the execution of an important project of common European interest'.

2.2. Applying the criteria to the free allocation of allowances under the EU ETS

In applying these criteria to our scenario, and to gain some sense of the Commission's previous general attitude towards this issue, we need to examine its earlier Decisions concerning the notification of national emissions trading schemes prior to the adoption of the EU ETS Directive. The closest analogue to the EU ETS is probably the UK's forerunner emissions trading scheme,[9] which was voluntary for participants, who were given an incentive to join the scheme by means of payments from the State. These payments clearly amounted to aid and were held to be such by the Commission. However, the Commission also went on to examine *per se* the free allocation of allowances to participants in the scheme:

> (b) The trading mechanism: The state allocates a limited number of transferable emission permits free of charge to the direct participants. The state thus provides these companies with an intangible asset for free, which can be sold on a market to be created. The fact that there will be a market is a sign of the value of the asset being allocated. This has to be considered to be an advantage to the recipient companies.
>
> The fact that companies will have to make expenses in order to realize the value of the allowances does not change the existence of an advantage, but can be considered a positive element in the assessment of the compatibility of the measure.
>
> This advantage distorts competition between companies. Companies able to make a profit from the allowances can use the profit for their business competing with other companies not having access to such a scheme. This can affect trade between Member States.
>
> The value of these permits is predicted to be considerable. By the envisaged arrangements, the State foregoes revenue, which could derive from auctioning the emission permits. One could argue that the voluntary nature of the scheme would hinder a different allocation of allowances than free allocation, as companies would not be likely to participate in such an auction. However, the State opted deliberately for a voluntary approach and by taking this option forewent [its] other option to gain revenue from an auction in the context of a mandatory scheme.
>
> The Commission therefore concludes that ... the trading mechanism [also] constitutes State aid under Article 87(1) EC.[10]

When searching for Commission State aid decisions when approving the national allocation plans (NAPs) submitted by the various Member States under the EU ETS, however, there is a significant dearth of material.

Examining the Commission's Decisions on the NAPs submitted for phase I, there are consistent references to the need to assess the allocation of allowances under the EC State aid rules (see, e.g., Recital 7 of the Commission's Decision on the UK's original NAP).[11] However, the 'assessment' is hardly extensive: 'On the basis of the information provided by the Member State, the Commission therefore considers that any potential aid is likely to be compatible with the common market should it be assessed in accordance with Article 88(3) of the Treaty'.[12] Further, in the Commission's earlier 'non-paper' of 1 April 2003,[13] the Commission indicated that:

> National allocation plans will constitute State aid under Article 87(1) EC and will therefore have to be notified to the Commission for assessment under State aid rules. Competition policy procedural rules will apply in this respect. The Commission intends to take at the same time the two decisions legally required on the Plan as regards the assessment as required in the common position and the State aid assessment.

However, the Commission does not seem to have adopted any separate State aid decisions dealing with the issues raised by the notification of the various NAPs for phase I. The most extensive comment to date on this issue is to be found in Recital 5 of the Commission's Decision on the French notification of its NAP:[14]

> Pursuant to criterion 5 [of Annex III], the Commission has also examined compliance of the French National Plan with the provisions of the [EC] Treaty, and in particular Articles 87 and 88 thereof [i.e. the provisions on State aid]. The Commission considers that the allocation of allowances free of charge to certain activities confers a selective economic advantage to undertakings which has the potential to distort competition and affect intra-Community trade. The allocation of allowances for free also appears to be imputable to the Member State and to entail the use of State resources to the extent that more than 95% of allowances are given for free and allows banking of allowances from the first to the second period. The Commission therefore at this stage cannot exclude that the plan implies State aid pursuant to Article 87(1) of the Treaty. The national allocation plan allocates excessive allowances to industrial activities. The Commission considers that this favourable treatment has not been duly justified by France and that the measure appears to grant an undue advantage to industrial activities, which would allow this activity to dispose of allowances without having to deliver a sufficient environmental counterpart. The Commission at this stage therefore cannot exclude that any aid involved would be found incompatible with the common market should it be assessed in accordance with Article 88(3) of the Treaty.

In spite of these criticisms, the Commission's final decision on the French NAP does not appear to have imposed any specific criteria or reached any formal decision relating to State aid, focusing instead upon other aspects in which the French NAP had been adjudged deficient according to the other (i.e. non-State aid) criteria laid down in the Annexes to the EU ETS Directive.[15]

Nevertheless, on the basis of the Commission's earlier Decision relating to the UK's national ETS and its tentative analysis in its Decision on the French NAP, it seems reasonably clear that the free allocation of allowances under the EU ETS does amount, *prima facie*, to State aid within Article 87(1) EC. Free allocation clearly involves the State foregoing revenue that might have been raised by the auctioning of such allowances and the grant of such allowances only to emitting installations may amount to a selective grant of an advantage (favouring them over other businesses) that may distort competition and affect trade between Member States where those in competition are established in different EU countries. Further, if it is established that opportunity costs are passed through (and the analysis in Sijm et al. (this issue) suggests that they most certainly are), then it seems clear not only that aid is granted by the free allocation of allowances, but also that it goes far beyond that expected simply from the free allocation of allowances in the first place. The extra element, beyond the value of the allowance itself, is the ability to use the fact of holding that allowance to pass through to customers the opportunity costs associated with holding that allowance. This last point (which relates to the question of proportionality) is highly significant for the assessment of the justifiability of such aid and will be considered in Section 3.2.5.

Earlier work on this topic (Merola and Crichlow, 2004) had suggested that an ETS at the *EU* level (rather than one adopted unilaterally at the *national* level) required a different assessment of the State aid criteria from that adopted by the Commission in the earlier Decisions relating to national systems. Specifically, it was argued, first, that the EU-wide grant of such allowances meant that no unilateral *advantage* was conferred upon undertakings under the EU ETS (Merola and Crichlow, 2004, pp. 34–36). Second, it was suggested that the selectivity criterion would also not be met under the allocation regime for the EU ETS, given that the Directive itself specifies the sectors covered by the scheme and does not allow sufficient room for Member States to derogate from this regime to amount to the *selective* grant of an advantage by the State to the undertakings involved.

On the first point, it is clear from the Commission's Decision on the French NAP notified under the EU ETS Directive (quoted above) that the Commission has taken the view that an advantage is conferred in such circumstances. This view is strongly bolstered by the discovery that opportunity cost pass-through is facilitated by free allocation (Sijm et al. this issue), as this involves a clear advantage received by those allocated allowances, and this is an advantage not intended to be related to the environmental goals of the scheme.

On the second point concerning selectivity, meanwhile, two comments may be made. First, insofar as different undertakings within each sector have different emission rates and caps assigned to them under each NAP, in accordance with their previous emissions record and their reduction targets, there is some degree of selectivity in the grant of the benefit within each sector. The response to this claim would no doubt be that this is, again, inherent in the EU-level adoption of the scheme and thus could not be described as 'selective' in the sense normally given to that term because it is not a selection made by the Member State, but at EU-level. The Member States remain ultimately responsible for adopting their respective NAPs, but their discretion in allocating allowances is severely curtailed by the terms of the EU ETS Directive. Merola and Crichlow (2004, p.36) did, however, accept that selectivity questions do remain with regard to that proportion of allowances not covered by the free allocation obligation. Without more, the point is clearly a finely balanced one, and one must accept the force of their argument overall.

However, the second point concerning selectivity is indeed something 'more': once again, the phenomenon of opportunity cost pass-through shows that the selectivity inherent in the EU delimitation of the sectors covered by the EU ETS actually is not merely limited to the advantage associated with holding the allowance itself, but extends to the further benefit received by virtue of holding the allowances – the ability to pass through the opportunity costs of holding such allowances (Sijm et al. this issue). This effectively exacerbates the extent of any selectivity inherent in the EU ETS to the extent that a clearly selective benefit is received by some within each sector (compare, for example, a coal-fired generator's receipt of allowances under the EU ETS with that of a wind-farm operator: the latter receives no allowances and thus no chance to pass through opportunity costs, while remaining in competition with the former in the sale of electricity generated). This also reinforces the conclusion that competition between those undertakings may be distorted and that trade between Member States may be affected.

Thus, it is suggested that the free allocation of allowances under the EU ETS does indeed amount, *prima facie*, to the grant of State aid under the rules of the EC Treaty.

2.3. Scenarios concerning free allocation and State aid law

In the light of this discussion, it is important here to distinguish two basic different relevant sets of circumstances for State aid purposes.

(i)   Would *continued* free allocation on the basis laid down in the current Directive conflict with EC State aid rules?
(ii) What State aid constraints are there in *amending* the allocation mechanism in the Directive (e.g. to allow free allocation to consumers in one form or another)?

These situations may require different treatment when examining the relevant procedures that must be followed to gain approval for any mechanism allocating allowances under an EU ETS in any form. The former situation, if it has not been notified properly to the Commission, may require action to regularize the position: otherwise, it is possible that any aid elements that have been granted without Commission authorization may have to be paid back. I return to this question in Section 4.3, where the possible shape of any legislative package in this area is considered briefly (e.g. securing both the amendment of the Directive and legal certainty for operators under the current regime). The latter situation, meanwhile, has consequences for the (re-)design of the EU ETS: as the current Directive makes clear,[16] the EU ETS does not itself operate as an exemption from the State aid rules in the Treaty and so Commission decisions concerning the application of any future EU ETS must also respect the procedural and substantive conditions of EC State aids law.

3. Justifying State aid granted by the free allocation of allowances

As mentioned in Section 2.1, the scheme of the EC Treaty provides that, assuming that there is aid involved, that aid must be *justified* on some accepted ground if the grant of such aid is to be compatible with the common market.

3.1. Background: the Commission's attitude towards State aid in this general area

In analysing the possible justification of State aid granted in the form of the free allocation of allowances under the EU ETS, it is important to have an appreciation of the Commission's general approach to the approval of the grant of aid for environmental purposes.[17] In its own words, this approach must 'satisfy a double imperative': it must ensure the competitive functioning of markets, while at the same time integrating environmental protection requirements into competition policy (in particular, focusing upon the internalization of the costs of environmental impacts). However, the Commission is prepared to allow aid:

(a)   in certain specific circumstances in which it is not yet possible for all costs to be internalized by firms and the aid can therefore represent a temporary second-best solution by encouraging firms to adapt to standards; and
(b)   where the aid may also act as an incentive to firms to improve on standards or to undertake further investment designed to reduce pollution from their plants.[18]

Nevertheless, it must be noted that the Commission's attitude has hardened in its 2001 Guidelines, even where environmental aid is concerned:

aid should no longer be used to make up for the absence of cost internalization. If environmental requirements are to be taken into account in the long term, prices must accurately reflect costs and environmental protection costs must be fully internalized. Consequently, the Commission takes the view that aid is not justified in the case of investments designed merely to bring companies into line with new or existing Community technical standards.

This is because the key factors – namely: the 'polluter pays' principle, the notion of internalizing such costs and the use of market instruments – have now long been promoted by EC environmental policy. The Commission's current view is clearly that companies have had long enough to adapt to such requirements and should no longer need aid to assist them in bearing such costs.[19] It is clearly arguable that the EU ETS falls squarely within this stricter analysis of the justification of environmental aid (which serves further to bolster the points made below (Section 3.2.5) concerning proportionality).

3.2. Evaluation of State aid: justifications for the grant of aid

3.2.1. Environmental grounds

Clearly, environmental justifications for the grant of State aid will be vital in this context.[20] Specifically, these justifications may fall under the headings of:

- 'projects of common European interest' (Article 87(3)(b) EC) ('the aid must be necessary for the project to proceed, and the project must be specific, well defined and qualitatively important and must make an exemplary and clearly identifiable contribution to the common European interest'),[21] or
- 'aid to facilitate the development of certain economic activities or of certain economic areas, where such aid does not adversely affect trading conditions to an extent contrary to the common interest' (Article 87(3)(c) EC).

It seems reasonably clear that, in our context, the EU ETS could be said to be a 'project of common European interest', since the Directive is a common action agreed by all the Member States to combat the common threat of global warming by endeavouring to incentivize the reduction of CO_2 emissions.[21]

Merola and Crichlow (2004) have argued that 'if the Commission applied Article 87(1) to the whole scheme, Article 87(3)(b) would authorize the entire allowance allocation scheme'. Under this approach, such an exemption would cover all emissions and make it unnecessary precisely to establish the proportionality of the aid to the environmental benefit to be secured under the EU ETS 'because the compensatory justification would be implicit in the fulfilment of the specific requirements of Article 87(3)(b), as indicated in paragraph 73 of the [Commission's] Guidelines'.[22] This claim illustrates the key importance of careful identification of the precise ground upon which any exemption is sought from the prohibition on the grant of State aid. This issue will be addressed in the discussion of the proportionality principle (Section 3.2.5), where it will be argued that proportionality must still be respected under the EU ETS.

3.2.2. Specific considerations concerning aid to facilitate 'investment in energy'

The Commission Guidelines also contain specific comments on aid to facilitate investment in energy.[23] While these provisions are not directly relevant to the exemption of any aid involved in the allocation of allowances granted under the EU ETS (unless Member States specifically attempt to argue that any such extra support amounts to the support of investment in renewable energy), they do, however, illustrate the Commission's amenability to environmental arguments concerning the promotion of energy produced from renewable sources. At the same time, it is clear from the Guidelines that the need for such support will require careful proof and justification in each individual case.

3.2.3. Specific guidelines concerning greenhouse gas reduction measures

Unfortunately, however, the specific provisions in the Guidelines concerning measures aimed at reducing greenhouse gases *pre-date* the EU ETS Directive:

> 70. In the absence of any Community provisions in this area and without prejudice to the Commission's right of initiative in proposing such provisions, it is for each Member State to formulate the policies, measures and instruments it wishes to adopt in order to comply with the targets set under the Kyoto Protocol.
>
> 71. The Commission takes the view that some of the means adopted by Member States to comply with the objectives of the [Kyoto] Protocol could constitute State aid [24] but it is still too early to lay down the conditions for authorizing any such aid.

Clearly, para. 70 is no longer fully applicable in this area, in the light of the EU ETS Directive. Nevertheless, given the Commission's attitude in its various Decisions on the NAPs submitted to it under the EU ETS Directive,[25] it seems clear that the Commission continued to consider (at least in principle and at the time that the NAPs were submitted to it for approval) that separate EC State aid control remained appropriate for such allocation of allowances, even after the advent of the EU ETS.

Further, and also unfortunately, the Commission's Decisions on the NAPs notified under the EU ETS Directive make no more than cursory and passing reference to the State aid question in relation to the allocation of emissions allowances under the Directive (see Section 2.2), so no detailed guidance is available from this source on the application of the environmental justification of such State aids either.

3.2.4. Do the environmental justifications apply here?

This question must be asked both in relation to the allowances allocated under the current EU ETS Directive and if some alternative form of free allocation were to be continued under a revised version of the Directive.

Concerning the continuing free allocation of allowances to 'operators of installations' only, as under the current Directive, does this raise State aid problems? Given the evidence discussed above concerning the pass-through of opportunity costs (Sijm et al. this issue), then the structure of analysis should be as follows:

(i)   Such allocation is acknowledged by the Commission to amount *prima facie* to State aid (as discussed in Section 2);

(ii)   Thus, the aid needs to be notified to the Commission, and found to be justifiable – here, one would rely upon environmental justification grounds;

(iii) It is clearly possible, in principle, to bring the current free allocation of allowances under the environmental grounds discussed above, *yet* it seems strongly arguable that the *extent* of the extra benefit received (due to the passing through of opportunity costs) would amount to a benefit that is disproportionate to any environmental gains made through the EU ETS.

The second of these points is significant, because failure to notify the aid renders its grant unlawful: this has consequences for possible court action to require the repayment of such aid (see Section 4.1.2). The last of these points raises the important question of the application of the EC law principle of proportionality in the State aids field: we must now consider the operation and significance of this element in the analysis.

3.2.5. The principle of proportionality
3.2.5.1. GENERAL CONSIDERATIONS
When the Commission takes a decision on the compatibility of any proposed grant of aid with the EC Treaty, it must respect the principle of proportionality. This is a general principle of EC law,[26] which is inherent in the EC Treaty and thus applies as a matter of law to the actions of the EC institutions (here, the Commission in approving State aid)[27] and to those of the Member States (when implementing or derogating from EC law: see, e.g., Tridimas, 1998, ch. 4).

Although the Commission has adopted its own Notice on *de minimis* aid and on thresholds of permissible aid (see Section 3.2.2), the EC courts are not bound by such Commission guidelines and may thus find that there is a breach of the principle of proportionality even in the face of the Commission's guidelines.[28]

Thus it is possible for proposed aid to be within the Commission's 'permissibility' thresholds and yet still contrary to the principle of proportionality.

3.2.5.2. THE APPLICATION OF THE PROPORTIONALITY PRINCIPLE
The basic structure of the approach required under the proportionality principle is as follows:

(i)   first, it must be established that there is a justifiable goal to be achieved [here, environmental protection by reducing CO_2 emissions];

(ii) second, we must ask: is the measure [here, the free allocation of allowances] suitable and *necessary* for achieving that goal; and

(iii) third, is the measure *proportionate* in achieving that goal? That is, even though the measures do achieve the justifiable goal, do they involve an excessive negative concomitant effect?

In practice, the key question will be the *standard* (i.e. the intensity) of review employed in asking what would amount to an 'excessive' negative effect: i.e. does it have to be the minimum negative effect possible, while still achieving the goal, or is a less strict standard appropriate?

3.2.5.3. IMPLICATIONS OF THE PROPORTIONALITY PRINCIPLE
In this scenario of allowances allocation, the argument is that the *policy choice* taken (i.e. free allocation) by the EC and/or the Member States is itself disproportionate. It is true that, in such cases, most courts (including the EC courts) tend not to review such choices too intensively (usually looking to see whether manifest error or manifest inappropriateness has been made out: see, e.g., Craig, 2003, pp. 625–628; Lenaerts and van Nuffel, 2005, paras 4-050–4-054).

However, note that in the State aids context we are also dealing with the *rights* of individuals to operate in a competitive market place without distortions due to aid granted by a Member State, which has not been approved by the EC. Where individual rights are concerned, courts are usually likelier to conduct a more intensive review of the measure in question, being satisfied only with measures that achieve the goal in view with a less distortive effect upon competitive conditions.

Here, the key point is that free allocation under the current regime effectively grants a windfall benefit to recipients of allowances, which is not related to the environmental gains that the EU ETS aims to secure: this is a good basis for an argument that such aid may be disproportionate.

So far as the argument (relating to justifying aid under Article 87(3)(b) EC) raised by Merola and Crichlow (2004) (noted in Section 3.2.1) is concerned, their point has some force in restricting the scope of the proportionality principle and its impact upon exemptions from the State aid rules. Clearly, while Article 87(3)(c) makes specific reference to the need to balance any scheme with the effect upon 'trading conditions' (a clear matter for proportionality), Article 87(3)(b) is not explicitly so constrained. The Commission's Guidelines refer to showing that the aid must be 'necessary' for the project of common European interest to proceed (Commission, 2001, para. 73), but do not expressly consider proportionality criteria. However, the force of this argument is significantly weakened by the phenomenon of the passing-through of opportunity costs (Sijm et al. this issue) associated with the holding of allowances under the EU ETS. This element could plausibly be said not to be 'necessary' for the implementation of the project in question. Even if it were to some degree necessary, the Commission's Guidelines cannot evade the application of the general legal principle of proportionality, particularly in circumstances where the windfall enjoyed via this pass-through of opportunity costs is so clearly unrelated to the environmental goals of the EU ETS. By contrast, the aid embodied in the free allocation method could certainly be found to be justified under Article 87(3)(b) or, indeed, under Article 87(3)(c), given its clear and close connection (indeed, 90% of allowances were *required* to be allocated freely) with the environmental goals of the current EU ETS. It is the extra benefit that the allowance confers which creates the difficulty and renders the proportionality principle of continuing relevance in the current situation. It is not sufficient in this context to suggest that the Directive's chosen method of free allocation inevitably creates the possibility of passing through the opportunity costs involved: as the Directive itself states (see in particular its Article 11(3), but also Recital 23 and Para. 5 of Annex III), its provisions must be applied by the Commission *subject to* the requirements of the EC State aid rules.

To ensure that such problems are not raised as against any successor scheme, care should be taken to avoid such extra benefits and accurately to link the allocation of allowances (and the benefits from receiving such allowances) with the environmental gains to be made from the EU ETS. Indeed, this approach fits best with the general approach taken by the Commission in its Guidelines on State aid for environmental purposes (as discussed in Section 3.1) and should thus, it is submitted, also commend itself to the Commission in the case of emissions allowances.

3.3. Allocation to consumers and other non-'installations'

3.3.1. General considerations

In summary, the general points concerning possible allocation of allowances to consumers are:

- The EU ETS Directive currently *requires* the free allocation of at least 90% of allowances;
- Only Article 3 and Annex I of the Directive specify allocation to installations;
- If amendment of the Directive were successful, this could allow (partial) allocation to consumers: e.g. a system could be set up that required residents to register with a trust fund for such

allowances. That trust fund would then receive the free allowances, sell them and then pay residents their share of the proceeds.

- Certain benefits would flow from the allocation of allowances to domestic consumers:
  - Allocation to the power sector only could be tailored to compensate losses
  - This would avoid the risk of regulatory intervention (e.g. in the form of some kind of windfall profit tax)
  - It would also avoid State aid problems
  - It could well increase support of consumers for the EU ETS
  - It would also ensure compatibility with Border Tax Adjustment.[29]
- Similarly, benefits could also be seen in the allocation of allowances to industrial consumers:
  - This would operate to compensate for the detrimental effects upon competition
  - Harmonization of the allocation criteria would be required, to ensure that distortions of competition (both within and between Member States) are minimized.

Meanwhile, proposals to introduce uniform allocation to all new entrants in the electricity sector (on a per kW or per kWh basis), without reference to whether or not they qualify as 'installations' under the current EU ETS Directive, would seem to be inconsistent with the Directive in its present form. The combination of Article 3(e) and Annex I of the Directive require installations to perform certain activities if they are to be covered by the Directive, and in the energy sector this only relates to 'combustion installations with a rated thermal output exceeding 20 MW'. Amendment of these provisions would require legislation (see Section 4.2.3). Such uniform allocation to new entrants could alleviate some of the difficulties of selectivity created by free allocation under the present regime, as it would not reserve the pass-through of opportunity costs to installations covered by the EU ETS. However, careful attention would need to be paid to the proportionality of such allocation in order to satisfy State aid rules (see Section 3.3.2.1).

3.3.2. Allocation to consumers or non-'installations': State aid considerations

If an amendment could be made to the Directive to allow allocation of allowances to consumers, would there also be State aid constraints on how to design those amendments?

If the problems raised by the pass-through of opportunity costs can be clearly established (Sijm et al. this issue), and if allocation to consumers can be shown to combat its problems, then there seems no reason why the same environmental justification grounds would not be applicable to the allocation of allowances to consumers: the environmental goals to be achieved would still clearly be justifiable, and the prevention of the 'pass-through problem' should mean that the benefit conferred is not disproportionate to the environmental gains made (subject, of course, to detailed working out of the system for allocation to consumers).

3.3.2.1. COULD WE ALLOCATE FREE ALLOWANCES TO INDUSTRIAL CONSUMERS IN SECTORS WITH LARGE ELECTRICITY CONSUMPTION OR TO OTHER NON-'INSTALLATIONS' (SUCH AS RENEWABLE ELECTRICITY GENERATORS)?

In principle, this should be possible (subject, naturally, to legislative amendment of the Directive to permit this approach). Care must be taken to ensure that, if allocation in this way were thought to face similar problems to the doubts expressed by the Commission re France's first NAP,[30] then the arguments for justifying that aid on environmental grounds (probably as promoting an important project of common European interest – Article 87(3)(b) EC (see Section 3.2.1)) are clearly explained. Questions of the proportionality of this response to the 'pass-through problem' would also need to be addressed, to ensure that the cure is not more painful than the ailment. For example, uniform allocation to all new entrant electricity generators on a kW (or kWh) basis would need careful calculation against the number of allowances already allocated, to prevent the system imposing yet further costs upon final consumers, simply in order to equalize conditions of competition between generators, while adding little or nothing to the achievement of the environmental goals of the EU ETS.

3.3.2.2 COULD WE ALLOCATE FREE ALLOWANCES TO TRUST FUNDS?

> For example, every resident of a country would register with a fund, thus determining the allocation of allowances to these funds. Then the allowances would be allocated to the funds in proportion to the number of members of the fund(s). The fund would then sell the allowances in the market and distribute the money to the members of the fund, either in one or two installations to be determined dependent upon the value of the allowances. Would we have a preference for deciding to allocate to citizens or to residents, given that different countries are involved: i.e. how could we comply with requirements to treat all EU citizens equally?

The basic issue here is the same as under Section 3.3.2.1 and concerns the environmental basis for justifying such aid.

So far as the point about equality of treatment of EU citizens is concerned, this can be accommodated within the framework for the application of a Directive in the various national legal systems. So far as the Directive (as amended) would allow NAPs to be drafted according to a set of common criteria but at the same time allowing for a degree of diversity between EC Member States concerning the *exact* characteristics and shape of their individual NAPs, different choices relating to the implementation of this new idea of allocation (to persons not designated as 'installations' under the existing Directive) would be an acceptable expression of subsidiarity (as per Article 5 EC). That is to say, there is a common goal to be achieved, the result of which is binding upon Member States (by virtue of Article 249 EC and the adoption of the EU ETS Directive, which specifies that common goal – establishing an EU ETS, etc), but leaving the choice of 'form and methods' of implementation to the Member States. So long as the Directive is not so prescriptive of the form and methods to be used,[31] then Member States remain free to choose methodologies (etc) that do not contradict the framework laid down in the relevant provisions (and Annexes) of the Directive.

At the same time, one of the points that has emerged during the assessment of NAPs (and the implementation choices made by the Member States under the EU ETS) has been the relative diversity of approaches involved and their possible distortive effect upon competition between undertakings in different Member States (both concerning the trading of allowances and in the undertakings' core businesses). If this came to be regarded as an unacceptable level of differentiation, then it would also be possible to adopt a Directive that gave Member States much less scope for creating diverging terms and conditions for allocation under the EU ETS. This is a matter to be decided upon during the negotiation process leading up to the adoption of any new EU ETS Directive.

4. Various procedural questions

It is important to make clear that the argument that free allocation of allowances under the EU ETS may constitute State aid under EC law may have important procedural consequences for the operation of the current system and for any moves to reform that system. This section discusses, first, the prospects for legal action in the courts to secure compliance with EC State aid law: this could be pursued before the EC courts, seeking to overturn the Directive itself or the Commission Decisions on the NAPs adopted under the Directive. Alternatively, if the allocation amounted to State aid but had not been properly notified under the relevant EC State aid procedures, then it becomes unlawful aid and potentially subject to actions in the national courts to seek or require recovery of that aid by the relevant Member State. The second and third sections address the possible amendment of the EU ETS, either via a 'regulatory committee' route or using a full EC legislative procedure. These routes to change the Directive and its application present both certain constraints and opportunities.

4.1. Possible judicial review? Action before the courts

4.1.1. Before the EC courts
So far as judicial review at the EC level is concerned, this may ultimately be an unfruitful avenue of attack. This is because it is entirely possible that, *even if* the ECJ were willing to hold invalid such Commission decisions approving NAPs (or even the EU ETS Directive itself), the consequence would be that the ECJ would maintain the decisions (and Directive) in force, pending their replacement. This would be because the ECJ would take the view that the goal to be achieved (establishing the ETS to meet environmental objectives) would better be achieved by maintaining the system in place pending the adoption of a new EU ETS, rather than by knocking the whole thing down and living without it in the interim.

A successful action for annulment leads the Court to rule that the act concerned is void (Article 231 EC) with general (*erga omnes*) and retroactive (*ex tunc*) effect, but there are qualifications to this basic principle:

- For example, if the aim of the action is to secure an act that imposes stricter limits: the Court will leave the act in place as imposing *some* limits, while ordering that a new act be adopted in accordance with the ruling;[32]
- Also, there is the possibility of avoiding the harsh effects of such retroactive voidness by qualifying the extent of the nullity: Article 231(2) EC. See, for example, the case concerning the Directive on students' rights of residence,[33] where the Directive continued in force until it was replaced by subsequent legislation. Equally, certain elements of the measure can be left in place – i.e. it is possible to impose temporal and scope restrictions upon the invalidity of the measure in question.

4.1.2. Before the national courts
Meanwhile, another avenue of challenge is the possibility of judicial review (or other court action) in any given Member State before their *national courts*. Such national courts may enforce the requirement that Member States must *notify* such aid (under Article 88(3) EC) and may not implement aid in the absence of having made such notification, so that they may 'find acts implementing aid measures to be invalid, suspend the implementation of unnotified aid [or] order its repayment …'.[34]

This raises the question of whether or not the Commission's tentative expressions of opinion in its Decisions on the NAPs for emissions allowances do indeed amount to Decisions sufficient to deal with the requirement that such State aid be notified to the Commission prior to its implementation by Member States. If the Commission does not act within two months of notification, the Member State may implement the aid. The aid then becomes an existing aid for the purposes of Art. 88(1) EC,[35] meaning that the Member State may implement it. However, note that the Commission still has a duty with regard to all existing aids to keep them under constant review: here, again, the question of the compatibility of such aids with the State aid rules may be raised by the Commission and may be the subject of a complaint by private parties to the Commission, requesting that it take action.

If it is held that no State aid notification was made at all, then a third party complainant may bring an action in a national court claiming that the grant of such allowances under any given NAP amounts to the implementation of a non-notified and non-approved aid scheme. Thus, all will turn upon whether or not the notification of the NAP and the Commission's Decisions are sufficient for State aid purposes to prevent national courts from treating the grant of allowances as unlawfully implemented State aid. In such a case, the general principle is that unlawfully granted aid must be recovered by the Member State:[36] such recovery procedures are based upon national law.[37] Insofar as the current NAPs notified to the Commission are available, a brief search through the NAPs produced no reference to the NAP involving the grant of State aid that would need specific exemption by the Commission. Furthermore, the relevant procedural Regulation (Regulation 794/2004/EC, [2004] OJ L140/1), which lays down the conditions for the notification of State aid, provides in its Article 2 that 'notifications of new aid pursuant ... shall be made on the notification form set out in Part I of Annex I to this Regulation'. It is clear that the NAPs were not notified to the Commission on this basis, suggesting that the (admittedly formal) argument that no proper State aid notification was made by the Member States of their respective NAPs is a very strong one indeed.

If a national court is not confident of making this assessment, however, there exists the possibility of making a reference to the ECJ under Article 234 EC for the interpretation of the relevant EC law principles (see, generally, Craig and de Búrca, 2003, ch. 11 and references cited therein). While it often takes some time to receive an answer to such questions, this would provide an authoritative interpretation of the position concerning the notified NAPs and their status under the procedural aspects of EC State aids law. Equally, it is possible that a national court will feel able to take its own decision on the question, which could lead to an order that unlawfully granted aid must be repaid by the recipient to the Member State. Given that EC State aid law applies in this fashion in all EC Member States, such a scenario could occur in any Member State where the EU ETS is properly implemented, with allowances allocated and the system up and running. Such challenges could be made to allowances already allocated under phase I, but the same reasoning would apply to any allowances granted under phase II if those grants were made without proper notification and clearance under the EC rules on State aid.

4.2. The possible 'regulatory' amendment of Annex III of the EU ETS Directive for phase II

4.2.1. Basis
This is possible by virtue of Article 22 of the EU ETS Directive (Directive 2003/87/EC [2003] O.J. L275/32):

Article 22 – Amendments to Annex III

The Commission may amend Annex III, with the exception of criteria (1), (5) and (7), for the period from 2008 to 2012 in the light of the reports provided for in Article 21 and of the experience of the application of this Directive, in accordance with the procedure referred to in Article 23(2).

Such changes could only take place for the next reference period, starting in 2008, following the procedure laid down in the Directive.

4.2.2. Procedure for such amendments

4.2.2.1. ARTICLE 21 OF THE DIRECTIVE

Any amendments must be made in the light of the reports by the Member States, which under Article 21 of the Directive they are required to submit to the Commission.

The Commission's December 2005 Report (Commission, 2005) in this area, adopted under Article 21(2) of the EU ETS Directive, remains largely silent on the question of allocation, apart from showing an inclination to encourage Member States to use the *auctioning* of allowances more widely and extensively in future (i.e. the 10% of allowances that are not mandatorily subject to free allocation in the next allocation round). If auctions were more widely used under phase II (post-2008), this would, to a limited extent, reduce the significance and extent of free allocation, with a concomitant effect upon the ability to pass through the opportunity costs involved. Nevertheless, since free allocation would still apply to at least 90% of all allowances, it is submitted that the proportionality of such pass-through effects would remain questionable at best.

4.2.2.2. THE 'COMITOLOGY' PROCEDURE

To make such amendments to Annex III, the procedure in Article 23(2) of the EU ETS Directive must be followed – this is a form of 'comitology' procedure.

'Comitology' is an EC decision-making process involving the delegation of power (to adopt decisions and standards, and sometimes to amend legislation) by the Council to the Commission, subject to the approval of a committee composed of Member State representatives.

There are three main forms of Committee procedure: the Advisory, Management, and Regulatory Committee Procedures. The current Comitology Decision is Decision 1999/468/EC.[38] Article 23(2) of the EU ETS Directive refers to the use of the 'Regulatory Committee Procedure' (under Article 5 of the Comitology Decision), under which the Commission submits a draft to the Committee, which adopts an opinion by qualified majority vote (QMV) (a form of vote weighting, under which a certain threshold of votes (representing a particular proportion of the Member States and their populations) must be met).[39] The measure cannot be adopted unless the Committee gives a positive opinion. If this does not happen, the Council can act by QMV to adopt, or, under one variant, by simple majority to block.

The Regulatory Committee Procedure is the one that grants the strongest role to the Committee. Thus, if amendments are to be proposed, it will be important to provide detailed reasons for both the Commission and the individual Member States for the necessity for such amendments, to ensure that:

- the Commission makes the appropriate proposals in its draft;
- the Regulatory Committee approves it by a sufficient majority to satisfy QMV; and
- even if the Committee does not approve the proposals, the Council does do so.

4.2.2.3. RESTRICTIONS UPON SUCH AMENDMENTS VIA THE REGULATORY COMMITTEE PROCEDURE

By the terms of Article 22 of the Directive, no amendments may be made to criteria (1), (5) and (7) as laid down in Annex III, *viz*:

(1) The total quantity of allowances to be allocated for the relevant period shall be consistent with the Member State's obligation to limit its emissions pursuant to Decision 2002/358/EC and the Kyoto Protocol, taking into account, on the one hand, the proportion of overall emissions that these allowances represent in comparison with emissions from sources not covered by this Directive and, on the other hand, national energy policies, and should be consistent with the national climate change programme. The total quantity of allowances to be allocated shall not be more than is likely to be needed for the strict application of the criteria of this Annex. Prior to 2008, the quantity shall be consistent with a path towards achieving or over-achieving each Member State's target under Decision 2002/358/EC and the Kyoto Protocol.

(5) The plan shall not discriminate between companies or sectors in such a way as to unduly favour certain undertakings or activities in accordance with the requirements of the Treaty, in particular Articles 87 and 88 thereof.

(7) The plan may accommodate early action and shall contain information on the manner in which early action is taken into account. Benchmarks derived from reference documents concerning the best available technologies may be employed by Member States in developing their National Allocation Plans, and these benchmarks can incorporate an element of accommodating early action.

It seems that the only potentially problematic element here may be criterion (5): thus, a clear explanation would be needed as to why the proposed amendments do not amount to undue favour for certain undertakings/activities, leading to concerns under the EC Treaty's rules on State aid. If the point were to redress such differentiation at present, then this would seem possibly to fit within criterion (5).

4.2.3. Inconsistency of Annex III, if amended as proposed, with the main body of the Directive?

This issue might be more problematic, were the Commission, the Regulatory Committee and/or the Council to take the view that it would not be possible to make the appropriate amendments to Annex III without this undermining the system and provisions of the main text of the Directive – and the main text could only be amended by legislation, adopted jointly by the European Parliament and the Council, after a process that could well be too lengthy to effect the required changes before the commencement of the next reference period.

It is certainly the case that the scheme of the EU ETS Directive very much assumes that 'operators of installations' are to be the recipients of allowances: see, e.g., the Commission's 'non-paper' of 1 April 2003 (Commission, 2003), which emphasized that:

It is important to note that, in accordance with Article 11, initial allocation of allowances can only be made to operators of installations covered by the scheme. Hence installations not covered by the scheme cannot be allocated any allowances, although they may purchase and hold allowances as any other person.

It is true that Article 11 of the EU ETS Directive refers only to 'the allocation of those allowances to the operator of each installation' (see Article 11(1) and (2)). The definition of 'installation' for the purposes of the Directive is contained in Article 3(e):

'installation' means a stationary technical unit where one or more activities listed in Annex I are carried out and any other directly associated activities which have a technical connection with the activities carried out on that site and which could have an effect on emissions and pollution.

The activities listed in Annex I are *not* open to change by use of a comitology procedure, as this is only specifically provided for where Annex III is concerned. This would seem to be a fairly conclusive argument against the possibility of amending Annex III to achieve allocation of allowances to parties that would not qualify as 'installations' under the Directive as currently worded. However, it should be noted that there is no specific statement anywhere in the Directive that *only* 'operators of installations', and no other entities, can be allocated allowances. If this could be argued, then perhaps an amendment of Article III could be effective. Alternatively, another argument might be that consumers are involved in 'directly associated activities which have a technical connection with the activities carried out' by the installation, although this clearly was not what was intended by the wording of Article 3(3) when the Directive was drafted[40] and may thus be unlikely to succeed.

On balance, and after careful consideration, it seems that the 'Annex III amendment proposal' may fall foul of the argument that it would lead to irreconcilable inconsistencies with the remainder of the EU ETS Directive as currently structured and worded. This suggests that, as a matter of the allocation process, it may require a change to the primary legislative text (by means of the full co-decision legislative process under Article 251 EC, involving the agreement of both the European Parliament and the Council) to secure the option of allocating allowances to those who currently are not 'operators of installations' under the EU ETS Directive.

4.2.4. Dealing with this inconsistency problem: alternative strategies

However, in phase II there may yet be a regulatory solution to this problem created by the rigidity of the primary legislative instrument (the Directive). This could be reached by a number of possible routes, perhaps the most promising of which would seem to be the application of EC State aid law as a basis for challenging any NAP that continued to grant free allowances to 'installations'. First, Member States would be well advised to notify future NAPs under both the EU ETS Directive *and* the specific EC State aids procedures. Then, any challenge could be brought by any Member State against a Commission Decision approving such an NAP, or the Commission itself could refuse to approve such a proposed NAP on the ground that any aid granted as a result of such free allocation of allowances was disproportionate in quantity to the environmental objectives to be achieved thereby. A Commission approval decision for a Member State's NAP could be made conditional upon some kind of claw-back by the Member State of the disproportionate aid elements associated with the ability to pass through opportunity costs to consumers. Naturally, if the undertaking receiving the allowances for each installation can show that such costs have not been passed through, then no claw-back would apply. It remains important to consider the State aid question here, because the Directive is, as highlighted throughout this article, specifically subject to the application of the EC Treaty's State aid rules.

4.3. Legislative action: amending the EU ETS Directive

Finally, a legislative strategy could be devised to deal with the issues raised by State aid law in this field. As with the current EU ETS Directive, the relevant legal basis under the EC Treaty for such legislation would be Article 175(1) EC, which would require a proposal from the Commission and the involvement and ultimate joint agreement of the Council and the European Parliament under the so-called 'co-decision' procedure of Article 251 EC. If this is the only way in which to achieve the desired changes, it is vital that moves begin as soon as possible: this process can be complex, hotly contested and lengthy before a workable legal instrument can be adopted. On the other hand, the process allows great scope for consultation, lobbying and the submission of observations by interested parties, which should make it possible for the key issues and consequences to be aired on a European level. Within the EU institutions, the Commission and the European Parliament will be key foci for any lobbying efforts, while the important role of the Council in the co-decision procedure means that lobbying at the national level to persuade national governments (who then sit in the Council) of the argument will also be vital.

Such a new Directive could conceivably be introduced to replace the current EU ETS Directive prior to the entry into its phase II in 2008; however, it seems that time constraints may prevent the formulation of an appropriate proposal by the Commission and its passage through the EC legislative process in time for adoption at EC level, let alone its implementation by the Member States.[41] Thus, any wide-ranging legislative solution may well have to wait until consideration is given to the continuation of the EU ETS beyond the end of phase II: these are matters of timing and the practical politics of the policy and legislative process.

So far as the specifics of any legislative 'package deal' are concerned, one model might be suggested that would tie up the loose ends, provide legal certainty under the current regime and allow amendments in allocation to be made going forward (whether for phase II (if adopted in time) or beyond phase II). This approach would involve the adoption of two legal instruments:

- first, a Regulation, which would immunize NAPs and the free allocation of allowances from possible challenges under EC State aid law, acting as a kind of block exemption from the prohibition on granting such aid and dating from the original grant of such allowances (whether for those already allocated under phase I or, going forward, if a similar situation arises under phase II allocation). This would avoid the uncertainty associated with possible challenges to NAPs in national courts (as discussed in Section 4.1.2);
- second, a new Directive or Regulation, amending the EU ETS to introduce different allocation mechanisms designed to avoid the pass-through problem (such as some use of auctioning or instead providing for free allocation to consumers).

The merit of this package deal would be to provide reassurance to operators under the current regime, while permitting the design of a transition from the old allocation arrangements to the new system as introduced under the new Directive.

5. Conclusions

This article has sought to assess the extent to which the EC legal rules on State aid affect the operation of the EU ETS and the actions of Member States under that regime. It has been shown that there is a strong series of arguments in support of the view that the free allocation of allowances under the various NAPs involves an element of State aid, which has neither been formally notified to, nor cleared by, the Commission under the EC Treaty. Even if it is found properly to have been notified, there are serious doubts as to whether the extent of aid granted satisfies the proportionality principle. As a result, the operation of the EU ETS may be subject to some legal uncertainty with regard to possible legal challenges to the current allocation of allowances. Going forward, any proposals to amend the operation of the EU ETS must take into account similar State aid considerations (particularly proportionality) and the experience gained from the working of the

EU ETS in the first phase up to 2008. The structural outline of a possible legislative package has been suggested, which could achieve the safeguarding of commercial and legal certainty under the current allocation regime, while at the same time providing a basis for amendment of the allocation mechanism under the EU ETS for phase II or beyond. The EC State aid law issue is a serious one and it needs to be taken into account by the Commission, the Member States and private parties in their future actions in this area.

Acknowledgements

The author would like to express his thanks to many colleagues for discussions relating to this subject, in particular to Dr Albertina Albors-Llorens, Prof. Alan Dashwood, Dr Karsten Neuhoff, Prof. Piet Jan Slot and Dr Rebecca Williams. As ever, however, responsibility for the final version and any errors therein remains with the author. All webpage references last visited 23 March 2006.

Notes

1 Directive 2003/87/EC (establishing a scheme for greenhouse gas emission allowance trading within the Community and amending Council Directive 96/61/EC) [2003] OJ L275/32.
2 In the EC Treaty itself, there are both automatic and discretionary exceptions from the prohibition, although both require Commission approval after notification of the aid by the Member State. Under the Treaty, legislation has been adopted to exempt various aids from the prohibition, in the style of the Block Exemptions used to give effect to the exemption in Article 81(3) EC. (See Joined Cases T-447/93 and T-448/93 AITEC v. Commission [1995] ECR II-1971.)
3 Case C-256/97 Déménagements-Manutention Transport SA (DMT) [1999] ECR I-3913: has 'the recipient undertaking receive[d] an economic advantage which would not have obtained under normal market conditions'?
4 See, e.g., Joined Cases 67, 69 and 70/85 Kwekerij Gebroeders Van der Kooy v. Commission [1988] ECR 219.
5 See, e.g., Case 730/79 Philip Morris Holland B.V. v. Commission [1980] ECR 2671 and Cases 296 and 381/82 Netherlands and Leeuwarder Papierwarenfabriek v. Commission [1980] ECR 809.
6 Favourable treatment granted to a given sector within the scope of general taxation will normally be regarded as an aid (Case 70/72 Commission v. Germany [1973] ECR 813) but may also be sometimes objectively justified as a response to market forces (Case 67/85 Van der Kooy [1988] ECR 219, although that justification was not established in the case itself).
7 See, e.g., Case 102/87 France v. Commission (Brewery loan) [1988] ECR 4067. This criterion is generally very easily found to be satisfied – indeed, such an effect is often assumed if the other criteria are met.
8 See also the EU ETS Directive, Recital 23 ('without prejudice to Articles 87 and 88' EC) and Para. 5 of its Annex III.
9 See also the Commission's Decision of 29 March 2000 (N653/1999) on Danish CO_2 quotas in the electricity sector (summarized in the Commission's Press Release IP/00/304, which is available at http://europa.eu.int/rapid/pressReleasesAction.do?reference=IP/00/304&format=HTML&aged=0&language=EN&guiLanguage=en and briefly discussed in (2000) EC Competition Policy Newsletter, No. 2, pp. 63–64). For discussion of the UK scheme see, e.g., Park (2002). Although compare the Commission's Decision of 25 July 2001, Belgian Green Electricity Certificates (Case N550/2000) [2001] OJ C330/3, in which the grant of 'green certificates' was held not to involve the transfer of State resources, since it amounted merely to an official proof of the fact that the relevant electricity had been produced from renewable energy sources. Similarly, the obligation to purchase a specified quantity of such certificates was held to be analogous to the purchasing. (Available (in French) at http://www.europa.eu.int/comm/secretariat_general/sgb/state_aids/comp-2000/n550-00_fr.pdf.) See, further, Merola and Crichlow (2004, pp. 33–34).
10 Commission Decision of 28 November 2001 (COM(2001) 3739 final), 'State aid No. N416/2001 – United Kingdom Emission Trading Scheme' (available at http://www.europa.eu.int/comm/secretariat_general/sgb/state_aids/comp-2001/n416-01.pdf), p. 9, para. V1(b).
11 Decision of 7 July 2004 (COM(2004) 2515/4 final), available http://europa.eu.int/comm/environment/climat/pdf/uk_final_en.pdf.

12 *Ibid*. This formulation is common to the majority of the Commission's Decisions on the various NAPs submitted to it for approval under the EU ETS Directive.

13 Available at http://europa.eu.int/comm/environment/climat/pdf/030401nonpaper.pdf.

14 Decision of 20 October 2004 (COM(2004) 3982/7 final), available at http://europa.eu.int/comm/environment/climat/pdf/france_final_en.pdf.

15 *Ibid*. Articles 2 and 3 of the Commission's formal Decision.

16 See the EU ETS Directive, Recital 23 ('without prejudice to Articles 87 and 88' EC), Article 11(3) and Para. 5 of its Annex III. Indeed, it seems unlikely that the relevant provision in the EC Treaty (Article 175(1) EC, which conferred power upon the EC to adopt environmental legislation such as the EU ETS Directive) would allow the adoption of any wholesale exemption that would not be compatible with the provisions on State aid.

17 See the Commission Guidelines [2001] OJ C37/3, esp. para. 14ff.

18 *Ibid*., para. 18.

19 *Ibid*., para. 19.

20 *Ibid*., paras 72–73.

21 Note that there will not be a common European interest in a scheme, 'unless it forms part of a transnational European programme supported jointly by a number of Governments of the Member States, or arises from concerted action by a number of Member States to combat a common threat such as environmental pollution' (Joined Cases 62 and 72/87 Executif Regional Wallon and S.A. Glaverbel v. Commission [1988] ECR 1573).

22 Merola and Crichlow (2004, p. 47).

23 Commission Guidelines [2001] OJ C37/3, para. 32.

24 See, e.g., the Commission's subsequent Decision on the UK's own national ETS, prior to the EC Directive, discussed above (see Note 9 and the accompanying text).

25 Discussed in Section 2.2.

26 See, e.g., Case C-331/88 R. v. Minister of Agriculture, Fisheries and Food and Secretary of State for Health ex p. Fedesa [1990] ECR 4023, Tridimas, 1998, chs. 3 and 4 and (generally) Ellis (1999).

27 See Case 730/79 Philip Morris Holland B.V. v. Commission [1980] ECR 2671, para. 17, where the ECJ made clear that the aid must be necessary for the achievement of the relevant objectives. As others (Merola and Crichlow, 2004) have noted, '[t]his criterion also means that all the aspects of the aid, and in particular the amount of the aid, must be reduced to a minimum. In addition, the duration, intensity and scope of the aid must be proportiona[te] to the intended objective'. See, also, the Commission's Decision in the matter that led to the Van der Kooy case (Decision 85/215/EEC on the preferential tariff charged to glasshouse growers for natural gas in the Netherlands, [1985] OJ L97/49 (for the ECJ's judgment on the appeal, see Note 4, above)), in which it was considered whether or not the aid was objectively justified in providing support to the horticultural purchasers to prevent them from switching to use coal as their energy source instead of natural gas. See also the Chronopost judgment (Cases C-83, 93 and 94/01 P Chronopost S.A. v. Commission [2003] ECR I-6993), where the 'market economy investor principle' usually applied in determining the notion of an 'advantage' was (in context) changed from the question of an investment in normal market conditions to the costs borne by another *public* company (paras 33–41) – this, too, could be argued to approximate to something of a proportionality criterion in that it allows a margin to the Member State in assessing what amounts to granting an 'advantage' to the recipient undertaking, dictated by the specific context in which the alleged aid was granted. See also Van Calster (Van Calster, 2000, p. 299), who asserts that '[t]he principle of proportionality plays an important role throughout the [Commission's] guidelines [on State aid for environmental purposes]' (although he was here referring to the previous 1994 incarnation of the guidelines on State aid for environmental protection there is nothing in the subsequent 2001 guidelines to suggest any change in his assessment of the significance of proportionality throughout the guidelines).

28 For an analogous point in EC antitrust law relating to anti-competitive agreements, see Case T-374/94 European Night Services Ltd. v. Commission [1998] ECR II-3141, para. 102: just as the fact that the parties' market share may exceed the Commission's *de minimis* threshold does not necessarily make any restriction of competition an 'appreciable' one under Article 81(1) EC, it is also possible that an agreement might fall below that threshold and yet still have an appreciable effect upon competition.

29 Ismer and Neuhoff (2004) and Hepburn et al. (this issue).

30 See Note 14, and the accompanying text: the point is the fear that excessive allocation to the industrial sector might be thought to favour that sector selectively, without the need for them to bear a concomitant environmental burden.

31 As one could argue that it currently is, given its specification of 'installations' as the only possible recipients of allowances, plus the detailed provisions in Annexes I and III of the EU ETS Directive. On the issue of harmonization, see generally Slot (1996) and Dougan (2000).

32 E.g., in Case 264/82 Timex Corp. v. Council and Commission [1985] ECR 849, the applicant sought the imposition of a higher level of anti-dumping duty imposed against the imports – pending a fresh decision, the old duty remained in force.

33 Case C-295/90 European Parliament v. Council ('Student rights of residence') [1992] ECR I-4193.

34 Evans (1997, p. 458, and the cases cited therein). See also, generally, Struys and Abbott (2003).

35 See Case C-44/93 Namur-Les Assurances de Crédit v. OND [1994] ECR I-3829 and Case C-99/98 Austria v. Commission [2001] ECR I-1101.

36 See Case 52/84 Commission v. Belgium [1986] ECR 89.

37 See Joined Cases 205-215/82 Deutsche Milchkontor GmbH v. Germany [1983] ECR 2633.

38 On QMV, see (e.g.) Dashwood and Johnston (2004, esp. pp. 1493–1500 and 1513–1516).

39 [1999] OJ 184/23.

40 As evinced by the Commission's document providing 'Replies to some frequently asked questions on the EC emissions trading proposal' (23 April 2002): available at http://europa.eu.int/comm/environment/climat/pdf/emissions_faq.pdf.

41 One solution to that Member State implementation problem would be the adoption of an EC Regulation (rather than a Directive), since this would apply in all Member States from its entry into force without the need for further legal implementation measures to be adopted by the Member States. The relevant legal basis for such action, Article 175(1) EC, permits the adoption of 'measures', which means that both Directives and Regulations may be adopted by the Council and the European Parliament, acting as co-legislators. On the one hand, given the concerns expressed in some quarters about the inconsistencies between allocation methods adopted under the NAPs of different Member States (see, e.g., Section 3.3.2.2), this method would have the additional benefit of setting uniform EC allocation rules (rather than the guiding principles in the current Annexes to the EU ETS Directive). On the other hand, securing agreement on such a Regulation may complicate the legislative process still further, causing delays and political compromises that may not be as much of an improvement over the current situation as one might hope. Also, justifying a far-reaching legislative measure such as a Regulation will require strong arguments for such action on the EC level according to the principle of subsidiarity under Article 5 EC.

References

Commission of the EC, 2000. Denmark: Commission approves tradable CO_2 emission permits for the electricity sector in Denmark for the period 2001–2003. EC Competition Policy Newsletter 2, 63–64.

Commission of the EC, 2001. Community Guidelines on State Aid for Environmental Protection. OJ C37/3.

Commission of the EC, 2003. The EU Emissions Trading Scheme: How to Develop a National Allocation Plan. Non-paper, 2nd Meeting of Working 3, Monitoring Mechanism Committee, 1 April 2003.

Commission of the EC, 2005. Further Guidance on Allocation Plans for the 2008 to 2012 Trading Period of the EU Emission Trading Scheme. COM (2005) 703 final, 22 December 2005.

Craig, P.P., 2003. Administrative Law, 5th edn. Sweet and Maxwell, London.

Craig, P.P., de Búrca, G., 2003. EU Law: Text, Cases, and Materials, 3rd edn. Oxford University Press, Oxford, UK.

Dashwood, A.A., Johnston, A.C., 2004. The institutions of the enlarged EU under the regime of the constitutional treaty. Common Market Law Review 41(6), 1481–1518.

Dougan, 2000. Minimum harmonization and the internal market. Common Market Law Review 37(4), 853–885.

Ellis, E. (ed.), 1999. The Principle of Proportionality in the Laws of Europe. Hart Publishing, Oxford, UK.

Evans, A.C., 1997. EC Law of State Aid. Oxford University Press, Oxford, UK.

Hepburn, C., Grubb, M., Neuhoff, K., Matthes, F., Tse, M., 2006. Auctioning of EU ETS phase II allowances: how and why? Climate Policy 6(1), 137–160.

Ismer, R., Neuhoff, K., 2004. Border Tax Adjustments: A Feasible Way to Address Non-participation in Emission Trading. CMI/DAE Working Paper 36.

Lenaerts, K., van Nuffel, P., 2005. Constitutional Law of the European Union, 2nd edn. Sweet and Maxwell, London.

Merola, M., Crichlow, G., 2004. State aid in the framework of the EU position after Kyoto: an analysis of allowances granted under the CO_2 emissions allowance trading directive. World Competition 27(1), 25–51.

Park, P., 2002. The UK greenhouse gas emissions trading scheme: 'a brave new world' or the result of hurried thinking? Environmental Law and Management 13(6), 292–299.

Sijm, J., Bakker, S., Chen, Y., Harmsen, H., Lise, W., 2005. CO_2 Price Dynamics: The implications of EU Emissions Trading for the Price of Electricity. ECN-C-05-081, Energy Research Centre of The Netherlands, Petten, The Netherlands.

Sijm, J., Chen, Y., ten Donkelaar, M., Hers, S., Scheepers, M., 2006. CO_2 Price Dynamics: A Follow-up Analysis of the Implications of EU Emissions Trading for the Price of Electricity, ECN-C-06-015, Energy Research Council of The Netherlands, Petten, The Netherlands.

Sijm, J., Neuhoff, K., Chen, Y., 2006. CO_2 cost pass-through and windfall profits in the power sector. Climate Policy 6(1), 49–72.

Slot, P.J., 1996. Harmonisation. European Law Review 21(5), 378–387.

Struys, M.L., Abbott, H., 2003. The role of national courts in state aid litigation. European Law Review 28(2), 172–189.

Tridimas, T., 1998. The General Principles of EC Law,. Oxford University Press, Oxford, UK.

Van Calster, G., 2000. Greening the EC's State aid and tax regimes. European Competition Law Review 21(6), 294–314.

www.climatepolicy.com

Auctioning of EU ETS phase II allowances: how and why?

Cameron Hepburn[1]*, Michael Grubb[2], Karsten Neuhoff[2], Felix Matthes[3], Maximilien Tse[4]

[1] St Hugh's College, Environmental Change Institute and Department of Economics, St Margaret's Road, Oxford OX2 6LE, UK
[2] Faculty of Economics, Cambridge University, Sidgwick Avenue, Cambridge CB3 9DE, UK
[3] Öko-Institut, Büro Berlin, Novalisstrasse 10, D-10115 Berlin, Germany
[4] Nuffield College, New Road, Oxford OX1 1NF, UK

Abstract

The European Directive on the EU ETS allows governments to auction up to 10% of the allowances issued in phase II 2008–2012, without constraints being specified thereafter. This article reviews and extends the long-standing debate about auctioning, in which economists have generally supported and industries opposed a greater use of auctioning. The article clarifies the key issues by reviewing six 'traditional' considerations, examines several credible options for auction design, and then proposes some new issues relevant to auctioning. It is concluded that greater auctioning *in aggregate* need not increase adverse competitiveness impacts, and could in some respects alleviate them, particularly by supporting border-tax adjustments. Auctioning within the 10% limit might also be used to dampen price volatility during 2008–2012 and, in subsequent periods, it offers the prospect of supporting a long-term price signal to aid investor confidence. The former is only possible, however, if Member States are willing to coordinate their decision-making (though not revenue-raising) powers in defining and implementing the intended pricing mechanisms.

Keywords: EU ETS; Auctions; Phase II allocations; Windfall profits

1. Introduction

Whether governments could or should sell emission allowances, instead of giving them out for free, was one of the most hotly contested aspects of negotiating the original EU ETS Directive. It resulted in the compromise – after determined intervention by the European Parliament to raise the threshold – that governments could auction up to 5% of allowances in phase I and up to 10% in phase II (the Kyoto first period of 2008–2012).

This compromise reflects two empirical facts about auctioning. The first is that economists almost unanimously recommend more auctioning. The second is that business tends to oppose it. The result is that despite all the academic recommendations, auctioning in emission trading

* Corresponding author. +44-1865-274965; fax: +44-1865-274912
E-mail address: cameron.hepburn@economics.ox.ac.uk

Box 1. Auctioning in the EU ETS – key findings

Auctioning in general:

- is likely to increase the macroeconomic efficiency of the EU ETS and offers scope to partially address its distributional impacts
- will have negligible competitiveness impacts
- reduces the distortions associated with free allocation and is correspondingly more compatible with EU State aid legislation
- will have a smaller impact on EU ETS prices than allocation cutbacks without auctioning
- will increase management attention and thus market efficiency

Auctioning may also provide a hedge against projection uncertainties, reduce price volatility, and increase investor stability. The recent EU ETS market collapse is a dramatic manifestation of uncertainty in emission projections. Reserving some allowances for periodic auctions:

- could assist transparency and liquidity
- offers a potential price cushioning mechanism (as in US transmission auctions), to create a more stable EU ETS market
- might facilitate ex-ante agreed target price ranges, thereby increasing predictability for investors

Auctioning poses no significant implementation difficulties:

- either ascending-bid or sealed-bid auctions could be used and based upon extensive experience, for example with securities auctions
- should be open to as wide a group of bidders as possible
- the concerns of small bidders can be addressed, for example through reserves guaranteed at the strike price

For the longer term (post-2012), auctioning could also:

- help protect industrial competitiveness by enabling WTO-compatible border-tax adjustments
- help provide a long-term carbon price signal by recycling revenue into carbon contracts

---

systems is the exception rather than the rule.[1] In phase I, only four out of 25 Member States used auctions at all, and in only one case were auctions fully employed to the 5% limit.[2] This contrasts sharply with, for example, the willingness of European governments to auction licences for the European 'third-generation' (3G) mobile telecommunications licences, where auctions raised enormous sums.[3] The difference in approach can largely be explained by three factors. First, emissions trading imposes costs on other sectors, producing strong lobbying by incumbents in these markets, whereas costs to other sectors by pricing the 3G spectrum were much smaller and less obvious. Second, emissions trading may affect national competitiveness in some export sectors. In contrast, competitiveness fears did not arise with the 3G auctions because international trade in spectrum licences (and downstream sectors) is obviously rather limited. Third, telecommunications is a fast-growing industry, where many powerful players were non-incumbents without the right to grandfathered allowances (Cramton and Kerr, 2002).

However, the political dynamics relevant to emissions allowance auctions may be changing. The great majority of participants in phase I (as measured by turnover or emissions) are making substantial profits from the system of free allocations, as economists had predicted. Additionally, there are now potential legal pressures arising from state aid considerations as a consequence of these profits (see Johnston, this issue). These considerations may increase the appeal of auctions. In this context, we re-examine the issues and arguments for and against auctioning, and also introduce some new considerations as follows: Section 2 reviews six 'traditional' arguments concerning EU allowance auctions; Section 3 considers how EU ETS auctions might be run, including an examination of the question of auction design; Section 4 examines some new issues, including whether auctions might reduce competitiveness exposure (through allowing border-tax adjustments); reduce price volatility, and support long-term price signalling.

2. The pros and cons of auctioning allowances

2.1. Economic efficiency, revenue recycling and the relationship with eco-taxation

Raising revenue from environmental policy is not a new idea. The classical recommendation is to tax activities with 'external' (such as environmental) costs, to make firms factor these costs into their decisions (Pigou, 1920). A secondary benefit of such eco-taxation, in addition to internalizing the environmental externality, is that the revenue raised can be 'recycled' to reduce other distortionary taxes on labour or capital in the economy.[4]

Despite the economic arguments for eco-taxation, implementation has been extremely patchy and highly contested.[5] The divergence between theory and practice has gradually led to a much deeper appreciation of the crucial importance of the political economy of instrument choice. Policy decisions are strongly influenced, for understandable reasons, by the creation and allocation of economic rents. Environmental taxes have struggled to win political acceptance because they attempt to combine two difficult feats: transferring the rents created by environmental constraints to the public purse, and providing incentives to change behaviour at the margins.[6] Attempting either feat alone, particularly the former, can generate strong opposition from powerful interest groups.

In addition to the political economy challenges, policies internalizing the carbon price (including taxes, and trading schemes whether the permits are grandfathered or auctioned) may have unwanted interactions with other taxes.[7] For instance, imposing a carbon price by a tax or trading scheme raises the price of energy and derived products, which (other things being equal) reduces real wages and therefore labour supply. Some considerations and studies suggest that this indirect 'tax-interaction' effect more than offsets the efficiency gains from revenue recycling, although the net effects remain disputed and context-dependent.[8]

But any policy that internalizes the carbon price *without* raising revenue (such as emissions trading with free allocation) suffers these tax-interaction effects without the benefit of the revenue-recycling effect (discussed above).[9] Because auctioning allowances does benefit from the revenue-recycling effect, it is almost certainly more efficient than free allocation, within the constraints of competitiveness effects. Thus, in practice, given that there is an emissions trading system in place, it is obvious that auctioning has the potential to improve the macroeconomic efficiency of the system.

Of course, efficiency considerations are merely the beginning, and we now examine five other considerations relevant to auctions, namely: the distribution of the economic rents created by CO_2 limits in the economy; competitiveness effects of auctioning compared to grandfathering; legal considerations; dynamic incentives; and transaction costs.

2.2. Rent distribution and equity considerations

Limiting CO_2 emissions puts a price on carbon and thereby increases production costs. Firms will pass a proportion of this marginal cost increase through to consumers. The proportion passed through depends upon the market structure.[10] When allowances are freely allocated to firms, some participating sectors will inevitably make profits.[11]

It is now beyond doubt that the electricity sector generally profits from free allowances under the EU ETS, unless it is subject to direct price regulation or a regulatory threat in concentrated markets, because generators pass costs on to electricity consumers, including non-ETS sectors and domestic consumers. Whether other participating sectors may similarly profit depends upon two main factors: whether they receive enough allowances to cover any increase in their cost base; and the constraints on cost pass-through placed by international competition.[12] In practice, of course, these factors vary considerably between sectors, and indeed, companies and facilities within sectors. Non-participating sectors with high electricity consumption (such as aluminium) will face substantially higher costs due to higher electricity prices, and yet are not compensated through the receipt of free allowances.

Not only does the ETS have significant distributional consequences between the various sectors (participating or not), it is also clear that most of the economic rents from the current arrangements ultimately accrue to shareholders of the profiting firms, who tend to be wealthier than the general population. As such, in aggregate the current arrangements transfer resources from the poor to the rich.[13]

One of the widest economic misconceptions about auctioning is that it would simply add costs which would be passed through to 'downstream' companies and consumers.[14] Yet if firms maximize profits, then even with free allocation they pass on the opportunity costs of allowances to downstream prices. Changing from free allocation to auctioning will have little impact on product prices.[15] However, because auctioning raises revenue that may be reallocated, it has, *prima facie*, the *potential* to correct distributional impacts.

If auction revenues are employed to reduce general taxes, the distributional impacts will depend upon the nature of these other tax changes: for example, a reduction in income tax would tend to shift revenue from the electricity consumer to the taxpayer, and if focused on the base rate might be somewhat progressive. Alternatively, direct dedication of the auction revenue to domestic consumers would give consumers an income stream that increases with higher CO_2 prices, thereby compensating for product (especially electricity) price increases. This might also increase public interest in and support for the ETS. Few generalizations are meaningful at this level, however, since each country will have different political preferences and considerations in the context of wider tax and consumer debates.

If revenues are earmarked within the business sector, distributional impacts will similarly hinge upon how these revenues are targeted. One example of national earmarking is the UK Carbon Trust, which receives revenues from the UK Climate Change Levy that is then used to support investment by UK companies in improving energy efficiency, and in the process of commercializing new and emerging low-carbon technologies. The aim is both to reduce energy costs for British companies and enhance their longer-term competitiveness by accelerating the use of advanced technology. In general, the use of CO_2 auction revenues to support R&D, demonstration projects, regional development bodies, and possibly also supporting infrastructure, is likely to be viable under State aid rules.

However, the use of auction revenues to mitigate the impact on downstream sectors (such as aluminium) on a larger scale is likely to be somewhat limited by State aid considerations (see below). Nevertheless, by introducing an additional degree of freedom, auctioning some fraction of allowances creates the potential for a more equitable distribution of the economic rents associated with emissions trading.

2.3. Competitiveness effects

Just as it is widely (but usually wrongly) assumed that auctions lead to increased costs on downstream consumers, it is also widely assumed that free allocation helps to reduce potential adverse impacts of the EU ETS on the competitiveness of European industry relative to countries without CO_2 controls.

However, many participating sectors, such as the electricity sector, are not directly exposed to foreign competition, so competitiveness concerns are not directly relevant. Exceptions may apply to closure and investment decisions, which are affected by the allocation of free allowances – as illustrated at the example of the power sector in Neuhoff et al. (this issue). Furthermore, although downstream industries are affected by increased electricity prices, it should be remembered that the electricity price increases they face should not differ much under grandfathering or auctioning.

Competitiveness concerns arise mainly in the sectors which (i) face significant cost increases, and (ii) are most exposed to competition from outside of the ETS. This includes industries such as cement, steel, non-ferrous metals and some chemical products. Although the shift from grandfathering to auctioning does not normally have much impact on costs at the margin,[16] it does affect the *gross revenues* of companies. Free allocation is essentially a one-off subsidy that helps companies maintain a good balance sheet in the face of higher operating costs. Auctioning reduces the scale of that subsidy. Alternatively, for companies which are not focused on near-term profit maximization, free allocation provides a subsidy to fund the protection of market share by under-pricing (e.g. limit pricing, see Smale et al., this issue), and auctioning reduces that capacity. As such, the general conclusion is that free allocation can act as a temporary subsidy to support firm balance sheets, but the choice between this and auctioning does not fundamentally change competitiveness in the longer term.

2.4. Legal considerations

As grandfathering and auctioning are mechanisms which allocate valuable assets, legal considerations are relevant. State aid considerations may place limits on the scope of free allocation. On the other hand, legal arguments might be proposed to support the view that firms have the 'right to emit', which cannot be taken from them, or that auctioning would adversely affect decisions that were made in reliance upon previous regulatory structures remaining in place.

The view that firms have a *right* to compensation for the establishment of, or changes to, the EU ETS, can be dispensed with rather quickly. It is clear that legislative bodies have the authority to change regulatory frameworks, particularly when regulated activities are harming others; indeed, there was never a 'right to emit' but only the freedom to do so until regulation provided otherwise. The argument that investors should be compensated for decisions made prior to the EU ETS (such as building a coal power station in 2000), relying upon the assumption that no new regulation would enter into force, is only marginally more persuasive – it is well established that if government has a good public-interest reason, it can restrain the use of an asset and there is no legal obligation to compensate as long as only the use is constrained but no expropriation performed.

Even if firms have no right to compensation, governments may wish to compensate adversely affected industry to enhance the credibility of their claims of investment certainty, and to continue to attract private-sector investment. However, without a specific justification, payments to industry may, *prima facie*, constitute State aid. A justification might be provided by analogy to the 'stranded cost regime' formulated and applied by the Commission under the 1996 Electricity Directive, which allowed for such compensation in the electricity sector. Similar arguments might be applied to other sectors.

If governments want to compensate investors for adjustment to regulation/legislation, this would motivate some free allocation of allowances during a transitory period to compensate investors who made investment decisions before there was any reasonable expectation of carbon controls. Different views exist about when this was. Most of those involved in the international process would argue it to have been 1990[17] or a couple of years thereafter.[18] Later relevant landmarks include the adoption of the Kyoto Protocol in 1997, the EU's Green Paper on emissions trading in 2000, and the EU's ratification of the Protocol and adoption of the ETS Directive in 2002. Whatever year is considered applicable, however, as time passes fewer and fewer investments will be able to make the claim that costs were sunk before a reasonable expectation of carbon controls.

Far from having a right to compensation, the balance of legal arguments seem heavily (and increasingly) weighted to the view that any such compensation is prohibited under State aid rules. Indeed, European competition law may create pressures to reduce the free allocations to industrial emitters so that they are proportionate with the (otherwise) forgone profits from prior to the introduction of ETS (Johnston, this issue).

Finally, requiring firms to pay for the right to pollute is consistent with the *polluter pays principle*, which starts from the premise that the right to a clean environment is owned by the public: from this basis, if firms wish to pollute the environment, they must purchase the right to do so from the public, rather than being given it for free.

The clear conclusion is, therefore, that legal principles are a very shaky basis from which to argue against auctioning. On the contrary, legal considerations suggest that auctions may be favoured over free allocations.

2.5. Reducing distortions and perverse dynamic incentives

An additional problem with free allocation is that it can lead to rather perverse dynamic incentives. For instance, if future allowances are allocated as a function of present emission levels, firms have an incentive to emit more now in order to extract a larger allocation in the future.[19] Similarly, if free allocation to existing installations is relatively generous, while allocations to new installations are more restrictive (as it is in many Member States) incentives are created for plant lifetime-extension rather than plant modernization or replacement.[20] These perverse incentives are eliminated by certain allocation mechanisms (e.g. benchmarking or once-and-for-all grandfathering), and such problems do not arise if allowances are auctioned.

This phenomenon is examined in two other articles in this Special Issue. In the electricity sector, Neuhoff et al. (this issue) demonstrate that the sheer value of free allocations in a sequentially negotiated trading system makes it hard to avoid some distortionary effects. Demailly and Quirion (this issue) also confirm that if allowances are allocated as a function of production whether contemporaneously (as in 'output-based' allocation) or in the future (as with updating), output choices are correspondingly distorted. Auctioning would obviously reduce or eliminate these effects.

2.6. Transaction costs of allocation processes

The final 'traditional' area of dispute concerns administrative costs. The phase I national allocation plans (NAPs) involved negotiation over allowances with a total asset value of almost €50 billion per year (assuming an average price of €20/tCO$_2$). Political decisions on how to allocate these assets between sectors and individual installations naturally creates intensive lobby activity by all participants in order to obtain the maximum possible share of the rents.[21] The time and energy devoted by companies, governments, and indeed consultancy and research sectors, to this enormous rent allocation process represents huge transactional costs.[22]

Estimates of transactional costs must account for the fact that the allocation process imposes significant risks upon both firms and government. Many firms fear being 'caught short', and these fears may be amplified by their lack of experience and confidence in trading on the secondary market and concerns about the future availability of permits. The government (and the public at large) run the risk that the allocation process will end up being unfair on some sectors, and overly generous to others. The government's response to this risk is to devote considerable resources to the process of 'allocation assessment'. Furthermore, transactional costs involved in free allocation are likely to increase in the future, as more complex allocation schemes (e.g. benchmarking) are employed to reduce other unwanted consequences.

In principle, auctioning more of the allowances reduces the volume of free assets open to lobbying, and therefore reduces the 'rent scrap' of these allocation negotiations. It would also help both firms and government manage their real and perceived risks – firms are less likely to be 'caught short' when they can buy permits at the next auction, and governments could redeploy their resources now spent on 'allocation assessment'. Of course, auctioning also involves administrative and other transaction costs. Thus, whether auctioning increases the overall implementation efficiency of the EU ETS may depend upon the design of the auctions, which we consider shortly.

2.7. Summary of the traditional arguments

Table 1 presents a summary of the arguments considered in this section. In addition to the reasons favouring some auctioning compared to 100% free allocation, it is notable that some

Table 1. Summary of issues

Issue	Favours
Static efficiency	Auctions
Distribution of rents	Auctions in theory, free allocation in practice
Competitiveness	Depends upon use of auction revenues
Legal considerations	Auctions
Dynamic incentives	Auctions
Transaction costs	Uncertain, favours auctions in medium term

auctioning might be preferred to simply cutting back free allocations by the same amount. If the market is liquid and – as considered below – auctions are open to all bidders, the choice between buying at auction and buying on the secondary market may make little difference to individual companies. However, at the economy-wide level, auctions release allowances into the market and thus do not raise the carbon price as much as cutbacks of the same quantity. They also have more desirable characteristics in terms of macroeconomic efficiency, distribution and lessening of perverse dynamic incentives, as discussed. We now examine how allowance auctions might be designed.

3. How to auction EU ETS allowances

The allocation of EU ETS allowances has several features in common with the sale of government securities such as T-Bills and Gilts, provided that Member States do not impose strong restrictions on participation.[23] In both cases there is a large number of potential bidders and a large number of identical goods which can subsequently be traded on a secondary market. Member States therefore have an opportunity to create a very competitive and efficient auction environment, as in the case of securities. Bearing in mind these similarities, we discuss some basic issues for the design of EU ETS auctions.

3.1. Multi-unit auction design

There are many possible formats for auctions of EU ETS allowances which can be divided into two broad types. These are *ascending-bid* auctions, in which bidders have the opportunity to raise their bids during the auction, and *sealed-bid* auctions in which bidders submit only their final offers. The preferred choice of format depends on the circumstances. For example, ascending-bid auctions may be easier to understand for inexperienced bidders and have been recommended for auctions of UK greenhouse gas emissions reductions in 2002 (Klemperer, 2004, p.135) and the New Entrants Reserve (NER) in phase I of the EU ETS in the UK (DTI, 2005).[24] However, in the case of EU ETS allowances, as long as Member States do not unnecessarily restrict competition in auctions (e.g. by allowing only one sector to participate in any given auction), there are many potential bidders and sealed-bid auctions should perform well.

In a sealed-bid auction, participating bidders submit confidential bids in the form of demand schedules, which specify how many permits a bidder would be willing to buy at any given price. These bids are added together to form an aggregate demand curve and a market clearing price is determined as the point at which aggregate demand equals supply. Winning bids are identified as those above the clearing price. Figure 1(a) provides an illustration of a sealed-bid auction, where P_C denotes the market clearing price. In Section 4.2 we discuss the idea of Member States

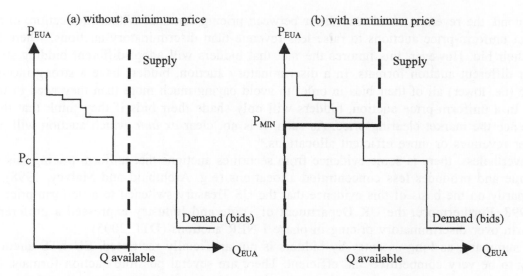

Figure 1. Market clearing price.

agreeing a reserve price for auctioned allowances. Figure 1(b) shows an example where this reserve price, P_{MIN}, binds. In the case shown, P_{MIN} is higher than the clearing price, so not all the allowances are sold at auction.

Two variants of the sealed-bid auction are the discriminatory and uniform-price formats commonly used to issue government securities. The two formats differ in the payments that winning bidders must make. In a uniform-price auction, every winning bidder pays the market clearing price. In a discriminatory auction, every winning bidder pays its own bid for the units it wins. For example a bidder who bids for 20 permits at €30 each and a further 10 units at €20 each pays a total of €800 if all the bids are above the market clearing price.[25]

Because both formats are now well established, Member States and potential bidders would be – or could easily become – familiar with the rules of either auction. Using these familiar formats would also address concerns about auctions being untested or over-complicated. Both discriminatory and uniform-price formats would be feasible and low-cost for Member States.[26]

There are two important considerations relevant to the choice between uniform and discriminatory formats. First, it is often argued that it is simpler for bidders to formulate bidding strategies in a uniform-price auction, promoting participation and competition. In a discriminatory auction, small or inexperienced bidders may find it difficult to anticipate the market clearing price and may be deterred from bidding for fear of making costly mistakes.[27] This might arise if secondary and futures markets are illiquid and there is a great deal of uncertainty over prices.[28] In the case of EU ETS allowances, one would expect greater uncertainty towards the beginning of a trading period (e.g. in the year 2008 for the 2008–2012 period) when fewer allowance trades will have occurred.

If low participation by smaller bidders is a concern, non-competitive bids could be permitted. A bidder who submits a non-competitive bid is guaranteed to win the desired units in the auction. In a uniform-price auction, the price is simply the market clearing price, while under discriminatory pricing the non-competitive price is an average of the conventional winning bids. Bidders can therefore limit risk by submitting non-competitive bids, particularly in discriminatory auctions.[29]

Second, the revenue raised may differ between pricing formats. Without reflection, one might expect uniform-price auctions to raise less revenue than discriminatory auctions, where bidders pay their bid. However, this ignores the fact that bidders will adopt different bidding strategies under different auction formats. In a discriminatory auction, bidders have a strong incentive to shade (i.e. lower) all of their bids in order to avoid paying much more than they need to for each unit. In a uniform-price auction, bidders will only shade their bids if they think that this may influence the market clearing price. As such, it is not clear *ex ante* which auction will produce higher revenues or more efficient allocations.[30]

Nevertheless, there is some evidence from securities auctions that uniform pricing raises *more* revenue and produces less concentrated allocations (e.g. Archibald and Malvey, 1998), and it was partly on the basis of this evidence that the US Treasury switched to a uniform-price format in 1998. Furthermore, the UK Department of Trade and Industry expressed a preference for uniform over discriminatory pricing in phase I NER auctions (DTI, 2005).

In summary, as long as entry by bidders is not artificially restricted, EU ETS auctions are likely to be very competitive and efficient. There are several possible auction formats, but the most likely candidates are the sealed-bid uniform-price and discriminatory auctions, used in sales of government securities. The limited evidence that we have slightly favours uniform pricing, especially as bidders appear to find uniform-price auctions more straightforward. If participation is a concern, then non-competitive bids may be used.

3.2. Eligibility and participation

The most important objectives of auction design are to promote competition and to encourage entry. Consequently auctions for EU ETS allowances should ensure the widest possible participation by bidders from all sectors. Artificially restricting participation to national buyers or specific sectors is likely to impair revenues and the efficient allocation of allowances.

Nevertheless, only one of the four governments that auctioned in phase I opened the auction to all EU bidders. Given that allowances are readily tradable, national or sectoral bidders will only benefit from restrictions on participation if auction prices are significantly lower than those in the secondary market. Despite the arbitrage possibility, prices at auction may be lower than on the secondary market if poor auction design facilitates non-competitive or collusive behaviour by bidders. The net result would be a reduction in revenue and an implicit subsidy for bidders.[31]

Increasing the number of eligible bidders is desirable because it is likely to lead to greater competition and higher auction revenues. However, even if they are eligible, small bidders are unlikely to participate directly in auctions because of the transaction costs involved in formulating and submitting bids. Moreover the institutions responsible for conducting the auctions face costs in dealing with each bidder (e.g. in ensuring compliance with capital requirements or securities regulations).

One option is to allow current dealers on the ETS secondary market to become 'primary dealers' who can bid on their own account or on behalf of clients. Because these dealers would participate more regularly than individual buyers, some transaction costs could be avoided. Small buyers might even be encouraged to participate via a dealer when they would not be willing or able to do so directly.

In order to prevent either primary dealers or their clients from manipulating the auction price, limits could be set on the size of any individual bidder's share of the allowances allocated in an auction. Manipulations of the secondary market (such as 'short squeezes') will probably not be a major consideration, as the proportion of allowances sold at auction will be relatively small.[32]

3.3. Allocation of free allowances

Obviously, auctioning allowances in phase II reduces the allowances that are available for free allocation. Governments must determine how the remaining free allocations are distributed between sectors. An obvious and simple approach is to reduce the allocation to all sectors by 10% (or the proportion chosen for auction). Nevertheless, given the differential pass-through of costs between sectors, as discussed in Section 2.2, it may be considered politically appropriate to compensate for undesirable distributional consequences by adjusting the allocation between sectors. For instance, sectors with higher rates of cost pass-through might receive a smaller share of free allocation, while others would receive a more generous allocation.

3.4. Auction periodicity

The principles

How often should auctions be performed? At one extreme, the entire allocation could be sold at the beginning of the 5-year period. Large infrequent auctions would minimize administrative and transaction costs and might also promote competitive bidding between bidders for whom this is the only chance to buy allowances at auction. However, we believe more regular auctions are advisable, for a number of reasons.

Smaller and more frequent auctions are likely to encourage participation by smaller bidders. For example, firms who wish to purchase at auction rather than on the secondary market may not have a large enough line of credit to purchase 5 years' worth of permits in advance. This is a substantial asset to hold on the balance sheet and one-off auctions might deter small bidders without 'deep pockets'. These bidders would still trade on the secondary market, but the auctions themselves would be less competitive.

By providing a steady injection of liquidity, more frequent auctions would limit the impact of any individual auction on market prices. Periodic auctions might also enhance price stability and the management of uncertainty, as discussed below in Section 4. Although market interactions are unlikely to be problematic for phase II, where only 10% of allowances can be auctioned, the impact on the market is likely to become more important if and as a greater proportion of allowances are auctioned over time.[33] Furthermore, smaller auctions reduce or eliminate any residual (and probably unjustified) concern that participants with market power would buy large fractions of the allowances and subsequently extract oligopoly rents on the secondary market. Multiple auctions would allow other players to adjust their bids in later auctions in response to any initial strategic purchasing by large players.

Auction frequency with 25 countries

Finally, periodicity also depends upon whether Member States coordinate their auctions. If Member States run their auctions independently, then staggering their timing would ensure a gradual release of liquidity. For instance, if all 25 Member States run quarterly auctions, there would be two allowance auctions every week, which seems too frequent. Even annual national auctions could result in an auction somewhere in Europe every 2 weeks. At the opposite extreme, Member States could collaborate and coordinate the timing of their auctions, as considered briefly below.

The ideal trade-off between ensuring a competitive auction with low transactions costs and providing steady liquidity is difficult to judge before we have gained more experience with allowance auctions. If auctions were to be based on experience with electricity markets, then a frequent uniform price auction (e.g. weekly), would allow small participants to directly acquire the allowances they need to cover their emissions in the auction.[34] High frequency would ensure that bidders pay a price close to the price on the secondary market at the time of emission, thus limiting risk exposure. In electricity markets this approach has been successfully implemented with low transaction costs (various pool type market designs).

If, on the other hand, EU ETS auctions were to be more guided by the experience of Treasury bill auctions, then less frequent auctions (e.g. 1–3 times a year) would be envisaged. A simple uniform price format might be employed, but less frequent auctions would also allow the use of a wider range of auction formats. Of course, a more complex auction format, requiring more careful preparation of the bid, would increase the costs for small players to directly participate in the auction. Very small players are therefore likely to obtain their allowances from intermediaries, who would provide risk hedging and other services, arguably at a cost reflected in lower auction revenue. This approach also has the benefit of supporting liquidity in CO_2 spot markets.

Finally, note that Member States could consider auctioning in advance; auctions for 2008–2012 allowances, for example, could and probably should be held before 2008 in order to help the market form price expectations.

3.5. Auction competition and coordination

In principle there is no reason why Member States should not hold auctions entirely independently of each other. The question of how actions in one country might affect others would then need to be considered; in effect, governments themselves might become active 'market players', judging the timing and volume of auctions in relation to market projections, including expectations about the auction decisions of other Member States – a kind of 'auction competition'. It is not clear how desirable it would be for the legal authorities responsible for forming the market to then become active players in it, and whether this might lead to conflicts of interest. How numerous auctions might interact with the auction method is another issue to be considered – especially if some of the auctions are very small, enabling large players to influence the outcome.

For these and other reasons, Member States might consider 'pooling' auctions under the same rules. In particular, Member States with fewer allowances to sell might decide to hold joint auctions and to divide the revenue according to their share of the supply. Coordinating the timing of auctions might also aid price stabilization.

The ultimate manifestation of this would be for all countries that hold auctions to pool together, in EU-level auctions. It is unlikely that Member States would give up revenues, but that is a separate issue; there would be nothing to prevent central EU institutions managing the auctions and returning revenues to Member States. De-linking decisions on auctions in this way from the revenues generated would avoid any potential conflict of interest. And to have some element of EU-level auctions may be inescapable for some of the more 'active uses' of auctioning, to which we now turn.

4. Active auctioning: hedging, pricing and border adjustments

Section 2 set out the main debates around auctioning, concluding that these offer strong arguments for a degree of auctioning, probably increasing over time. Section 3 indicated that there are no significant operational problems in conducting such auctions. In our view, however, these are not necessarily the only interesting and important benefits of auctioning. In addition to the distributional and incentive properties, there may be other important practical roles for auctions in the context of the EU ETS that have as yet been inadequately considered, and we now examine these issues.

4.1. Management attention

Economic analysis tends to assume that firms maximize profits. This assumption drives the result, noted in Section 2.2, that cost increases passed through to consumers should depend on the marginal cost increase – driven by the carbon price – not directly by the method of allocating allowances. In practice, although an assumption of narrow profit-maximization is not egregiously wrong, it is an idealization that obviously does not fully capture reality. The behaviour of people and firms embody considerable inertia and they often use heuristics and 'rules of thumb'.[35] One relevant example from the energy sector emerges from the experience with financial transmission rights in north-eastern USA. There it was found that the free allocation of transmission rights dampened the industry response to price signals. To increase responsiveness subsequently, all transmission rights were auctioned and revenues returned to the initial owners of the rights.

If the allowances given to firms cover the bulk of their emissions, there is no risk exposure and few cash flows. In these conditions, the EU ETS may well be handled by environmental compliance departments, particularly in smaller companies, rather than moving up to affect investment, operational and strategic decision-making. Indeed the design of the EU ETS and its focus on facilities itself reflects its origins in EU environmental regulation, with emphasis upon compliance. In these conditions, the current arrangement largely allows companies to carry on

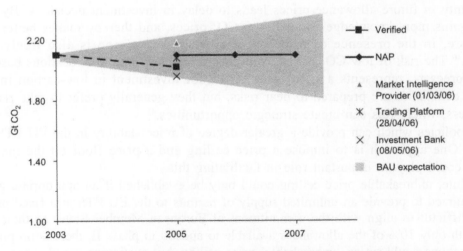

Figure 2. Uncertainty on emissions from installations covered by the EU ETS.

emitting as they would have in the absence of the scheme. Worse, it may foster a psychology that firms must put their main emphasis upon lobbying for all the allowances they project to be needed, rather than on considering or implementing their real opportunities for abatement, particularly in sectors characterized by smaller firms or lower energy intensity.

Thus, the effectiveness of the trading system might be substantially improved by mechanisms which prompt an active response from management. Two options would appear to grab management attention, namely cutbacks in allocation and auctioning. Allowance cutbacks are also emerging as a way of addressing the profits accruing to the power sector.[36] Given lobbying, market uncertainty and price volatility, as well as the macroeconomic dimensions considered in Section 2, auctioning might well be seen as the preferred method. Auctioning could help to get the desired response to the regulation, as the increased financial flows may shift management attention to include allowance costs when optimizing production decisions.[37]

4.2. Auctioning and price stability in phase II

Since the EU ETS market opened in January 2005, prices have been quite unstable: they rose more than expected, had a couple of periods of volatility in the range €20–30/tCO$_2$, crashed in Spring 2006 as real data on verified emissions for 2005 were released, and at the time of writing are oscillating wildly as governments debate options for shoring up the price. The fundamental cause is that the projections upon which allocations were based embodied far greater uncertainty than was acknowledged, and the cutbacks were well *within* the range of the uncertainty.

This is illustrated dramatically by Figure 2, which compares verified emissions (for 21 of the 25 countries covered by the EU ETS)[38] – the declining line from 2003–2005 – with actual allocations for 2005–2007, and estimates made in the run-up to the data release. Allocations exceeded emissions by close to 100MtCO$_2$; the gap could easily have been even bigger.[39] Yet, *even as late as Spring 2006*, there were retrospective estimates from a leading provider of market intelligence that turned out to be completely wrong. The uncertainty in the original projections upon which NAPs had been based was, of course, far wider still. This gives some indication of the uncertainty inherent in predicting emissions and abatement responses – and hence, of prices and costs.

Uncertainty in future allowance prices leads to delay in investment decisions. By waiting, a company gains more knowledge about future CO$_2$ prices, and thereby makes better decisions. Furthermore, in the presence of price uncertainty, risk aversion is also likely to reduce investment.[40] The risk of low CO$_2$ prices, or even a price crash due to allocations based on high emission forecasts, represents a significant hurdle for investment in low-carbon investments. Obviously, companies are prepared to bear risks, but they generally prefer to take risks in their core business, where this can create strategic opportunities.[41]

Clearly, policies which can provide a greater degree of price stability in the EU ETS would be valuable.[42] One approach is to impose a price ceiling and a price floor on the market,[43] and auctioning could play an important role in facilitating this.

An absolute, unbreakable price ceiling could only be established if an appropriate government institution agreed to provide an unlimited supply of permits to the EU ETS at a fixed price, which would be difficult to align with the commitment of European Member States to their cap under Kyoto.[44] With only 10% of the allowances available to auction in phase II, there is no practical way in which auctions could set an 'unbreakable' price ceiling, but auctioning could reduce the risk of price spikes if some allowances were held in reserve and only released on to the market in the event that price went above some predetermined level for a certain duration. A limited auction capacity of this nature would, however, have to address potentially serious problems of gaming the system.[45]

Auctions probably offer a more ready and 'game-proof' approach to supporting, although not dictating, a price floor.[46] Governments could agree that part of the allowances held back for auction would be sold above a reserve price (e.g. €15/tCO$_2$). Given the limited volume (because of the 10% maximum under the Directive), this could not *guarantee* a particular price floor, but it could make a useful contribution to price stability. There are two main cases to consider.

(a) *Tight market*. If external supply of JI and CDM credits is limited or constrained (perhaps by additionality criteria), and if abatement is also limited or expensive, the participating sectors may want to purchase all of the auctioned allowances. In this case the reserve price in the auction, P_{MIN}, translates to a price floor for ETS. Figure 3 illustrates this idea. In Figure 3(a), without auctions, the EUA price P^* is determined by the point at which the demand curve crosses Q_{Kyoto}. In Figure 3(b), 10% of the allowances are removed from circulation, and auctioned back at or above the reserve price, P_{MIN}. A proportion of the auctioned allowances remains unsold, and the EU ETS price now equals P_{MIN}.

(b) *Loose market*. Second, if supply of JI and CDM credits increases significantly or large emission reductions are achieved in the ETS sector, then the allowance price could drop below the reserve price of the auction, as illustrated in Figure 4. The auction reserve price still increases the EU ETS price from P^* to P_A^* (compare Figures 4(a) and 4(b)), because the withdrawal of 10% of the allowances from the market ensures that the price is higher than it would have been otherwise.

Setting an auction reserve price would only have no impact in two unlikely situations. First, with very weak emission targets (or extremely cheap abatement) the allowance price might drop to

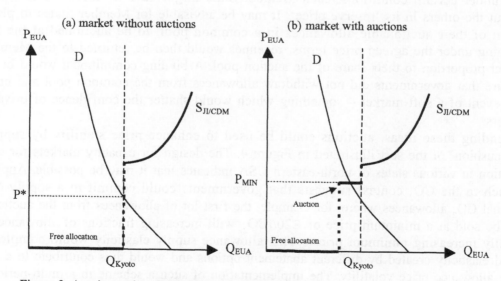

Figure 3. Auctions when JI/CDM supply is **not** important.

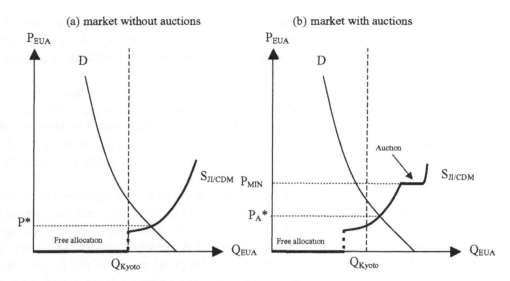

Figure 4. Auctions when JI/CDM supply is important.

zero, even if only 90% of the allowances are available.[47] No company would purchase at auction, and the price would remain at zero. This theoretical possibility, however, seems highly unlikely.

Second, if ETS prices are already well above the reserve price, P_{MIN}, then the reserve price is irrelevant – the allowances will be sold at a clearing price above P_{MIN}. Nevertheless, even in this situation, auctions provide indirect beneficial effects, including greater price stability *ex ante*, and hence increased investment in low-carbon technologies.

Using reserve-price auctions to increase price stability is a simple mechanism that could improve the performance of the scheme, but it would require commitment and coordination between Member States. This is an area in which 'auction competition' might be problematic, since, under certain conditions, each Member State might have an incentive to fractionally undercut the others in its 'reserve price'. It may be advisable for Member States to place some fraction of their auctionable allowances in a common pool, to be auctioned at the EU-level auctioning under the agreed price terms; revenues would then be returned to the Member State in direct proportion to their share of the auction pool. A binding commitment would be required to ensure that governments did not withdraw allowances from the common pool and undercut it in the event of a soft market – something which would shatter the confidence of private-sector investors.

Extending these ideas, auctions could be used to enhance price stability by supporting a 'price cushion' of the sort illustrated in Figure 4. The design for capacity markets for electricity generation in various states of north-eastern USA indicates that it may be possible. Applying this approach to the CO_2 context suggests that governments could commit to a supply curve for additional CO_2 allowances where, for example, the first lot of allowances from the auction budget might be sold at a minimum price of €20/tCO_2, with increasing fractions of allowances sold at gradually increasing minimum prices. This allowance supply elasticity would complement the demand elasticity created by different abatement options and would thus contribute to a reduction in CO_2 allowance price volatility. The implementation of such a scheme in a multi-period, multi-country auction would, however, require careful consideration. Initial price stabilization might reduce the incentive of market participants to hedge their decisions, potentially exposing them to even higher risk in the case that all available allowances are auctioned and prices become more peaky.

In sum, the foregoing analysis suggests that within the current EU directive, auctions might play a useful role in serving to support a cushion for prices, reducing volatility and increasing investment security.

4.3 The feasibility of long-term price signals

The economics literature sets out a strong case that, in the context of a problem such as climate change, fixing prices is more efficient than capping quantities.[48] The essential argument concerns the relative sensitivities of the benefits of mitigation, and the costs of control under uncertainty. If the marginal costs imposed by a given quantity constraint are very sensitive to the level of constraint (steep marginal cost schedule), but the marginal benefits of abatement are relatively insensitive to the amount (a flat marginal damage schedule),[49] then price-oriented controls are more efficient.[50] Pizer (2002) finds that a price-oriented approach for near-term CO_2 controls could yield enormous net social benefits. In contrast, an equivalent absolute emissions cap is far less attractive – if the cap turns out to be wrong, the economic costs could rise sharply and offset the environmental benefits.

In practice, there are several reasons why pure price instruments are still rarely applied to environmental problems.[51] Given the political realities, the best feasible approach may be to design emissions trading systems to address price uncertainties. In a multi-period system like the EU ETS, allowing banking and borrowing creates several interesting possibilities, as discussed by Newell et al. (2005). For instance, parties might agree that the stringency of targets in the next period automatically depends upon the revealed price in the current period, with the relationship being defined by the agreed target price.[52]

Auctions offer some additional approaches to providing a basis for a clear, long-term carbon price signal. First, the mechanisms discussed above could be used to create a long-term 'price floor'. This could be implemented by auctioning all allowances with a reserve price equal to the price floor, coupled with a government commitment to repurchase allowances at the price floor. If credible, a price floor would increase investor confidence in the profitability of low-carbon technology investments.

Second, Helm and Hepburn (2005) propose that the revenue from auctions could be recycled to industry in a technologically neutral way that provides long-term carbon price certainty. They outline a scheme in which national governments would sign 'carbon contracts' under which the government would pay the private sector a fixed price (to be determined by another auction) for the supply of emissions reductions over a long time horizon, such as 20–30 years. A key feature of the scheme is that the 'carbon contract' auction would be technology-neutral, so that the government would be able to avoid the fraught process of 'picking winners'. Winning a carbon contract would provide low-carbon innovators with a reliable forward revenue stream which could be employed to secure project finance.[53] Note that the use of carbon contracts would not prevent governments from subsequently implementing a more stringent climate policy, if appropriate.[54]

Auctioning EU ETS allowances would provide the Treasury with the public funds to pay for carbon contracts.[55] This would be politically appealing – spending auction revenues on long-term carbon contracts would represent genuine revenue recycling to industry in a manner that enhances the environmental effectiveness of the EU ETS,[56] and also provides a much needed long-term price signal.

4.4 The feasibility of border-tax adjustments

A final dimension of auctioning is its relationship to competitiveness through the use of border tax adjustments. It is difficult for energy-intensive sectors to pass through the (opportunity) costs of CO_2 allowances to product prices if these prices are set in international markets. Persistent price differences might, therefore, drive new investors to regions not covered by stringent emission trading schemes, as discussed more fully in Grubb and Neuhoff (this issue).

If the effective CO_2 price differs between regions post-2012, investment in energy-intensive industries is likely to gravitate towards regions with lower CO_2 prices. Clearly, a stringent CO_2 policy is only possible, in the mid-term, if it does not undermine the competitiveness of a region or country. To protect competitiveness, energy-intensive sectors might be excluded from the ETS, but this would weaken the overall scheme. Alternatively, the allocation methodology of free allowances could be redesigned to reduce the impact of CO_2 prices on product prices. But this would distort investment and operation incentives and severely restrict substitution effects to less carbon-intensive products, seriously undermining the effectiveness of the ETS in delivering CO_2 emission reductions.

Border-tax adjustment (BTA) may be a preferable solution to facilitate the longer term extension of CO_2 policies in the absence of global agreement (Biermann and Brohm, 2003). To make BTA compatible with WTO principles, tariffs must be set at the average costs of CO_2 allowances, excluding opportunity costs. Average costs are only significant with auctions, and thus a move to auctions is required to facilitate BTA. Ismer and Neuhoff (2004) suggest the following approach to address frequently voiced concerns about WTO compatibility (Esty, 1994). Suppose a company producing one widget, with the best available technology, emits X tonnes of CO_2 and consumes Y MWh of electricity in the process. Emission trading increases the costs of this company by X times the allowance price and Y times the price increase of electricity due to emission trading. An auditing body will determine the factors X and Y for the best available technology of the relevant product groups, thus minimizing administrative efforts (Zhang, 1998). The auditing body would consult with industry, ensuring a balanced result between the differing interests of domestic and foreign industry. Any exporter out of the area covered by the emission-trading scheme will now be reimbursed for these costs. Older or less efficient plants will also be compensated at the level of the best available technology. On the flip side, a tariff at the level of these costs is levied on imports. This reinstates a level playing field for companies irrespective of the domestic CO_2 policy.

The joint implementation of stringent CO_2 trading with this type of border-tax adjustment will leave companies in foreign countries slightly better off than the absence of any scheme, while domestic companies are slightly worse off. The joint implementation thus addresses concerns resulting from the analysis of independent implementation of border-tax adjustment (Charnovitz, 2004). The joint scheme achieves the objective of facilitating unilateral internalization of CO_2 costs, as simulated for the cement sector (Demailly and Quirion, this issue), without discriminating against foreign producers.

However, WTO regulations mean that companies could only be compensated for the *real* costs they incur as a result of the regulation – not for the marginal costs or opportunity costs that follow from free allocation. Thus, companies could only be compensated up to the level of actual, average costs incurred, whereas the competitiveness issue is more to do with the impact of marginal costs of prices, at least when firms seek to maximize profits. Auctioning helps to bring average cost impacts in line with the marginal costs, and thus would enable a greater level of border-tax adjustment more aligned with any actual price differentials. To implement effective BTA, a prerequisite for WTO-compatibility is auctioning.

5. Conclusions

The traditional arguments for and against auctioning, reviewed in Section 2, support two widely known conclusions, namely that (i) auctions are almost certainly in the public interest, but (ii) political economy considerations have to date presented serious obstacles to the implementation of auctioning within the EU ETS on any significant scale. The winds may be changing, however, and more recent signs are that governments are keen to find approaches to resolve these political challenges.

If auctions are employed in phase II, Section 3 of this article provides some broad guidance on how this might occur. Sealed-bid auctions are likely to be appropriate, and both discriminatory and uniform-price payment rules are feasible. Auctions could be conducted at relatively frequent intervals (every 6 months or so) over the 2008–2012 commitment period. Market power is not expected to be a significant problem as long as Member States do not impose artificial restrictions on entry.

Perhaps the most interesting possibilities for auctions, though, go beyond the usual benefits of static and dynamic efficiency. Section 4 discussed the potential for auctions (and the resulting revenues) to provide several new benefits, including (i) an increase in the environmental effectiveness by focusing management attention on carbon; (ii) an amelioration of competitiveness considerations, either by direct support or by legitimizing border-tax adjustments; (iii) a clearer long-term price signal, through recycling the revenues into carbon contracts; and (iv) an improvement to price stability if Member States agree to coordinate auctions by including an auction price floor.

One can only speculate whether these additional considerations will increase the political support for greater use of auctioning in phase II. Certainly, as targets become more demanding, efficiency becomes more and more important and the appeal of auctioning will correspondingly increase. The creative deployment of auctions to increase efficiency, stabilize prices, and help to address competitiveness issues would be feasible, and could yield substantial social benefits.

Acknowledgements

Financial support from UK Research Council project TSEC is gratefully acknowledged. Thanks also go to Billy Pizer, Paul Klemperer and two anonymous referees for their helpful comments.

Notes

1   The US government auctions only 2.8% of allowances under its SO_2 programme (McLean, 1997).
2   Denmark auctioned 5% and used the revenue to purchase JI/CDM credits, Hungary auctioned 2.4%, Lithuania auctioned 1.5%, and Ireland auctioned 0.75%, with European-wide eligibility, to cover the administrative costs of the scheme.
3   In the year 2000, the UK auction raised €39 billion (Klemperer, 2004) and the German auction almost €100 billion (1 billion = 1,000 million).

4   This corresponds to a very simplistic statement of the 'double dividend' hypothesis. Various definitions are used in the literature, sometimes inconsistently, including 'weak', 'intermediate' and 'strong' forms. This terminology is avoided here. Tax-interaction effects are discussed later.

5   See, e.g. Helm (2005).

6   A 2006 Special Issue of the *Energy Policy Journal* (34(8)) analyses the European experience with eco-taxation and points to deeper underlying issues about the degree of public understanding and trust in political processes. A Swedish survey also underlines that attitudes to carbon taxation are directly related to the degree of trust in politicians, more even than an individual's own exposure to the taxes (Hammar and Jagers, 2006).

7   See Bovenberg and de Mooij (1994), the critique by Fullerton (1997) and the reply by Bovenberg and de Mooij (1997), as well as Bovenberg and van der Ploeg (1994), Goulder (1995), Parry (1995) and Bovenberg and Goulder (1996).

8   Parry (2003) finds that the tax-interaction effect dominates the revenue-recycling effect. This would be expected from the optimal tax theory result that broad taxes produce lower efficiency losses than narrow taxes (e.g. Diamond and Mirrlees, 1971a, 1971b). In practice, the net impact depends on a wide variety of assumptions about the current tax base, whether the economy is modelled as a fully deployed equilibrium, etc (IPCC, 2001, chs 7 and 8).

9   See Goulder et al. (1997, 1999), Parry et al. (1999) and Fullerton and Metcalf (2001). The tax interaction effect could provide an argument for a carbon price that is below the Pigouvian level. It is not an argument for not raising revenue.

10 See the companion articles in this issue by Smale et al., Demailly and Quirion, and also Hepburn et al.

11 Indeed, Smale et al. (this issue) suggest that *most* participating sectors will profit.

12 There is some indication that non-power sectors with significant emission levels are also able to pass through a proportion of the marginal cost increase. See, for instance, de Leyva and Lekander (2003).

13 Parry (2003) points out that in the USA the top income quintile owns 60% of all shares, with the bottom income quintile owning less than 2%. A survey commissioned by Wall Street Europe concludes that in the USA 60% of households have equity ownership, while in Europe this number is only 18%. Likewise, while in the USA 50% of the population has more than €50k private ownership, excluding property, this compares to only 15% in Europe. (GfK Custom Research Worldwide, Sep/Oct 2004, 14,383 people in 18 countries.)

14 Cramton and Kerr (2002) note that in the US cellular communications licence example, prices happened to fall when the scheme shifted from free allocation to auctions because of an increase in competition.

15 Some cost differential might be expected by the logic in Section 2.5 on the perverse dynamic incentives created by repeated free allocations. The fact that the assumption of profit maximization does not fully capture reality is discussed in Section 4.1.

16 As already noted, an exception may apply when the allocation method has perverse dynamic effects, as discussed in Section 2.5.

17 The publication of the IPCC's First Assessment Report and the UN General Assembly Decision to launch negotiations on tackling climate change.

18 The UN Framework Convention on Climate Change, which agreed on the nature of the problem and the need for action led by industrialized countries, was signed at the Rio Earth Summit in June 1992 and ratified by the US Senate later the same year, and entered into force a year later. It was also in the period 1990–1992 that the EU developed proposals for a carbon tax, later made conditional on action by other countries.

19 Additionally, if the rules provide for higher allocations to dirtier new entrants, then entrants have an incentive to construct more carbon-intensive facilities than is economically efficient.

20 This is analogous to the 'ratchet effect' in economic theory (Freixas et al., 1985) and clearly reduces the efficiency of the trading scheme.

21 The need for lobbying may exacerbate the dynamic incentive effects discussed in Section 2.5 if firms make inefficient investment decisions to improve their bargaining position for free allowances.

22 The relative paucity of published academic work on this huge scheme is evidence of this process – most academics and think tanks are caught in extensive consulting exercises for either government or industrial participants on the rent allocation, rather than devoting their attention to forward-looking studies on how to create innovation, least-cost abatement and appropriate institutional changes.

23 Eligibility and participation issues are considered in Section 3.2.

24 The 2002 auction of emissions reductions was a reverse auction in which bidders competed to sell reductions to the government. Concerns about encouraging entry led to the use of a descending-bid auction format (the mirror image of ascending bids in a standard auction). The fact that this was the first ever auction for greenhouse gas reductions and the relatively small scale of the market meant that small bidders could have been deterred by the costs of having to formulate

a strategy in a sealed-bid auction. (The small scale of the auction meant that having a non-competitive bid facility of the kind that would mitigate these concerns would be impractical.) The government was keen to promote entry, both to increase competition in the auction itself and to ensure a liquid secondary market (Klemperer et al., forthcoming).

25 An alternative type of sealed-bid auction is the Vickrey auction, where a winning bidder's payments equal the bids of the losers who would have won in the absence of his participation. The winner thus pays the opportunity cost of his bid. Vickrey auctions are of great interest to academic auction theorists and have been shown to have desirable theoretical properties (Ausubel and Cramton, 1998). However Vickrey auctions are much harder for participants and the public to understand, and as long as bidders have very little market power, uniform-price auctions produce similar results.

26 This is not to say that alternatives should not be considered, or that either option is necessarily the preferred auction format for every Member State. However the low costs of such formats (e.g. compared with ascending bids) and the fact that Member States can draw on the experiences of securities markets suggest that discriminatory and uniform-price auctions should be thoroughly examined.

27 One possible problem is the 'winner's curse'. The value of winning a tradable allowance is similar for bidders because they will all face the same resale price on the secondary market. In this kind of 'common value' auction, the bidders estimate what this price will be and bid accordingly. However the most likely to win is also the most likely to have overestimated the price, and bidders need to shade their bids to account for this.

28 In the UK, index-linked securities (gilts) are sold in a uniform-price auction, while conventional gilts are sold using discriminatory pricing. The Debt Management Office explicitly attributes this decision to the greater uncertainty surrounding prices of index-linked gilts and the illiquidity of secondary markets.

29 If non-competitive bids are permitted in securities auctions they typically comprise a small proportion (about 10–20%) of the issue.

30 There is also the possibility of 'demand reduction' in uniform-price auctions (Ausubel and Cramton, 2002).

31 This is then equivalent to partial grandfathering, and the various arguments discussed in Section 2 are applicable. If such subsidies are justified in some manner, there would be better ways of delivering them than by distorting the auction design.

32 US Treasury auctions restrict bidders to 35% of supply in any auction, but these rules have occasionally been circumvented. In 1991 Salomon Brothers admitted to submitting fraudulent bids in the names of their clients in order to squeeze short sellers in the 'when-issued' market.

33 Auctioning permits all at once would increase liquidity in the secondary market. However, since only 10% of allowances will be sold at auction, this is unlikely to be a major concern.

34 A discriminatory price auction with non-competitive bids could also be used.

35 As documented and analysed more fully in the growing literature on behavioural economics. For specific examples see Gigerenzer and Goldstein (1996) and Gigerenzer (2003). Of course, the use of heuristics *per se* is not *necessarily* inconsistent with profit maximization.

36 Allowance cutbacks to power generators would reduce total allowances, increasing the allowance price. In contrast, auctioning would not have this effect. As such, downstream sectors should clearly prefer auctioning to an equivalent allocation cutback.

37 Auctions might also raise shareholder awareness of carbon costs, and alert them to the possibility of savings through abatement, resulting in greater pressure on managers to reduce emissions.

38 It is assumed that Poland, the main unknown, has an 18% excess allocation, similar to Hungary and the Czech Republic.

39 Big gas price increases during 2004–2005 led to a switch back to coal in power generation, increasing emissions. This indeed was the principal factor behind the initial increase in CO_2 prices. Had gas prices stayed low, emissions from the dominant power sector would have been lower and the gap between emissions and allocations probably even larger.

40 These are classic results of real option theory. See Baldursson and von der Fehr (2004) for a more sophisticated discussion of the impact of risk aversion.

41 Furthermore, asymmetries in risk hedging and allocation have an impact. Utilities in the power sector (with a more conservative risk profile and relatively restrictive allocations) have needed to buy from other sectors, which were under no pressure to sell surplus allowances. This sellers' market arguably inflated prices. Auctions on a regular basis (e.g. biannually) would improve, both directly and indirectly, the liquidity of the market, by reducing this type of problem.

42 The ability to bank allowances from phase II into subsequent periods can in theory contribute to price stability; in practice, given the present fundamental uncertainty about the nature of post-2012 commitments, this may remain a marginal consideration for much of phase II (we return to the topic in the following section).

43 In the limit, if the ceiling and the floor are equal then obviously the allowance price would be fixed, and what was a 'quantity instrument' would now effectively become a 'price instrument'.

44 On price capping, see, e.g., Pizer (1997, 2002), Aldy et al. (2001), McKibbin and Wilcoxen (2002) and Jacoby and Ellerman (2004). The EU directive prohibits *ex-post* adjustment of national allocation plans; hence national governments could not sell additional allowances after the submission of these plans.

45 For example, market players might artificially create a price spike to prompt the release of allowances into the market. The experience with speculative attacks on currency and exchange rate controls provides some important lessons.

46 An absolute price floor in the EU ETS could be established if a government institution agreed to *purchase* an unlimited number of permits at a fixed price. If sellers are guaranteed this floor price by selling to the government, the market price will not fall below the floor. Treasuries, however, are typically reluctant to sign up to such financial liabilities.

47 This would be reflected in Figure 3 by the demand curve shifting down to cut the axis in the free allocation area.

48 Weitzman (1974) and Roberts and Spence (1976) provide the canonical theory. Pizer (2002) and Hoel and Karp (2001, 2002) apply the theory to climate change, accounting for the fact that greenhouse gases are a 'stock pollutant' not a 'flow pollutant'.

49 Note that assuming a flat marginal benefits curve does not imply that damages from climate change are small. It simply implies that damage from climate impacts do not *change* rapidly as a function of additional emissions. Assuming a flat marginal damage curve is probably accurate over a short period (e.g. 5 years), because climate damages are a function of the *stock* of greenhouse gases in the atmosphere, rather than the flow of emissions. This assumption is less appropriate over longer time-frames, and Hoel and Karp (2002) show that capping quantities becomes more attractive as the relevant policy time horizon is increased.

50 See Hepburn (2006) for a simple presentation and review of the 'prices vs. quantities' literature with an application to policy questions in health, transport, defence and the environment.

51 As noted above, taxes combine several politically difficult problems in one, and their history (as with the European carbon tax proposals of the early 1990s) is patchy and limited. Newell et al. (2005) examine some of the problems from a theoretical perspective. At the international level, the difficulties that would be faced in trying to establish a harmonized, long-term, credible global carbon tax are obvious.

52 Newell et al. (2005) develop the mathematics of these approaches in detail.

53. This could lead to the development of a more sophisticated forward market for long-term allowances, in which low-carbon innovators could hedge against future low prices by taking a short position (i.e. agreeing to provide reductions).

54 Additional policies would not erode the credibility of the contract, which is so crucial in climate policy (Helm et al., 2003), because the price set in the long-term carbon contract is fixed and would not be affected by changes in the stringency of other climate policies.

55 Alternative financing structures are possible. For instance, the government could require the emission reductions to be fungible with the EU ETS, such that the liability under the carbon contracts can be offset by selling the allowances on to the EU ETS. Alternatively, the transmission systems operator could purchase the emission reductions under the carbon contacts, so that if any liability materializes it can be passed through to customers via transmission charges.

56 To get a rough sense of the potential improvement in environmental effectiveness offered by recycling auction revenues into long-term carbon contracts, consider the following highly imperfect back-of-the-envelope calculation. If 50% of a Member State's emissions are covered by the EU ETS, then auctioning 10% of phase II allowances is equivalent to auctioning 5% of the applicable Kyoto limit. Now suppose that the prices paid in the auction are similar to the prices the government pays for emissions reductions delivered under the carbon contract. If the carbon contracts required delivery for 2008–2012, the government would thereby achieve an additional 5% reduction in emissions. Of course, the point of a long-term carbon contract is to extend beyond 2012, so they would deliver less than a 5% reduction over the first commitment period, but would also deliver emissions reductions after 2012. The net present value of the emissions reductions delivered should be within an order of magnitude of a 5% reduction in the first commitment period.

References

Aldy, J.E., Orszag, P.R., Stiglitz, J.E., 2001. Climate change: an agenda for global collective action. Conference on The Timing of Climate Change Policies, Pew Center on Global Climate Change, October.

Archibald, C., Malvey, P.F., 1998. Uniform-Price Auctions: Update of the Treasury Experience. United States Treasury Working Paper.

Ausubel, L.M., Cramton, P., 1998. Auctioning Securities. University of Maryland Working Paper.

Ausubel, L.M., Cramton, P., 2002. Demand Reduction and Inefficiency in Multi-Unit Auctions. University of Maryland Working Paper.

Baldursson, F.M., von der Fehr, N.-H.M., 2004. Price volatility and risk exposure: on market-based environmental policy instruments. Journal of Environmental Economics and Management 48, 682–704.

Biermann, F., Brohm, R., 2003. Implementing the Kyoto Protocol without the United States: The Strategic Role of Energy Tax Adjustments at the Border. Global Governance Working Paper 5, The Global Governance Project, Potsdam, Germany.

Bovenberg, A.L., Goulder, L.H., 1996. Optimal environmental taxation in the presence of other taxes: general-equilibrium analyses. American Economic Review 86(4), 985–1000.

Bovenberg, A.L., de Mooij, R.A., 1994. Environmental levies and distortionary taxation. American Economic Review 84(4), 1085–1089.

Bovenberg, A.L., de Mooij, R.A., 1997. Environmental levies and distortionary taxation: reply. American Economic Review 87(1), 252–253.

Bovenberg, A.L., van der Ploeg, F., 1994. Environmental policy, public finance and the labour market in a second-best world. Journal of Public Economics 55, 349–390.

Charnovitz, S., 2004. Trade and Climate: Potential Conflicts and Synergies. Beyond Kyoto: Advancing the International Effort Against Climate Change. PEW Center on Global Climate Change.

Cramton, P., Kerr, S., 2002. Tradable Carbon permit auctions: how and why to auction not grandfather. Energy Policy 30, 333–345.

Demailly, D., Quirion, P., 2006. CO_2 abatement, competitiveness and leakage in the European cement industry under the EU ETS: grandfathering versus output-based allocation. Climate Policy 6(1), 93–113.

DTI [Department of Trade and Industry], 2005. EU ETS: Planning for Auction or Sale. Prepared by Environmental Resource Management (ERM) and Market Design Inc. (MDI), August 2005.

Diamond, P.A., Mirrlees, J.A., 1971a. Optimal taxation and public production. I. Production efficiency. American Economic Review 61, 8–27.

Diamond, P.A., Mirrlees, J.A., 1971b. Optimal taxation and public production. II. Tax rules. American Economic Review, 61, 261–278.

Esty, D.C., 1994. Greening the GATT: Trade, Environment and the Future. Institute for International Economics, Washington, DC.

Freixas, X., Guesnerie, R., Tirole, J., 1985. Planning under incomplete information and the ratchet effect. Review of Economic Studies 52(2), 173–191.

Fullerton, D., 1997. Environmental levies and distortionary taxation: reply. American Economic Review 87(1), 245–251.

Fullerton, D., Metcalf, G., 2001. Environmental controls, scarcity rents, and pre-existing distortions. Journal of Public Economics 80, 249–68.

Gigerenzer, G., 2003. Fast and frugal heuristics: the tools of bounded rationality. In: Koehler, D., Harvey, N. (Eds), Handbook of Judgment and Decision Making. Blackwell, Oxford, UK.

Gigerenzer, G., Goldstein, D.G., 1996. Reasoning the fast and frugal way: models of bounded rationality. Psychological Review 103, 650–669.

Goulder, L.H., 1995. Environmental taxation and the double dividend: a readers' guide. International Tax and Public Finance 2, 157–183.

Goulder, L.H., Parry, I.W.H., Burtraw, D., 1997. Revenue-raising vs other approaches to environmental protection: the critical significance of pre-existing tax distortions. RAND Journal of Economics 28, 708–731.

Goulder, L.H., Williams, R.C., Burtraw, D., 1999. The cost-effectiveness of alternative instruments for environmental protection in a second-best setting. Journal of Public Economics 72, 329–360.

Grubb, M., Neuhoff, K., 2006. Allocation and competitiveness in the EU emissions trading scheme: policy overview. Climate Policy 6(1), 7–30.

Hammar, H., Jagers, S.C., 2006. Can trust in politicians explain individuals' support for climate policy? The case of CO_2 tax. Climate Policy 5(6), 611–623.

Helm, D., 2005. Economic instruments and environmental policy. Economic and Social Review 36(3), 205–228.

Helm, D., Hepburn, C., 2005. Carbon Contracts and Energy Policy: An Outline Proposal. Oxford University mimeo, October.

Helm, D., Hepburn, C., Mash, R., 2003. Credible carbon policy. Oxford Review of Economic Policy 19(3), 438–450.

Hepburn, C., 2006. Regulation by prices, quantities or both: a review of instrument choice. Oxford Review of Economic Policy 22(2), forthcoming.

Hepburn, C., Quah, J.K.-H., Ritz, R.A., 2006. On Emissions Trading and Firm Profits. Oxford University Department of Economics Discussion Paper.

Hoel, M., Karp, L., 2001. Taxes and quotas for a stock pollutant with multiplicative uncertainty. Journal of Public Economics 82, 91–114.

Hoel, M., Karp, L., 2002. Taxes versus quotas for a stock pollutant. Resource and Energy Economics 24, 367–384.

IPCC, 2001. Climate Change 2001: Mitigation. Cambridge University Press, Cambridge, UK.

Ismer, R., Neuhoff, K., 2004. Border Tax Adjustments: A Feasible Way to Address Nonparticipation in Emission Trading. Cambridge Working Papers in Economics CWPE 0409. CMI Electricity Project Department of Applied Economics, Cambridge, UK.

Jacoby, H.D., Ellerman, A.D., 2004. The safety valve and climate policy. Energy Policy 32, 481–491.

Johnston, A., 2006. Free allocation of allowances under the EU emissions trading scheme: legal issues. Climate Policy 6(1), 115–136.

Klemperer, P.D., 2004. Auctions: Theory and Practice. Princeton University Press, Princeton, NJ.

Klemperer, P.D., et al., 2006. Auctions for Environmental Improvements: The UK ETS Auction. Nuffield College Working Paper.

de Leyva, E., Lekander, P.A., 2003. Climate change for Europe's utilities. McKinsey Quarterly 1, 120–131.

McKibbin, W.J., Wilcoxen, P.J., 2002. The role of economics in climate change policy. Journal of Economic Perspectives 16(2), 107–130.

McLean, B.J., 1997. Evolution of marketable permits: the U.S. experience with sulfur dioxide allowance trading. International Journal of Environmental and Pollution 8(1/2), 19–36.

Neuhoff, K., Keats Martinez, K., Sato, M., 2006. Allocation, incentives and distortions: the impact of EU ETS emissions allowance allocations to the electricity sector. Climate Policy 6(1), 73–91.

Newell R., Pizer, W., Zhang, J., 2005. Managing permit markets to stabilize prices. Environmental and Resource Economics 31, 133–157.

Parry, I.W.H., 1995. Pollution taxes and revenue recycling, Journal of Environmental Economics and Management 29, S64–S77.

Parry, I.W.H., 2003. Fiscal interactions and the case for carbon taxes over grandfathered carbon permits. Oxford Review of Economic Policy 19(3), 385–399.

Parry, I.W.H., Williams, R.C., Goulder, L.H., 1999. When can carbon abatement policies increase welfare? The fundamental role of distorted factor markets. Journal of Environmental Economics and Management 37, 52–84.

Pigou, A.C., 1920. The Economics of Welfare. McMillan, London.

Pizer, W.A., 1997. Prices vs. Quantities Revisited: The Case of Climate Change. RFF Discussion Paper 98-02, Resources for the Future, Washington DC.

Pizer, W.A., 2002. Combining price and quantity controls to mitigate global climate change. Journal of Public Economics 85, 409–434.

Roberts, M.J., Spence, M., 1976. Effluent charges and licences under uncertainty. Journal of Public Economics 5, 193–208.

Smale, R., Hartley, M., Hepburn, C., Ward, J., Grubb, M., 2006. The impact of CO_2 emissions trading on firm profits and market prices. Climate Policy 6(1), 31–48.

Weitzman, M., 1974. Prices vs. quantities. Review of Economic Studies 41(4), 477–491.

Zhang, Z.X., 1998. Greenhouse gas emissions trading and the world trading system. Journal of World Trade 32(5), 219–239.

*For Product Safety Concerns and Information please contact
our EU representative GPSR@taylorandfrancis.com Taylor & Francis
Verlag GmbH, Kaufingerstraße 24, 80331 München, Germany*

T - #0195 - 270225 - C0 - 262/190/9 - PB - 9781138002005 - Gloss Lamination